AF600062

PASTORS,

THEIR RIGHTS AND DUTIES

ACCORDING TO THE

NEW CODE OF CANON LAW.

A DISSERTATION

SUBMITTED TO THE FACULTY OF THE SACRED SCIENCES OF THE CATHOLIC UNIVERSITY OF AMERICA

IN PARTIAL FULFILLMENT OF THE REQUIREMENTS FOR THE DEGREE

DOCTOR OF CANON LAW

By CHARLES J. KOUDELKA, J. C. L.
Catholic University of America

1921.

Imprimatur:

† JOS. M. KOUDELKA, D. D.,
Episcopus Superiorensis.

Die 8 Junii, 1921.

PASTORS

THEIR RIGHTS AND DUTIES

ACCORDING TO THE

NEW CODE OF CANON LAW.

INTRODUCTION.

The pastoral office has ever been one of the greatest importance and dignity. When we consider its origin in the New Testament, we see the outstanding figure of Jesus Christ arising upon the horizon as the 'Pastor Bonus.' "I am the good shepherd. The good shepherd giveth his life for his sheep." John, X. II. When we consider its end, we hear the cry of millions of souls thirsting for salvation. And if we consider its reward, the words of the Holy Ghost through Daniel give us an answer: — "They that instruct many to justice (shall shine) as stars for all eternity." Daniel, XII, 3.

The parish priest takes a great part in this sublime office and, consequently, shares also in the blessings which it brings. He is to be the follower of Jesus Christ as the good Shepherd, he is to heed the cry of these thirsting souls and then he may also securely hope to realize the words of Daniel and enjoy the happiness of heaven. His duties, indeed, are many and his responsibilities great. The Bishop gives him a number of souls, entrusts them to his care. These, then, are the field of his pastoral labor, these he must bring Home. Like the general of old, who used to lead the warriors into battle, the pastor must lead his people into the spiritual fray. He should not demand of them anything which he himself is not willing to undergo. Like the pilot, who guides the ship through calm and storm, the parish priest must direct his flock safely into the Heavenly Port. He must watch the route and see that all is clear and safe ahead. But the pastor's duties do not end here. There are also other sheep that are not of his flock—these he must seek out and bring into the one true fold.

In order that every pastor might know what his rights and duties are, the Church has taken great pains to determine and define them for him even to the smallest detail. And wisely so, for even the smallest details are of great significance where there is question of souls. But if the Church took so much trouble to do all this for the pastor is it not, accordingly, the duty of the pastor to study and know these matters and put them into practice? This study will necessarily entail much time and labor but the importance of the office demands that this time and labor be spent.

Information regarding these rights and duties of pastors may be gathered from the various works on Moral Theology, Canon Law and Pastoral Theology. But most of these works were compiled before the New Code of Canon came into effect and, therefore, do not contain the New Legislation in all its changes. For this reason, have I taken it upon myself, with the help of God, to gather this matter and to treat of this subject as it is today, according to the New Canon Law. I do not presume to give a complete and exhaustive treatment of the matter in hand but hope to give the parish priest a working knowledge of the subject with reference to the more important and frequent rights and duties. Moreover, this is a canonical dissertation on the subject and, consequently, questions of moral theology, will not be treated, except in so far as they are necessary to explain the law.

It may also be well to state here that in many places canons treating of benefices will be quoted as proofs for matters pertaining to parishes.

What is written in these pages is written in complete subjection to the teaching authority of the Catholic Church and with a hope that these lines may prove of some value in increasing the effectiveness of our parish priests.

CHAPTER I.

A Short History of the Parochial Office.

It is not my intention to give a detailed history of the parochial office. The subject of my dissertation does not demand this nor will time allow it. Consequently, the following points are to serve merely as a short review of the origin and progress of the parochial institution, pointing out the time of its origin, the nature of its institution and the scope of its powers together with a brief resume of its expansion and progress.

When we look into the history of the parochial office, we notice that controversy upon controversy arose about various points. Thus, certain writers tell us that the parochial office dates back to the time of the seventy two disciples of Jesus Christ, others that nowhere can certain signs of it be found before the third or fourth century. On the one hand we are asked to believe that this office was instituted by Christ, on the other that it is of mere Ecclesiastical institution. Again, some writers claim that the parish priest has external jurisdiction, others deny him this power altogether. Were we to treat these points in detail, the time and space allowed for this whole dissertation would not suffice to do them justice.

There were some writers who held that, the period of time to which we must look for the origin of the parochial office is that of the seventy two disciples, that they formed a third hierarchy in orders and that they possessed external jurisdiction "vi officii ex jure divino". This opinion "iam reprobata et nostra aetate penitus antiquata, quatenus aliquid veri continet, manifeste non attendit differentiam et officium parochialem, quod denuo ab officio pastorali Episcopi non satis distinxit; insuper ex origine et vicissitudine historica officii parochorum evidenter refutatur". (1). Other canonists agree with him, in fact, there is no canonist at present who could successfully uphold the opposite view. Consequently, the parish priests cannot be the successors of the disciples of Christ and we will have to look elsewhere for their origin.

Excluding the opinion just refuted, there is still much diver-

1. Wernz, F. X. Jus Decretalium. vol. II. p. 688 sq.

gence among the canonists as to the exact time when the parochial office actually came into existence. In the early days of the Church's existence, when the number of Catholics was as yet very small, there were no parishes whatever. This is certain. There was but one church in the whole diocese and that was cared for by the Bishop himself with the assistance of several priests. These priests were not pastors in any sense of the word for they were not even allowed to say Mass apart from the Bishop. (2) This same discipline was maintained even later when there were more churches in the diocese. The priests were still obliged to assist at the Holy Sacrifice of the Mass in the cathedral as before, on all Sundays and Holydays of Obligation. As Marius Lupus says: "Idem servatum peraeque fuisse, postquam praeter unum primum templum proprie dictum, in urbibus aedificari coeptae sunt aedes; nam nihilominus ad eam solummodo in qua Episcopus sacra faciebat accurebant, ibique tantum celebrabatur synaxis." (3)

It is no easy matter to determine the exact time when the diocese began to be divided into parishes. As Bohmerus put it: "Those who have written "ex professo" on this subject, rather obscure it than clear it up." (4)

The best we can hope to do here is to give the views of some of the writers and let the reader choose for himself from among them. Thomassinus thinks that parishes started in the middle of the fourth century, while Marius Lupus says that they originated somewhat sooner. It seems safe to say, however, that certain signs of parishes and of parish priests cannot be found before the fourth century. This is the opinion of Thomassinus, (5) Bouix, (6) Wernz, (7) and Vecchiotti. (8) One fact that all agree upon is that the first parishes were started in country places and not in the cities. Thus Dionysius Petavius tells us that: "hujus-

2. Bouix, D. Tractatus de Parocho. Pars. I. c. 6. p. 44 .

3. Marius Lupus, De Paroeciis ante annum 1000 A. D. diss. 2. cap. 5. p. 173. edit. Bergoni, apud Bouix, D. 1. c. p. 16-17.

4. Bohmerus. Ius Parochiale. sect. 2. c. 2. p. 63. apud Murray, L. Present Juridical status of Parishes in the U. S.

5. Thomassinus. Vetus et nova Eccl. Disciplina, p. 1. l. 2. c. 21.

6. Op. cit. p. 22. aqq.

7. Wernz, op. cit. vol. 2. p. 689.

8. Vecchiotti. Institutiones Canonicae. p. 328

modi ergo paroeciarum institutum, vel ut vulgo loquuntur, parochiarum, dixi in animadversiones ad Epiphanium, prius in agris et extra urbes, quam in urbibus usurpatum videri." (9) The East possessed a resident clergy sooner than the West. City parishes were formed later, but those in Episcopal cities did not appear until the year 1000 A. D. It seems quite certain that this was the case in all such cities with the exception of Rome and Alexandria. The episcopal church was, during all this while, the only parish church in the whole city and all the faithful had to come thither to fulfill their parochial duties.

But even in those places where parishes were started in the fourth century their multiplication was not very rapid. From the fifth to the eighth century many chapels were built but these could not be called parish churches, since they were dependent upon the principal church of the village or hamlet. After the eighth century they spread more quickly and in the eleventh century they also arose in the episcopal cities. This change in the cities mentioned came about through a certain state of affairs which we need not speak of here. The first steps in this direction were taken in Gaul, later in Italy.

As a matter of fact the parochial boundaries of parishes were not strictly determined even at this time. The Parish priests ministered to anyone that came to them without asking whether he belonged to their parish or not. This state of affairs lasted until the fifteenth century. The Council of Trent took cognizance of it and consequently decreed # "in iis quoque civitatibus, ac locis, ubi paroeciales ecclesiae certos non habent fines, nec eorum rectores proprium populum quem regant; sed promiscue petentibus sacramenta administrant; mandat Sancta Synodus episcopis, pro tutiori animarum eis commissarum salute ut, distincto populo in certas propriasque parochias, unicuique suum perpetuum peculiaremque parochum assignent, qui eas cognoscere valeat, et a quo licite sacramenta suscipiant; aut alio utiliori modo, prout loci qualitas exegerit, provideant. Idemque in iis civitatibus ac locis, ubi nullae sunt parochiae, quamprimum fieri curent; non obstantibus quisbuscumque privilegiis et consuetudinibus, etiam imme-

9. Dionysius Petavius. Theologica Dogmata, De Ecc. Hierarchia. lib. 2. C. XII. vol. 7. p. 633.

morabilibus." (10) This order of the Council gave rise to many new parishes and to the determination of their boundaries in a stricter manner. In many places the law of Trent could not be carried out in its fullness, e. gr. here in the U. S., but, even in such cases, care was taken that the discipline should conform to the prescribed law as much as possible according to the circumstances of the places. (11) In this way something like harmony was brought about throughout the whole world.

At present our Country is also governed by the common law of the Church. Parishes are to be erected according to the ruling found therein. Every diocese is to be divided into parishes and these parishes are to be cared for by parish priests. C. 216. In this way the spiritual welfare of the people can best be taken care of.

Referring to the controversy regarding the jurisdiction of parish priests much need not be said here. It is certain that the parochial office does not need external jurisdiction "ex natura sua", for facts show that it is very valuable and effective without it. Divine law does not grant parish priests this prerogative, because the office is not of divine institution. Neither does Ecclesiastical law give them such powers, since we cannot prove that the Church ever conferred such a distinction upon the pastors. The teaching of canonists and the practice of the Church throughout the world do not acknowledge any such jurisdiction in the parish priest.

We must bear in mind, however, that the external jurisdiction spoken of here means the legislative, judicial and coercive authority taken together. We do not wish to deny that pastors have the power of dispensing from matrimonial impediments in certain cases and circumstances, or from the law of fast and abstinence, etc. Still, this cannot be called external jurisdiction in the strict sense as we use it here. The parish priest has some of these powers, but he had them already before the New Code came into effect and yet, we do not find any canonist saying that pastors had external jurisdiction under the old law.

10. Conc. Trid. Canones et Decreta. ses. XXIV. c. 13. et c. 14. p. 194.
11. Conc. Plen. Balt III. C. V. # 32. p. 21.

CHAPTER II.

Parochus.

"Parochus est sacerdos vel persona moralis cui paroecia collata est in titulum cum cura animarum sub Ordinarii loci auctoritate exercenda." C. 451 #1.

This is the definition of a parish priest as found in the New Code. In the first place no one can become a pastor unless he be a priest or a moral person. Today, therefore, no physical person, who is not endowed with the sacerdotal character, can be validly appointed to such a position. Canon 154 confirms this statement by saying: "Officia quae curam animarum sive in foro interno sive in externo secumfert, clericis nondum sacerdotio initiatis conferi valide nequeunt." Beside Canon 453 expressly states that only such as belong to the sacred Priesthood can be validly appointed pastors, i. e. actual pastors. The wisdom of this legislation is easily seen when we consider the duties of a pastor. Still, this ruling is a new one. The Church did not always insist upon this quality in the parochus. In the twelfth century Pope Alexander III. decreed that no one ought to be admitted to such a position unless he be at least a sub-deacon: "dispensative tamen in minoribus ordinibus constituti consueverunt assumi; dum tales sint, quod intra tempus possint in presbyteros ordinari." (1) According to a decretal of Pope Boniface VIII (1294—1303) it is evident, that no sacred orders were necessary. (2) Moreover, some authors assert, that not even minor orders were demanded as of necessity for the validity of the appointment. Thus Fagnanus says: "Nam parochiales conferuntur etiam clericis primae tonsurae." (3) All that was necessary in such cases was, that the appointed one be ordained to the priesthood within a short time. This "short time" was interpreted to signify "one year". (4) The Council of Trent did not make any change in this regard and so, even after this time, the sacerdotal character was not a necessary requisite for the validity of the appointment. Now, however, there can be no

1. In Capite Praeterea 5, tit. de aetate et qualitate 14. lib. decretalium.

2. C. 8. De Praebendis 4, lib. III. in 60.

3. In Capite Praeterea, de aetate et qualitate, 8.

4. Pirhing "Jus Canonicum nova methodo explicatum" tit. XIV. lib. I. decretalium n. 41.

question about this. The New Code insists that pastors, whenever they are physical persons, be priests. The Bishops themselves cannot dispense from this quality for it is a matter of common law and, consequently, unless Canon 81, can be made use of, they cannot dispense.

But a parish is not always given to a physical person. It is not of infrequent occurence that parishes are given to moral persons, especially to religious communities. In such cases the moral person cannot be the actual pastor but merely the habitual parish priest. C. 452. The moral person must, in such cases, provide a vicar into whose hands the actual care of the souls is placed. For example, when a religious community is given a parish, not all the priests pertaining to that community can be allowed to take part in the actual care of the people. This would be a confusing and inefficient way of caring for their spiritual welfare. For this reason the Church insists that, in such cases, the actual charge of the parish be given to a vicar. C. 471#4. This vicar may be presented to the Ordinary of the place by the moral person but it belongs to the Ordinary to appoint him. In certain cases the Ordinary may appoint the vicar without any previous presentation on the part of the moral person. C. 471#2.

A parish is to be committed "in titulum." What does this mean? Father Augustine explaines this term in the following manner:—"A title may be defined as "the legitimate cause of possessing what otherwise does not belong to one." It plays a conspicuous part in prescription and possession. To hold a parish in title, or a title to a parish, therefore, means to be the owner or possessor of the parish. However, no parochus can be styled the owner or possessor or the proprietor of a parish.... here title must be restricted to possession by a legitimate cause." (5) —

The third point in the definition of the parish priest contains his duties. It is, in short, the care of souls. This is the all-important office of the pastor.

The fourth and last point explain his power. The power which the pastor possesses by virtue of the office which he holds

5. Augustine, C. A. Comm. on Canon Law. vol. 2. p. 510.

is an ordinary power. He acts not as a representative of the Bishop but in his own name. He acts "ex officio" and not "ex delegatione". Therefore it follows, that the Ordinary cannot diminish or take away his power to such an extent as to make it practically worthless. Still, the parish priest must always keep in mind the last part of canon, i. e. that he exercises all his power under the authority of the Ordinary of the diocese. Father Augustine again remarks: "It follows that the institution of the parish priests or pastors of souls, in this limited sense, is not of divine origin and that it is circumscribed by, and dependent upon, the authority of the Bishop." (6) The priest owes obedience to the Ordinary as to his superior. When the pastor is negligent in the fulfillment of his duties the Ordinary can punish or remove him.

Pastors are either territorial, national or personal. That parish priest is territorial who receives his subjects by reason of territory. National pastors are those, who receive their people by reason of nationality without regard to the boundaries of other parishes. Although even these parishes have certain defined limits, still they do not observe the territorial limits of all other parishes but include territory also belonging to other parishes which are territorial. Thus, an Italian parish may embrace territory belonging to two or three English speaking parishes. A personal pastor is one who is appointed for a certain number ot persons or for some family, e. gr. the pastor of a royal family. Such parishes i. e. national and personal, may not be constituted now without an Apostolic Indult. Those that now exist cannot be changed to territorial without consulting the Holy See. C. 216#4.

Parish priests are either removable or irremovable. This does not mean that some can be removed and that others are absolutely permanent. The distinction is made in the stability of the two classes. The removable pastors are more easily removed than the irremovable ones, but both the one and the other can and may be removed according to law when the case demands it. C. 454#1—2. However, neither can be removed

6. Augustine, 1. cit. p. 511-512.

"ad nutum Episcopi" as was the case in regard to some heretofore. Nor can either be removed without a canonical cause and the use of the prescribed canonical form. There is one exception to the above rule. Pastors belonging to religious societies, whether exempt from the jurisdiction of the Ordinary of the place or not, are always removable "ad nutum" both of the Ordinary and of the religious Superior. But when one of these proceeds with such a removal he is to notify the other of that action but no reasons need be given to the other. C. 454#5. Although religious may not be subject to the ordinary in other matters, they are subject to him in matters pertaining to the management of the parish. And so, even though the religious superior resides in the same house with the religious pastor, the Ordinary may visit and correct the latter in parochial matters just as he visits and corrects his own diocesan parish priests. C. 631#I. If it should happen that the Ordinary and the religious Superior disagree upon certain orders that have been given to the religious pastor regarding parish work, the commands of the Ordinary prevail over those of the Superior. C. 631#2.

Canon 451 goes on to tell us who are equal in law to pastors (in so far as the rights and duties are concerned) and who fall under this name in Canon Law. They are not real pastors as those mentioned above, but still have the same rights and duties as the real parish priests have, and any ruling made for the pastors also applies to them unless the contrary is expressly stated. Such then are I. quasi-pastors, who have charge of quasi-parishes, and 2. parochial vicars, who possess full parochial powers. C. 451#2.

Just as dioceses are divided into parishes so Prefectures Apostolic and Vicariates Apostolic are divided into quasi-parishes. The rectors who have charge of parishes are called pastors, while those in charge of quasi-parishes are called quasi-pastors. C. 216 #1 and 3. These last are all removable. C.54#4.

Now, who are to be included under the name of vicars with full parochial powers? Vicars can be reduced to the following classes: — 1. Vicars, who have charge of a parish of which a moral person is the habitual pastor. C. 471; 2. Vicar oeconomus, C. 472-475; 3. Vicar Substitutus, C. 474; 4. Vicar Adiutor, C.

475; 5. Vicar Cooperator, C. 476. Their rights and powers will be stated as we proceed to discuss them. Bear in mind, however, that only such as possess full parochial powers are to be classed under the name "parochus" according to canon law.

1. Those vicars, who are placed in charge of parishes which were given in charge of religious communities or other moral persons, possess all the rights and duties that fall to a real pastor. These are theirs by common law, by the diocesan statutes or by lawful custom. C. 471#4. Any ruling, therefore, made for pastors is also binding upon them in the same manner, unless the contrary be expressly stated. The same canonical causes and the same form must be observed in their removal as is to be used and observed in the removal of parish priests. However, if the vicar be a religious, then he is, again, removable as religious parish priest are. C. 471#3; C. 454 #5.

2. Whenever a parish becomes vacant through the death or removal of a pastor, a priest is to be placed in charge of it until the new parish priest has been appointed. The priest put in charge during this interregnum is called a "vicar oeconomus". C. 473#1. He also has all the rights and duties that belong to the regular pastor as far as the care of souls is concerned. Nevertheless, this vicar may not do anything that would be to the prejudice of the rights of the pastor of the parish itself. C. 473#2.

3. At times the pastor may leave the parish for a time, e. gr. on account of ill health, for a vacation, etc. According to canon 465#4-5 if such a leave be for more than a week, a capable substitute must be provided. These substitutes are called "vicarii substituti". C. 474. Such vicars have all the rights and duties pertaining to the parish priest himself unless the Ordinary or the pastor reserve some of these.

4. Whenever a pastor becomes too old and feeble to care for the parish properly, or when he is affected with some permanent malady which hinders him in the fulfillment of the parochial duties, a helper should be given him by the Ordinary of the Diocese. Such helpers are called "vicarii adiutores". C. 475#1. If such a helper takes the place of the pastor in all things he has also all the rights and duties of the pastor, except that of

applying the Missa pro populo. This last duty always remains with the parish priest himself. But if the assistant supplies the pastor only in some of the parochial duties he does not possess all the rights and duties of the parochial office but merely those contained in the letters of appointment. C. 475#2.

5. Finally, when a parish becomes too large and the people too numerous for one priest to take care of, an assistant is to be sent there. Such assistants are called "vicarii cooperators". C. 476 #1. If necessary, more than one such assistant may be sent. These vicars do not possess all the rights and duties of the pastor's office, but merely those determined by the diocesan statutes, the letters of appointment or by other letters of the Ordinary or finally by the pastor himself. C. 476#6. These assistants may be appointed to assist in the whole parish or only in a part of it. C. 476#2. But the appointment will always extend to the whole parish unless the contrary is expressly stated. The Missa pro populo is not of obligation for these assistants. C. 476#6. The pastor has also a right to be heard before these cooperators are sent to him and the non-observance of this ruling makes the appointment invalid. C. 105; C. 476#3. Of course, the Ordinary need not ask any permission or stand by the wishes of the pastor as long as he gives him a hearing. C. 105.

All the vicars mentioned above save those under number one are removable "ad nutum Episcopi vel Vicarii Capitularis, non autem Vicarii Generalis sine mandato speciali". C. 477. If they are religious they are removable according to canon 454#5, i. e. "ad nutum tam loci Ordinarii, monito Superiore, quam Superioris, monito Ordinario, aequo iure, non requisito alterius consensu; nec alter alteri causam iudicii sui aperire multoque minus probare tenetur, salvo recursu in devolutivo ad Apostolicam Sedem."

CHAPTER III.

The Appointment of Pastors.

The Church is a perfect society. "For a society to be perfect two conditions are necessary:—1. The end which it proposes to itself must not be purely subordinate to the end of some other society; 2. the society in question must be independent of other societies in regard to the attainment of its end." (1) The Catholic Church has these two essential conditions as is evident from the words of Pope Leo XIII. in his encyclical "Inmortale Dei" (Nov. 1, 1885):—"The Church is distinguished and differs from civil society; and what is of highest moment, it is a society chartered as of right divine, perfect in its nature and its title to possess in itself, and by itself, through the will and loving kindness of its Founder, all the needful provisions for its maintenance and action. And just as the end at which the Church aims is by far the noblest of ends, so is it's authority the most excellent of all authority, nor can it be looked upon as inferior to the civil power, or in any manner dependent upon it." If this is true, and we know that it is, then it is certainly repugnant to have anyone outside of the Church conferring any of its offices.

Moreover, the Church is a hierarchical society, "in qua regimen est penes apostolos eorumque successores, non penes populi multitudinem." (2) Consequently, the concession of ecclesiastical offices is a part of the ecclesiastical government. Therefore, no one, who does not belong to this hierarchy or who is not legitimately authorized by it to do so, can confer any of the ecclesiastical offices.

Again, the Church is an absolute monarchy. The Pope rules with full and supreme power. He has the full disposition of all the offices of the Church. It is only when he relinquishes in part this authority to others that they may validly confer some of these offices. No one be he cleric or of the laity, can validly dispose of any of the Church's offices against the will of the Roman Pontiff.

---

1. Joyce, G. H. verbo "Church" in the Catholic Encyclopedia, vol. 3. p. 760.
2. Wernz, F. X. Ius Decretalium, vol. 2. tit. 15. p. 52.

Now as Wernz says: "quod ex natura Ecclesiae Catholicae deductum est, id luculenter comprobatur positivis Ecclesiae declarationibus." (3) The New Code restates what was already contained in the older legislation in this regard:—"Officium Ecclesiae nequit sine provisione canonica valide obtineri." C. 147#1. This being true, the parochial office, being an ecclesiastical office, cannot be secured without this canonical provision. The same canon goes on to tell us what is meant by the "provisio canonica." It says that it is a "concessio officii ecclesiastici a competente auctoritate Ecclesiastica ad normam sacrorum canonum.. C. 147 #2. Canon 455 part 1 determines this provision in reference to parishes still more. It states who is the competent authority in this case. The only persons able to make such a provision are the Holy See and the Ordinary. The Holy See possesses this prerogative over all the parishes; the Ordinary enjoys it only in connection with those parishes situated within his diocese, which were not reserved to the Holy See. All contrary customs are done away with and, consequently, "neve sinantur in posterum reviviscere." C. 5.

Parishes are either collative, elective or patronal. 1. The collative or free parishes are those to which a pastor is appointed freely by the competent superior, i. e. the appointment is made without any previous election or presentation on the part of others. 2. To the second class i. e. the elective, belong such parishes to which some other person has the right of electing the candidate. The appointment, however, is always made by the Holy See, if the parish be reserved to it, or by the Ordinary of the place. 3. The patronal parishes are those in which the presentation of a candidate is left to the Patron. By presentation the candidate acquires a "ius ad rem" but not as yet a "ius in re". The latter right is secured only through the appointment itself, which is to be made by the "auctoritas competens."

The right of election and presentation has not been taken away by the New Code. This is clear from canon 455 part I, where the law points out who is competent to appoint pastors, whereupon it adds "salvo privilegio electionis aut praesentationis,

3. Wernz, F. X. 1. c. tom. 2, pars, 2, tit. 15, p. 52.

si cui legitime competat." Thus for example, the right of presentation belongs to religious superiors for most of the parishes entrusted to their care. This, however, only if their constitution grants them this right, for the Code expressly says:—"cui ex constitutionibus id competit." C. 456. The appointment again, as in all other cases, belongs to the Holy See or to the Ordinary, as the case may be.

A parish is not to be left vacant for more than six months after the Ordinary receives word of its vacancy. An exception may be made when on account of circumstances it becomes advisable for the Ordinary to postpone the appointment for a longer time. C. 458; C. 155.

Who may be appointed to the parochial office as actual pastor? In the first place the person appointed must be a priest. No one, who does not possess the sacerdotal character, can validly be appointed. C. 453#1. Besides this, other qualities are also necessary although not for the validity of the appointment. Such qualities are "sit insuper bonis moribus, doctrina, animarum zelo, prudentia, ceterisque virtutibus ac qualitatibus praeditus, quae ad vacantem paroeciam cum laude gubernandam iure tum communi tum particulari requiruntur." C. 453#2. The New Code also introduces a change here as to the age of the candidate for office. In previous legislation the age of twenty four was demanded. Bouix tells us:—"Omnino certum est constituti non posse in parochum, nisi qui annum vigesimum quintum attigit, id est, inchoavit; atque hac deficiente aetate, irritam prorsus et nullam fore parochiae provisionem." (4) The new law states that only such can be appointed as are priests. Now, no one should be ordained to the priesthood before the twenty fourth year has been completed. C. 974. Thus far then the law is the same. But what about a case where the candidate is ordained with a dispensation before this age of twenty four has been attained? The law merely states that the priesthood is necessary and, consequently, even if the candidate is ordained before the canonical age he may be validly appointed as pastor.

What should be the "doctrina" of the candidate. The New

4. Bouix, D. Tractatus de Parocho, p. 333.

Code does not legislate in detail here. But since this same quality was demanded in the old law we may use that as a form for the interpretation of the new, since canon six tells us, that those parts of the New Code which are the same as the old legislation are to be interpreted according to the old. Bargilliat says of this qualification under the old law:—"Parocho ea scientia necessaria est qua verbum Dei praedicare et Sacramenta rite administrare valeat. Haec etiam aestimatur ex conditione paroeciae cui praeficiendus est." (5).

As to the other qualities, such as conduct, zeal for souls, prudence, etc., nothing more need be said here. The Ordinary will have to judge whether the candidate possesses the sufficiently to make a successful pastor and it will depend upon him to decide whether the candidate is fit or not. Besides these qualities prescribed by the Code others may be added by the particular laws of the diocese or province.

In selecting the pastor the Ordinary must choose the one most fit. C. 459#1. The collator is to show no partiality or personal feeling toward one or the other candidate. This binds him "graviter onerata conscientia." He must take into consideration not only what the person knows, but also the other qualities and virtues which are required in order that the parish be governed with success. C. 459#2.

The manner of seeking information as to the various candidates is not left to the judgement of the Ordinary. The old law prescribed a certain form which was to be used and the New Code contains similar legislation in this regard. However, the form prescribed by the New Code differs from that of the old. The new law follows: The documents, which are found in the diocesan archives, are to be examined. These papers include all the references to the candidate's conduct, his records of previous examinations, especially those annual tests passed immediately after Ordination.

If satisfactory and sufficient information cannot be secured in this way, recourse may be had to secret communication with those who know the candidates, even with such as live outside

5. K. Bargilliat, Praelectiones Juris Canonici, vol. II, p. 14.

of the diocese. C. 459#3 p. I. If the candidates are equal in all other things, the one standing highest in the examinations passed immediately after ordination according to canon 130, is to be chosen. C. 459#3, p. 2. Finally a special examination is to be made by all candidates in the presence of the Ordinary and the Synodal examiners. C. 459#3 p. 3. Such priests as have distinguished themselves in sacred Theology, e. gr. licentiates and doctors of Theology, who received their degrees at some Catholic university, as well as professors in this branch, although they have no degree, may be exempted from this examination. However, this is not left to the discretion of the Ordinary alone but must be decided with the consent of the examiners. C. 459#3 p. 3. After this procedure had been completed the Ordinary is bound to give the parish to such a one as is found most fit. C. 459#1. Now let us look at what the old law had to say in this regard.

According to the Council of Trent a "concursus" was required before any parish could be conferred. (6) The discipline of this concursus was more definitely settled by the various Pontiffs especially by Pope Benedict XIV. in his constitution "Cum Illud", (Dec. 14. 1742.) This was known as the particular concursus. Some diocese or countries used another form of selecting their pastors and that was known as the general concursus. Are these forms abolished by the New Code? No, because the law expressly states that:—"in regionibus in quibus paroeciarum provisio fit per concursum sive specialem ad norman const. Benedicti XIV, Cum Illud, 14 Dec. 1742, sive generalem, haec forma retineatur, donec Sedes Apostolica aliud decreverit." C. 459#3 p. 4.

Now, then, what is the method to be followed here in the U. S.? Are we to follow the general law laid down in the New Code or are we to follow one of the forms used under the old legislation? This all depends upon the form in use here previously.

The discipline regarding the examination and the selection of candidates for the parochial office is set down in the II. and III. Councils of Baltimore, and is as follows:—"Each candidate

6. Conc. Tridentinum. ses. XXIV, c. 18, de ref.

was to make an examination before the Bishop and two priests selected by the Bishop. Moreover, no one could be a candidate unless he labored in the diocese for at least five years previous. Regulars who lived in these provinces for five years were not bound by this regulation. (7). The Third Council of Baltimore went further than this and prescribed a concursus for those candidates who sought an irremovable rectorship. As the Fathers of the Council said: "Volumus tamen, ut Episcopi facultate gaudeant, pro prima vice, omisso concursu Rectorés inamovibiles designandi quos magis dignos et idoneos coram Deo judicaverint, praehabito consilio Consultorum suorum." (8) Consequently, the Bishops could choose the first irremovable rector without any concursus as long as they heard the Consultors. But, thereafter, all candidates for such a rectorship had to pass a concursus. One other exception was made here, i. e. that the concursus could be waived in favor of an ecclesiastic, whose learning was well known or whose services to the Church were worthy of special notice, provided the Bishop took counsel with the synodal or prosynodal consultors. (9) From all this we see that as far as the U. S. is concerned we had the concursus for our irremovable rectorships and, consequently, that will remain "donec Sedes Apostolica aliud decreverit". C. 459#3 p. 4. For the others the general law of the New Code will have to be made use of. It will be well to explain the concursus for the irremovable pastorates as it was and is to be carried out.

The method to be used for the concursus is defined in the acts and decrees of the III. Council. It is in form substantially the same as that prescribed by the Council of Trent and more fully determined by the constitution of Pope Benedict XIV. Several minor changes were introduced to accommodate it to the state of affairs found here in the United States.

One of the conditions laid down by the Fathers was that only such candidates would be allowed to make the examination as were of good morals, had exercised the ministry successfully

7. Concilii Plen. Balt. II. Acta et Decreta, tit. III, #126 p. 79-80.

8. Concilii Plen. Balt. III. Acta et Decreta. tit. II, #37, p. 23.

9. Conc. Plen. Bolt. III. l. c. tit. II. #57, p. 57-58.

within the diocese for at least ten years and had charge of a parish, as simple priests, for at least three years or had otherwise given signs of ability to govern a parish with success. (10) Particular legislation regarding the concursus follows:—

1. The concursus for an irremovable rectorship must be made before the Bishop or his Vicar General and at least three examiners, who are to be chosen from among those constituted like synodal and pro-synodal examiners (according to Chapter 3 of Third Plen. Council of Balt.) There must always be at least three examiners unless this number cannot be had on account of the small number of priests within the diocese. #42.

2. When a mission, enjoying the right of irremovability, becomes vacant, this fact is to be made known to the clergy of the diocese by the Bishop. At the same time he is to tell them that a competitive examination will be held for that place At least ten days time should be allowed, so that those who would wish to enter this concursus, could indicate their intention and ask permission of the Bishop to compete. At the same time testimonials or documents concerning their qualities and fitness should be sent in to the Chancellor of the Diocese, or to the person designated by the Bishop. #51. The limit of 10 days may be extended to twenty days by order of the Bishop. And according to a decree of the S. Congr. of the Propagation of the Faith, our Bishops received faculties to extend this time to thirty complete days on account of "dioecesium amplitudinis, sive locorum distantiae, sive gravissimorum negotium, quae assiduam Episcoporum solicitudinem exigunt." (11) After the time set by the Bishop had passed, no more papers should be received. The Bishop is then to decide who shall be allowed to enter the concursus. #42 — #43.

3. The examination "de scientia" is to be held both in writing and orally. Questions are to be given in Moral Theology and Dogma, in Liturgy and Canon Law, and should take up such parts as are more necessary aund ought to be

10. Conc. Plen. Balt. III. l. c. #43, p. 26.

11. Decretum apud p. ciii Conc. Plen. Balt. III., l. c.

known. A question or two from the cathechism should also be given in order to find out with what skill the candidate can explain christian doctrine and to ascertain the method he follows. Moreover, each of the candidates must write a short sermon on any text assigned by the examiners. This text is to be taken from the Gospels. #44.

4. In the written examinations the same questions and cases as well as the same sermon text are to be given to all. A certain defined period of time should be given for the fulfillment of each. #45.

5. In order that none of the candidates could hope to pass without knowing what is supposed to be known, the examiners are told to do their duty with religious exactness. #46.

6. All the candidates are to assemble in one room or hall and the Bishop should appoint a prefect over them. No one besides this prefect and the candidates, together with the Bishop and the examiners, is to be allowed into the room during the examination. Likewise no one is allowed to retire before the test has been completed, except in a case of necessity. #47.

7. The Bible, the Council of Trent and the Corpus Juris Canonici, together with a concordance, are the only books allowed as helps to the competitors. All other books or pamphlets are prohibited. If any one is caught cheating he shall be expelled and excluded from further competition. After eacn candidate has written all that he desires, he is to sign the papers and hand them in to the prefect. The chancellor of the concursus, the Bishop or his Vicar and the examiners must also sign each of the candidates' papers. #48.

8. The oral examination cannot be held unless the Bishop or his substitute and at least three examiners are present. # 49.

9. The examiners must weigh carefully the practical knowledge of each candidate as shown in his explanation of christian doctrine as well as his skill in adapting himself to the mental capacity of the young. In the written examinations

they must also consider the opinions of the different competitors, their use of suitable words as well as the perspicuity and beauty of language in the sermons. #50.

10. Consideration must be taken not only of the learning of the candidates but also of the other qualities required in a successful parish priest, and so the Fathers of the III. Council thought it wise to embody the following decree:—'Probe igitur advertant examinatores, accurato examine sibi inquirendam esse, non solum de concurentium scientia ac doctrina; sed eandem immo forte maiorem conferendam esse industriam in alias perscrutandas dotes animarum regimini consentaneas. Ne igitur gravi suo munere desint, literarum peritiae scrutinio minime neglecto, deligenter inquirant de ceteris qualitatibus regendae ecclesiae necessariis de aetate scilicet, de anteactae vitae ratione, mundis antea exercitis, gravitate et honestate morum, prudentia, temporalium rerum administrandarum peritia, obsequiis Ecclesiae hactenus praestitis; qui demum tales sint, ut oves suas Verbo et exemplo pascere queant." (12) Information regarding these qualities can be taken from the papers sent in by the candidates before the examination as well as from other reliable sources. #31.

11. The examiners are not competent to select the pastor, nor should they even pass judgment as to which of all the candidates is most fit. All that they are required and allowed to do is to decide who among these competitors are fit for the office in question and to report the names of such to the Bishop. The Bishop alone then chooses "quem ipse digniorem in Domino censuerit." But he can take counsel with the examiners before his selection is made. #32.

12. Judgment as to the fitness of the candidates must be made by the examiners before they leave the place of examination and separately from the Bishop or his substitute. This judgment may be passed by means of a secret ballot or openly. "Congruentius tamen videtur, ut examinatores inter

12. Conc. Plen. Balt. III., l. c. #51, p. 28.

se suffragia communicent, qui ad acta referri possit, qui approbati, qui reprobati fuerint." #53.

13. The Bishop or his substitute have no vote in this judgment of the examiners unless the ballots are evenly divided or in case of "vota singularia". In such cases then the Bishop's vote is the decisive one and must be made known to the examiners before their departure since this pertains to the completion of the examination. In this manner judgment is passed upon each and every candidate and they are found fit or unfit. Suspension of judgment is not allowed. #54.

14. After the examiners had passed their judgment the parish in question must be given to one of those found capable. #55.

15. In case the Bishop alone knows of some certain defects in one or the other candidate and this defect is sufficient to render him unworthy, he may pass over such a person and select another. #56.

If any of the candidates are not satisfied and appeal "a mala relationis examinatorum vel ab irrationabili iudicio Episcopi" this appeal can be made "in devolutivo" only and not "in suspensivo", i. e. the one who received the parish continues in office until the case is decided against him. An appeal of this kind must be accompanied with all the records of the concursus just held "et judex, nisi illis visis et gravamine comperto, sententiam non pronunciet." (13) The judgment of the higher judge must be based completely on these records. The same constitution goes on to say—"Quia vero a publica indictione, usque ad diem habiti concursus, tantum temporis intercessit, quantum satis fuit commode exhibendis necessaria iuribus, *attestationibus, requisitis, aliisque, meritorum, documentis;* idcirco ut quaevis via fraudibus, praecifatur, volummus, ac districte mandamus, ne dd. attestationes, fidem tam iudiciales quam extra-iudiciales, et documenta quaecumque studiose conquisita, et post concursum, ut aiunt, expiscata, ullo modo recipiatur. Non obstantibus supra memoratis litteris a Congr.

13. Pope Benedict XIV, cons.t "Cum Illud" #7, p. 146 apud Collectanea S. Congr. De Prop. Fide.

Concilii Tridentini interprete anno 1721 editis, quibus, ad praemissorum effectum in has parte derogamus, illis tamen in reliquis una cum omnibus in eis contentis, firmiter in suo robore permansuris." (14)

Whenever the Bishop passes over one man and grants the office to another for reasons known to himself alone, he should notify the judge of appeals of this reason, when one of the others makes an appeal. This should be done by a personal, secret letter to the judge and the latter is then held by the seal of secrecy in regard to this matter. If the Bishop suspects the judge of appeals, the reason need not be sent to him but preferably to the Prefect of the S. Congregation of the Council. This, also, must be done by secret letter. If the judge of appeals decides in favor of the Bishop's choice, no further appeal can be had. If, on the contrary, he decides against the Bishop, the priest, who received the office, has the right of appealing to another judge, retaining, in the meantime, the parish secured through the concursus. The sentence of this second judge is final. If the present incumbent of office receives a favorable sentence here the case is settled and he retains the position. If the second judge also decides against the Bishop's choice the election is null. (14)

This then is the legislation of the Fathers of the Baltimore Councils, supplemented in part from the constitution of Pope Benedict XV. The supplements are also implicitly included in the Acts and Decrees of the Council since it is there expressly stated that appeals are to be governed by that constitution. #36.

Besides this legislation regarding the particular concursus the Acts and Decrees of the III. Plen. Council of Baltimore also contain certain rulings in regard to the general concursus. The latter differs from the former in this, that the examination as to learning is to be held at stated times each year, whether there is any vacancy or not at that time. The standing of the candidates is determined here in reference to "doctrina" and preserved for future use. The other qualities are not examined until

---

14. Benedict XIV, const. "Cum Illud" #6 apud 1. cit. p. 146.

a vacancy occurs. All those passing the test "de doctrina" are considered fit subjects in that regard for any rectorship within the next six years. If they desire to be candidates for such positions again after that they must make another concursus. This form, called the general concursus is to be used only when the diocese is confronted with such circumstances as make it very hard to hold the particular concursus whenever an irremovable pastorate falls vacant. (15)

What then is the form to be used here in the United States? According to the old law both the particular and the general concursus were used here for the selection of irremovable rectors and, consequently, those forms are to be retained as before in the selection of irremovable pastors, until the Holy See decides otherwise. C. 459#3 p. 4. But what about the removable pastorates? The candidates were not held to any concursus before but were obliged to make an examination before the Bishop and two priests. This cannot be called a concursus. Consequently, these will be appointed henceforth according to the form found in the New Code and explained above.

According to the common law then candidates are to be examined everytime before a parish is given them. Some exceptions were given by the Pontifical Commission for the authentic interpretation of the New Code on the 14th of November, 1920, as follows:—The first question asked was, whether a priest must make this examinaton every time he receives a new parish or whether it is sufficient to undergo it before the first parish is received? The answer received was as follows:—"Ad Ium; Ad Iam partem providebitur in 2a. Ad 2am partem, affirmative, si translatio fiat proponente ac suadente Ordinario; negative, si fiat ad instantiam parochi, nisi Ordinarius cum examinatoribus synodalibus iudicet idoneitatem adhuc perdurare, eamque esse sufficientem ad novam parochiam." Other questions proposed were the following:—"Utrum examini subjiciendus sit parochus remotus a paroecia qui, ad tramitem canonis 2154, transfertur ad aliam paroeciam." Respondetur; "negative". "Utrum pariter examini subjiciendus sit parochus qui ex officio transfertur ad

15. Conc. Plen. Balt. III. l. cit. #59 p. 30.

aliam paroeciam, ad tramitem tituli XXIX, libri IV, canonum 2162-2167." And the response came, "Negative". "Quid agendum si clerici, quos Ordinarius idoneos reputat, nolint examini subiacere, quod forte non semel accidet pro minoribus paroeciis." The answer given was:—"Quatenus non sit provisum per responsionem ad Ium dubium, Ordinarius recurrat as S. Congregationem Concilii." Again it was asked:—"Utrum periculum, de que in canone 996##2 et 3, dummodo coram ipsomet Ordinario et examinatoribus synodalibus fiat, sufficere possit saltem ad provisionem pro prima paroecia." Answer:—"Negative; nisi examen versetur etiam circa ea omnia, de quibus interrogandus sit clericus de paroecia providendus." Finally the Commission was asked:—"Utrum examen, de quo in canone 130#1, sufficiat ad provisionem paroeciarum toto tempore quo sacerdotes illud subire tenentur, dummondo coram Episcopo et examinatoribus synodalibus fiat." And the response came back:—Negative; salvo tamen praescripto #2 eiusdem canonis." (16)

After the concursus had been completed and the appointment made the priest proceeds to take the parish. This is done according to the form prescribed by particular law or approved legitimate custom unless the Ordinary dispenses from this procedure for some good reason. In that case the dispensation takes the place of the form to be used. C. 1444 #1. The Bishop determines the time within which the parish must be taken. If the one appointed does not take it within that time and there is no legitimate impediment to hinder him, the Bishop can declare the parish open again, presuming that the one appointed renounces the place to which he was sent. C. 1444,#2. C. 188,#2. If the person designated cannot take possession of the parish by himself he may appoint someone else to take possession of it for him, but for this a special mandate must be given the proxy by the one appointed. C. 1445.

Before a pastor takes possession of his parish he must make a profession of faith. C. 1443, 1406 #1 p. 7. Any custom

16. "Dubia soluta in Plenariis Comitiis Emorum Patrum. Solutiones datae Romae, 24, Nov. 1920.

against this ruling is null, since the New Code expressly states:—"reprobatur quaelibet consuetudo contra canones hujus tituli." C. 1408.

No distinction is made here between the removable and irremovable pastors. Consequently, as long as the law does not distinguish neither should we make any such distinction and, therefore, all pastors must make this profession.

The fulfillment of this last obligation is of a personal nature. It cannot be made through another. The following canon expresses this very clearly:—"Obligationi fidei professionem emittendi non satisfacit qui eam per procuratorem—emittit." C. 1407. Moreover, it must be made before the Ordinary or his delegate, who cannot be a layman. C. 1407.

When is the profession to be made? Every time a pastor obtains a new parish, whether this be within the same diocese or not. C. 1406 #2. As to the exact time when it should be made we must see Canon 461. The law there says that the obligation must be fulfilled either before or in the act of taking possession of the parish. But is this necessary for the validity of the possession? My opinion is that it is merely demanded for the liceity. This seems to be implied in the canon which treats of penalties for those who neglect to make the profession without a just reason. There the law says, that such a person should be warned and a reasonable time given him within which it must be made. If, after this warning the pastor fails to make the profession within the specified time, the Superior may even deprive him of the parish. In the meantime the pastor is not allowed to make use of the fruits of the parish. C. 2403. Treating this canon logically one has to admit that the profession is necessary merely for the liceity of the assumption of the parish. For, if the pastor cannot take possession validly without making the profession why should that canon speak of depriving him of it. One cannot deprive another of something which he has not. Moreover, the penalty is to be used only when the pastor fails to make the profession without a just reason.

As soon as the priest takes charge or possession of the parish he becomes the pastor of that parish. C. 461. From then on the rights and duties, that fall to the portion of a pastor, according to law, are also his and he is responsible for the flock entrusted to his care.

CHAPTER IV.

General Rights and Duties.

The care of souls demands hard and constant labor on the part of the parish priest. As a shepherd, ever watchful of his flock, the pastor must be on guard against every harmful influence from within as well as from without. He must be ready to assist "his people". He is their "dux viatorum", leading them onward and upward to the home of eternal bliss. As a pilot directs his ship, so the pastor must guide his people to that longed-for heavenly port. A father, an adviser, a director and what not must he be to them. Varied is the program of his duties. Exalted indeed is his position but great also its responsibilities. Great will be his reward if faithful and true but severe the penalties if he be negligent. To him the congregation was entrusted, he must do his part to lead it on the right road. He must be willing to give all, aye, even his life, as Christ did, if that be demanded of him.

The rights and duties of the pastor are numerous and varied. He must administer the sacraments, preach, teach catechism, look to the services in the parish church, care for the temporal affairs of the parish, etc. And, moreover, he is to take a lively interest in the non-catholics living within his territory. C. 1350 #1. The fulfillment of all these functions presupposes a certain amount of knowledge, which the successful pastor is to possess. Besides this, charity and prudence must play a great part in the performance of his duties. Again he is not to seek his own glory or worldly reward but do all for the greater honor and glory of God. His life must be one of continual good example to the people. The honor and glory of God and the salvation of souls his only aim. He should, like St. Paul, become:—"Omnibus omnia, ut omnes facerem salvos," (1) and not "quaerens quod mihi utile est, sed quod multis, ut salvi fiant." (2) As Barbosa says:—"Qui ad aliorum salutem procurandam invigilant, propri-

1. 1. Cor. Chap. IX, v. 22.
2. 1. Cor. Chap. X. v. 33.

um peccatorum veniam impetrant, Dei gratiam conciliant, virtutem, meritum et gloriam sibi exaugent." (3)

We shall now proceed to treat the different rights and duties of the pastors under separate headings and it shall be my aim, as far as possible, to place all the legislation pertaining to each subject respectively under its particular division. Regard will be taken not only of those rights and duties which a parish priest has directly toward his people but also to those which flow indirectly from these. The divisions will be treated concisely, yet so that the information may not be misleading.

3. Barbosa, A. De Officio et potestate Parochi. C. III, #12, p. 42.

CHAPTER V.

Rights and Duties in Particular.

As was stated in the last chapter the rights and duties of parish priests will be treated under separate divisions, with an end to collect all the legislation, pertaining to each subject, under that respective section. The matter under consideration is the following:#1. Residence; 2. Missa pro Populo; Catechising and Preaching; 4. The Sacraments; 5. The Sacramentals; 6. Divine Worship; 7. Ecclesiastical Burial; 8. Temporal Administration.

Part I. RESIDENCE.

"Parochus obligatione tenetur residendi in domo parochiali prope suam ecclesiam". C. 465 #1. As Father Augustine remarks:—"This canon is nothing else but the embodiment of the Tridentine decrees and of the current practice, with some mitigation." (I.) This law of residence is binding upon all priests, whether removable or irremovable. The habitual pastors, however, are an exception, and in their case the vicar must observe this law. The obligation of residence is a personal one and cannot be fulfilled through another, even if the people be better served through the substitute. (2) Moreover, a mere material residence is not sufficient to satisfy this law, it must be a formal one. What is the difference? A material residence is that where the pastor actually stays in his parish house, while a formal residence is a "commoratio assidua, seu ferme continua, in ecclesia seu loco beneficii, servitii ecclesiastici personaliter praestandi causa." (3) Hence, he who merely stays within the parish and does not perform the duties incumbent upon him, fulfills the obligation in as far as the material residence is concerned but he cannot be said to reside there in the sense of the canons. The residence must be "laboriosa". When the law prescribes residence it wishes to use the term in its proper signification. C. 18. Consequently, a pastor merely staying near the parochial church would not be fulfilling

1. Augustine, C. A. Commentary on Canon Law, Vol. II, p. 546.
2. Barbosa, A. De officio et Potestate Parochi, Pars. I. Cap. VIII. p. 69.
3. Bargilliat, M. Praelectiones Juris Canonici. vol. II, p. 364.

the law. Material residence is not sufficient in the exercise of his duties.

The New Code states that the parish priest must live near the parochial church and in the rectory of that parish. However, this is not so binding as to admit of no exception. Circumstances may demand a change from the common law. Still, this change cannot be made by the pastor himself but only with the permission of the Ordinary of the diocese. The place of residence even then must be close to the church of the parish. In all cases it must be such as to enable the pastor to fulfill his obligations without detriment to the welfare of his people. Nor may the pastor live outside of the parish even with the permit of the Ordinary for the latter himself cannot dispense and allow the pastor to live so far from the parish that he be unable to exercise his duties properly and thus cause harm to the parishioners. (4)

The pastor must, consequently, live in the parish and near to the parish church. But can he never leave the parish? The law concerning this point is very well defined in the New Code. Canon 465 answers this question in the following manner:—

#1. "Parochus obligatione tenetur residendi in domo parochiali prope suam ecclesiam; loci tamen Ordinarius potest iusta de causa permittere ut alibi commoretur, dummodo domus ab ecclesia paroeciali non ita distet ut paroecialium perfunctio munerum aliquid inde detrimenti capiat."

#2. "Eidem abesse permittitur per duos ad summum intra annum menses sive continuos sive intermissos, nisi gravis causa, iudicio ipsius Ordinarii vel diuturniorem absentiam requirat vel breviorem tantum permittat."

#3. "Dies quibus parochus piis exercitiis vacat ad normam can. 126, non computantur, semel in anno, duobus vacationum mensibus, de quibus in #2."

#4. "Sive continuum sive intermissum sit vacationem tempus, cum absentia ultra hebdomadam est duratura, parochus, praeter legitimam causam, habere debet Ordinarii scriptam licentiam et vicarium substitutum suo loco relinquere ab eodem Ordinario

4. Blat, A. Commentarium Textus Codicis Iuris Canonici. Lib. II. De Personis, Pars. I. cap. IX, p. 430.

probandum; quod si parochus sit religiosus, indiget praeterea consensu Superioris et substitutus tum ab Ordinario tum a Superiore probari debet."

#5. "Si parochus repentina et gravi de causa discedere atque ultra hebdomadam cogatur abesse, quamprimum per litteras Ordinarium commonefaciat, ei indicans causam discessus et sacerdotem supplentem, eiusque stet mandatis."

#6. "Etiam pro tempore brevioris absentiae parochus debet fidelium necessitatibus providere maxime si id peculiaria rerum adiuncta postulent."

In the first place, then, every pastor has a right to two months vacation in every year, and it matters not whether he takes them at one time or during shorter periods, e. gr. two weeks at a time. But, this does not mean that each pastor can take such a vacation at any time without any regard for the Ordinary of the diocese. The law states expressly that when the Ordinary has sufficient cause he may shorten this period. The gravity of the cause is to be decided by the Ordinary alone. For the same reason the Ordinary may also prolong the vacation. This already implies that the Ordinary must be informed of one's intention and desire to leave the parish. And the law confirms this and adds that. the "written permission" of the Ordinary is necessary even when the time to be taken is shorter than two months, aye, for every period of more than one week.

Another point that must not to be overlooked is, that a pastor must provide a suitable substitute to take his place when he leaves for more than a week. The substitute must be approved by the Ordinary, and if the pastor be a religious, the substitute needs also the approval of the religious Superior. In the same way, the religious pastor must also habe the written permission of the Ordinary and religious Superior before he may leave the parish.

All permissions must be in writing. But the law also provides for such cases where this permission cannot be secured in time. In such cases the pastor, who is called away suddenly for some grave cause, must write to the Ordinary and explain the reasons for leaving, stating also the name of the vicar taking his place. The Bishop will, thereupon, give his instructions to such a pastor and these instructions must be obeyed. Consequently, if the Ordinary does not consider the reason for leaving sufficient he may recall the parish priest and the latter will be obliged to return at once.

The spiritual retreat made by the priests annually is not being counted into the two months vacation allowed to pastors.

This much about vacations or leaves of more than a week. The last part of the canon proceeds to legislate about absences of less than a week, i. e. "ad summum 7 dierum". Even in such cases, the law says, the pastor must provide for the wants of his parish. This is the more necessary when there is danger of sick calls, etc., during his absence. Still, it will not be necessary to provide a substitute, in the sense that another priest must live in that parish. The pastor may ask the neighboring priests to look after the congregation during his absence. Of course, if the circumstances are such that a neighboring priest could not or would not take care of the parish during this time, a substitute ought to be secured if possible, especially when there is danger of sick calls during that time.

The pastor who leaves for one of these short vacations needs no permission from the Ordinary unless this be demanded by the diocesan statutes. Some dioceses restrict the absence of a pastor without permission to two or three days. In such cases, then, permission will have to be secured from the legimate authority in the diocese.

Penalties against those pastors who violate the law of residence are to be found in C. 2381 as follows:—"Qui officium, beneficium, dignitatem obtinet cum onere residentiae, si illegitime absit:—1. Eo ipso privatur omnibus fructibus sui beneficii, vel officii pro rata illegitimae absentiae, eosque tradere debet Ordinario, qui ecclesiae vel aliovi pio loco vel pauperibus distribuat. 2. Officio, beneficio, dignitate privetur, ad normam can. 2168-2175." The law is very strict in this regard.

To be absent "illegitime" means to be absent without the permission required above. This legislation holds good not only in cases where the general law of the Church is transgressed but also in the violation of the particular law of the diocese. (5) By the very fact that one leaves the parish illegitimately or remains away longer than allowed the pastor is deprived of the revenues which he derives from the parish. This loss is to be measured in proportion to the length of time he is absent and to the sum which corresponds to the time he spends away illegitimately. Father Blat explains this in the following manner:—"pro rata illegitimae absentiae, scilicet: distributis fructibus annualibus vel mensualibus in dies anni vel mensis, "privatur fructibus" qui respondeant diebus quibus modo praedicto absit." (6) When the sum has been computed it is to be sent to the Ordinary and he will distribute it according to the law and his own judgement. There is no necessity of informing the pastor that this recompense must be made, for the law expressly states that, he is deprived of these fruits "ipso facto".

The second part of the canon quoted above directs us to another set of canons which treat of the procedure against clerics who violate the law of residence. In the first place the ruling directs the Ordinary to warn the negligent pastor of his duty. In the meantime, the pastor is held to pay the expenses which arise from the provisions made for the parish during his absence. The admonition sent by the Ordinary shall also include the time within which the pastor must return as well as the penalties which he is liable to incur by continuing this illegitimate absence. If necessary the Ordinary may also state that unless the pastor returns "legitimo impedimento non detentus" within a specified period of time, the parish will become vacant "ipso facto", as determined in C. 188 # 8. C. 2168. The Ordinary shall, thereupon, wait for his return or for a letter from the pastor. When the time specified in the admonition elapses and the pastor does not return nor send an explanation of his absence, the Ordinary shall investigate to ascertain whether the admonition sent by him was received and whether it could have been answered during this time. If it is evident that the pastor failed to return or answer through his own fault the Ordinary may declare the parish vacant.

5. Blat, A, O. P. opus. cit. Pars. III, p. 708.

6. Blat, A, O. P. op. cit. pars III, p. 708.

C. 2169 and 2149. If the investigation reveals that the pastor could not answer, the time for answering or returning should be extended. C. 2149 #2. If the pastor received no admonition, another letter should be sent to him and a new specified period of time given for his return. If the pastor fails to return or answer during this second period of time the Ordinary may proceed to declare the parish vacant.

If, however, the pastor returns after the first admonition, or, upon the non-reception of the first, after the second admonition, what is to be done? Is the case closed thereby? Presupposing that the absence was illegitimate he necessarily loses the fruits of the parish for that time "pro rata illegitimae absentiae". But besides this penalty, the ordinary can inflict upon him other punishments as he sees fit, according to the pastor's culpability, C. 2170.

Still another supposition is possible. The pastor may not return after the first warning but send a letter to the Ordinary, stating reasons for his departure and absence. In such cases the Ordinary is to take the reasons into consideration. In this he must be aided by two examiners. These three are to see whether the alleged reasons are sufficiently grave to excuse the pastor. In case it be thought advisable they may even start an investigation to ascertain whether the causes given are true or not. C. 2171. If after this careful consideration the reasons are found to be unsatisfactory, the Ordinary shall order the pastor back to his parish, and set a definite time within which he must return. C. 2172. If the parish priest does not return even then but sends more reasons for his absence, the following course of procedure is to be taken: —Either the pastor is removable or irremovable. If he is a removable pastor these new reasons need not be considered nor need the Ordinary give the parish priest another opportunity. He may proceed at once to the declaration of the vacancy in that parish, as soon as the time set for the return elapses. If the pastor should return after the second warning, the Ordinary may punish him with a salutary penalty according to the gravity of the offence and order him never to leave the parish again without written permission under the penalty of "ipso facto" privation of office. If the pastor however, is an irremovable parish priest and sends in reasons a second time, the Ordinary is obliged to consider them anew, as before, using the same examiners as in the first case. When these new causes are again found unsatisfactory, then, as the law states, ignoring all other arguments or reasons, the Ordinary shall order the irremovable pastor to return withing the time set in this third notification, informing him also that, unless that is done, privation of office will follow immediately and "ipso facto". Should the pastor return after this new notification and within the time prescribed, the Ordinary may punish him as above and give him the same precept of observing the law of residence hereafter. If the pastor should fail to return even after this third admonition but sends further reasons the Ordinary need not consider them and may proceed to deprive the irremovable pastor of his parish. C. 2174.

As a closing canon to this section of the Code we find the following legislation:—"Neutro in casu Ordinarius beneficium vacare declaret, nisi postquam, perpensis una cum examinatoribus discessus rationibus quas clericus forte allegaverit, eiusdem Ordinarii licentiam in scriptis ab eodem clerico peti potuisse constiterit." C. 2175. This canon is to serve as a precaution against hasty and unconsidered action on the part of the Ordinary. He must always take into consideration both the reasons produced for the departure and the possibility of securing permission before the leave. Aided by his two examiners the Ordinary must determine whether the pastor could have asked for permission had he so desired before going away from the parish, and, again, he must take into consideration the reasons sent in afterwards. The guilt of the pastor must be well established before the Ordinary proceeds to privation of office.

The law of residence is, indeed, an important one. Whoever takes it lightly and cares not how often he leaves his people nor for how long a time, should take cognizance of the penalties to which he becomes liable. Illegitimate absence deprives him of his parish revenue during that period and, consequently, he cannot make it his own without committing a sacrilege. The Ordinary will not refuse permission to leave when the causes are good and it can be granted without detriment to the welfare of the people. If the pastor is refused permission and he deems it unjust, he may have recourse to the competent superior. This recourse, of necessity, is "in devolutivo" and not "in suspensivo", i. e. he is bound to remain in the parish until the case is decided in his favor and the permission is granted. The competent authority for recourse here in the U. S. is the *Apostolic Delegate at Washington, D. C.*

Part. II. MISSA PRO POPULO

"Omnis namque pontifex ex hominibus assumptus pro hominibus constituitur in iis, quae sunt ad Deum, ut offerat dona et sacrifica pro peccatis." (1) "Iamvero si omnis pontifex pro hominibus consituitur, ut per se sacrificia offerat pro peccatis, a fortiori dicendum id venit de parochis relate ad suum gregem, pro qua speciatim constituitur in iis quae sunt ad Deum, ut offerat dona et sacrificia." (2) And again we find the following solemn words uttered by the Council of Trent:—"praecepto divino mandatum sit omnibus, qui curam animarum commissa est, — — pro his sacrificium offerre." (3) From all this it is evident that, Bishops, who have full care of souls, who are entrusted with all the ordinary means which the Church possesses for the sanctification and salvation of souls, are held by this divine law spoken of by the Council. But what about the parish priest? He has neither full care of souls nor is he entrusted with all these means, possessed by Bishops, for the sanctification and salvation of souls. Is he, then, also bound by the divine law mentioned above? The answer to this question can be found in the decision of the S. Congr. of the Council, given as a response to certain doubts which were proposed by the "Episcopus Wratislaviensis", as follows:—"Soli Episcopi iure divino absoluto tenentur ad sacrificium pro populis offerendum: . . . . Ceteri autem, qui curam animarum habent, praeter Episcopos, non habent velut proprium sibique inhaerens pastoris officium ex divino iure, sed illud exer-

1. I. Hebr. Ch. V. v. I.

2. S. Congr. Concilii, 14 Dec. 1872 apud. Thesaur. Resol. S. C. C. vol. 131, p. 559.

3. Conc. Trid. Canones et Decr. ses. XXIII. c. I. de ref. p. 153.

cent ex ecclesiastica delegatione et institutione, intra quosdam limites. Quamobrem quum de his, parochis ceterisque, dicitur incumbere illis onus ex divino praecepto applicandi Missam pro Populo, intelligendum est de iure divino, non absoluto sed hypothetico." (4) Our pastors are not of divine but merely of ecclesiastical institution and for that reason possess only that authority and exercise merely those functions which the Church assigns to them. The Church has given priests the cure of souls in the internal forum and also declared that they must apply Mass for the people. "In this way" as Father Slàter, S. J. says; they come hypothetically under the divine law which commands all who have the care of souls to offer sacrifice for their flocks." (5) Without taking up the fact of the pastor's jurisdiction, this point remains certain, that the Church has given parish priests the cure of souls to a certain extent and has ordered them to apply the Holy Sacrifice for them on certain days. In this way the pastors come under the divine law in a certain sense.

That pastors are bound to apply the Mass pro populo cannot be doubted. The New Code expresses this duty in the following manner:—"Applicandae Missa pro populo obligationis tenetur parochus ad norman canonis 339." C. 466 #1. From this it is clear that each and every pastor, be he removable or irremovable, must say Mass for the people at certain times. The obligation imposed upon him is: I. special; 2. real; 3. temporal; 4. personal; and 5. local.

1. The obligation of saying Mass for the people is a special obligation. By this is meant that the obligation is his "not in virtue of orders or of benefice or of revenues, but of the pastoral office and of the quasi-contract in justice made by the pastor when assuming the cura animarum." (6) The following consideration will bear this out. A pastor may have a parish which is not a benefice and, still, he is bound to offer up the Holy Sacrifice for his people. That this obligation does not flow from orders received by the priest is evident from the fact that other

4. S. Congr. Conc. 13 Julii 1918, apud Acta. A. Sedis vol. IX, Feb. 1, 1919.

5. Slater, Thos. S. J. apud. Amer. Eccl. Review vol. 62, p. 635.

6. Kaiser, Alb. C. PP. S. apud Amer. Eccl. Review. vol. LXI. p. 364.

priests, possessed of the same Holy Orders, are not held by this obligation. Finally, it is not a duty arising from the revenues of the parish, since the Code expressly states that, it must be fulfilled "omni exiguitate reditum . . . remota." C. 339 #1. As Ferraris tells us:—"Parochus non ratione sustentationis, sed ratione officii tenetur sacrificium pro populo applicare." (7) The Sacred Congregation of the Council expressed itself in this maner:—"Una est SS. Congregationum Romanorum et Doctorum sententia, obligationis Missam pro populo applicandi causam sitam esse omnino in pastorali officio." (8)

2. The Obligation of applying Mass for the people is a real obligation. By this is meant that whenever the pastor is unable to apply it himself he must have it said and applied for the people by ancther. (9) It is not a duty that passes when the day, on which it is supposed to be said, elapses. And the Masses omitted must always be supplied unless a condonation had been received from the Holy See. This has ever been the teaching of canonists and this is the legislation today:—"qui obligationi de qua in superioribus paragraphis non satisfecerit, quam citius pro populo tot applicet Missas, quot omisit." C, 339 #6. The obligation is one of justice and cannot be omitted without incuring the responsibility of making restitution either by saying the Mass later or having it said by some one else as soon as possible. Moreover, it is not left to the pastor to choose when he will supply it. St. Alphonse teaches that a postponement of two months would constitute grave matter. Other theologians also hold that theory. The saying of this Mass is just as important as any Mass for which a stipend had been received and with these latter a postponement of two months is considered "materia gravis". (10) No custom is able to excuse from this real obligation. For, when the question was put before the S. Congr. of the Council, whether any custom, which would excuse a pastor from applying this

7. Ferraris, L. Bibliotheca canonica, etc. vol. V. verbo Missa, p. 757.

8. S. Congr. Concilii, 13 Julii, 1918, apud. A. A. Sedis, Feb. 1919.

9. Noldin, H. S. J. Summa Theol. Mor. juxta Cod. Jur. Can. lib. 3. p. 210.

10. Sabetti-Barrett, Comp. Theol. Mor. p. 61. Noldin, H. op. cit. p. 219. Lehmkul, Theol. Mor. vol. 2. p. 145.

Mass for the people on Sundays and other prescribed days, could become a legitimate custom, the S. Congregation answered:—"Negative." (11)

3. The obligation of applying the Missa pro populo is of a temporal nature, in the sense that it must be applied on certain days. The New Code tells us on what days this is to be done:—"Omnibus dominicis aliisque festis diebus de praecepto, etaim suppressis." C. 339 #1. Consequently, the pastor must follow these instructions. The law is very definite now, and all those bound by it can easily find out the days specified for the fulfillment of this duty.

This was not the case at all times. After the Council of Trent there arose various opinions as to exactly how often this obligation binds. Some held, that those pastors who received large (pingues) revenues, must offer Holy Mass for their people every day, while those parish priests, who received small (tenues) revenues, need say it only on the feast days. Thus, the obligation, from its temporal aspect, was made to depend entirely upon the quantity of the revenues of the pastors. This caused much confusion. What was to be considered a large revenue? Theologians differed in the explanation of this term and consequently, abuses gradually crept in. Some theologians again held that it sufficed to apply this Mass whenever the people were obliged to attend Mass and, on other days, only according to the custom upheld in the various regions. This again caused divergence according to the different places, especially after the suppression of some of the feasts began. Still other theologians held that the number of days on which this obligation is to be fulfilled was to be left to the judgment of prudent men. But even prudent men differed. Finally, some went so far as to declare that the pastor was not obliged to apply the special fruits of the Mass for the people at all, but that it would be sufficient to offer up the general fruits for all the people and especially for those present. According to this opinion the pastor could then take a stipend for each of these Masses and apply the special fruit of that Mass for the intention desired. Pope Benedict XIV. took notice

11. S. Congr. Concilii. Mechlinensi, 25 Sept. 1847.

of this state of affairs and of the variety of opinions held the world over and he saw the abuses creeping in. Consequently, he thought it necessary to issue an Encyclical in order to correct the prevailing abuses and set up one standard for all. "Quapropter non modo opportunum," he says, "verum etiam necessarium duximus encyclicam hanc epistolam ad vos scribere, per quam sublata demum diversarum, in quas scriptores abierunt, opinionum varietate." (12) For this reason the encyclical "Cum Semper" points out the days when the obligation of applying the Mass for the people must be fulfilled. Among other things he says: "Idcirco opportunum censemus fraternitatibus vestris declarare, Nobis abunde satisfactum fore, vobisque proinde satis esse posse, dum ii qui animarum curam exercent, sacrificium Missae pro populo celebrant, atque applicent in Dominicis, aliisque per annum diebus festis de praecepto, cum praedicti Dominici aliique festi dies ii sunt in quibus juxta praeceptum conc. Tridentini, ses. V. cap. 2, et sess. XXIV, cap. 4, quilibet animarum curae praepositus 'populum sibi commissum salutaribus verbis pascere debet, docendo ea quæ scire omnibus necessarium est ad salutem"; (12) The Pontiff then proceeds to state that, in many places some of the feasts have been suppressed and, on that account, are no more days on which the people have to attend Mass. On this account there are doubts as to when the Missa pro populo must be said. Thereupon he says:—"statuimus et declaramus quod etiam iisdem festis diebus, quibus populus Missae interesse debet et servilibus operibus vacare potest, omnes animarum cura gerentes missam pro populo celebrare et applicare teneantur." (13) Thus Benedict XIV. foreshadowed the rule about suppressed feasts. In fact, this decision tells us, as the New Code does today, that the Missa pro populo must be said also on those days when the people are no more bound to attend Mass or abstain from servile work. The New Code practically repeats the words of that celebrated constitution "Cum Semper".

It may be of practical value to enumerate these days. When

12. Bened. XIV. "Cum Semper" loc. cit. p. 742.

12. Benedict XIV. const. "Cum Semper" 19 Aug. 1744 apud Ferraris vol. V. p. 742.

13. Bened. XIV. "Cum Semper" loc. cit. #7.

the question was asked of the "Pontifical Commission for the Authentic Interpretation of the New Code" as to what was meant by the "suppressed feasts" in canon 339, the answer came:—"nihil hac in re per Codicem iuris canonici immutatum esse a disciplina huc usque vigente." (14). This did not seem sufficiently clear for some Bishops and so they sent a petition to the S. Congr. of the Council asking it to repeat authoritatively the suppressed feasts. An answer came on the 28th of Dec. 1919 as follows:—"Feriae II et III post Dominicam Resurrectionis D.N.I.C. et Pentecostes; Dies Inventionis S. Crucis; Dies Purificationis B. M. Virginis; Dies Annunciationis B. M. Virginis; Dies Nativ. B. M. Virginis; Dies Dedicationis S. Michaelis Archangeli; Dies Nativitatis S. Joannis Baptistae; Dies SS. Apostolorum Andreae, Jacobi, Ioannis, Thomae, Phillippi et Jacobi, Bartholomaei, Matthaei, Simonis et Judae, Mathiae; Dies S. Stephani Protomartyris; Dies SS. Innocentium; Dies S. Laurentii Martyris; Dies S. Sylvestri, Papae; Dies S. Annae, Matris B.M.V.; Dies Patroni Regni; Dies S. Patroni Loci." (15) These then are the suppressed feasts. The feasts of obligation are enumerated in canon 1247 as follows: "Dies festi sub praecepto in universa Ecclesia sunt tantum:—Omnes et singuli dies dominici, festa Nativitatis, Circumcisionis, Epiphaniae, Ascensionis et Sanctissimi Corporis Christi, Immaculatae Conceptionis at Assumptionis Almae Genitricis Dei Mariae, Sancti Ioseph eius sponsi, Beatorum Petri et Pauli Apostolorum, Omnium denique Sanctorum." Here in the U. S. only the Sundays and six of the feasts are of obligation. But this does not make any difference as far as the obligation of applying the Mass for the people is concerned. If in any part of the Church certain of these days are not of obligation, the Bishops and pastors are nevertheless under the obligation of applying the Holy Sacrifice for their people on those days. (16) Considering all these things, the following is a complete list of the days on which the Missa pro populo must be said:

---

14. Feb. 17, 1918. apud Acta Apost. Sedis, vol. 58, p. 170.

15. C. Concilii, Dec. 28, 1919, vol. XII. Feb. 2, 1920 p. 43 in Acta Apost. Sedis.

16. Slater, Thos. S. J. in Amer. Eccl. Review. vol. LXII, p. 638.

1. All Sundays of the year...............
2. Circumcision of Our Lord J. C. ....Jan. 1
3. Epiphany ....Jan. 6
4. Purification of the B. V. M..............Feb. 2
5. St. Matthias, Apostle.....................Feb. 24
6. St. Joseph................................Mar. 19
7. Annunciation of the B. V. Mary...........Mar. 25
8. Easter Monday and Tuesday..........
9. St. Phillip and James.....................May 1
10. Finding of the Cross.....................May 3
11. Ascension of Our Lord...............
12. Pentecost Monday and Tuesday.......
13. Corpus Christi.......................
14. Nativity of St. John the Baptist............June 24
15. St. Peter and Paul, Apostles...............June 29
16. St. James, Apostle........................July 25
17. St. Anne, Mother of B.V.M................July 26
18. St. Lawrence, Martyr......................Aug. 10
19. Assumption of the B. V. Mary.............Aug. 15
20. St. Bartholomew, Apostle..................Aug. 24
21. Nativity of B. V. Mary....................Sept. 8
22. St. Matthew, Apostle......................Sept. 21
23. Dedication of St. Michael, Archangel.......Sept. 29
24. St. Simon and Jude, Apostles..............Oct. 28
25. All Saints.................................Nov. 1
26. St. Andrew, Apostle.......................Nov. 30
27. Immaculate Conception of the B.V. Mary.....Dec. 8
28. St. Thomas, Apostle.......................Dec. 21
29. Nativity of Our Lord......................Dec. 25
30. St. Stephen, Protomartyr..................Dec. 26
31. St. John, Apostle and Evangelist...........Dec. 27
32. Holy Innocents............................Dec. 28
33. St. Sylvester, Pope........................Dec. 31
34. Patron Feast of the Country or Kingdom
35. Patron Feast of the Place.............

In the United States the patron feast of the country is that of the Immaculate Conception of the Blessed Virgin Mary.

On these days and only on these is the pastor obliged to say the Mass for the people. To transfer the obligation to another day the permission of the Ordinary is necessary, which may be given by him for any just cause. C. 466 #4. This is a change from the old law. Formerly, according to the constitution "Cum Semper" of Pope Benedict XIV., the Ordinaries had the faculty of allowing such a transfer for one cause only, to wit:—"Quia vero propria nonnunquam experientia satis agnovimus aliquos esse parochos adeo pauperes, ut ferme ex eleemosynis, quas a fidelibus pro Missarum celebratione accipiunt, vivere coguntur; eos vero, qui ecclesia parochiali vacante, ad animarum curam exercendam sub vicarii seu oeconomi minime deputantur, aliquibus in locis adeo illiberaliter tractari, ut exigui redditus ipsis constituti, et pauca incerta emolumenta eisdem obvenientia aegre ad eorum vitae necessaria sufficiant; quod iis quoque non raro evenire solet, qui in aliquibus ecclesiis, habituali cura apud alios manente, actuali tantum exercitio addicti; proinde cum istis severe nimis agi videtur si in diebus festis, quibus potissimum hujusmodi occasio se offert, eisdem vetitum esset eleemosynam pro applicatione Missae recipere. Idcirco, Nos, tam istorum quam illorum inopiam summopere miserantes, eisdem quantum Nobis integrum est consulere volentes; quamvis, ut supra dictum est, omnes et singuli praedicti teneantur diebus festis missam pro populo celebrare et applicare; attamen, quod pertinet ad praedictos parochos egentes, unicuique vestrum facultatem concedimus, cum iis, quos revera tales esse noveritis, opportune dispensandi, ad hoc ut, etiam diebus festis hujusmodi eleemosynam ab aliquo pio offerente recipere, et pro ipso sacrificum applicare, quatenus id ab eo requiratur, libere et licite possint et valeant; dummodo ad necessarium populi commoditatem in ipsa parochiali celebrent, ea tamen adjecta conditione, ut tot missas infra hebdomadam pro populo applicant, quot in diebus festis infra eamdem hebdomadam occurentibus, juxta peculiarem intentionem alterius benefactoris obtulerint." (17) From this we see that poverty was the only cause on account of which a pastor could be excused from that obligation by the Ordinary. Today the New Code simply states

17. Benedict XIV. Const. "Cum Seper l. c. p. 742.

that it may be done for any just cause. Doctor Kinane, commenting on this phrase in the new law, says:—"Hitherto the Ordinary could permit this transference of the obligation only in one particular case, viz. when a parish priest who was very poor received a large stipend for the application of a Mass on a Sunday or Holyday. Now he can do so not only in this case, but also whenever any reasonable cause for this transference exists, as for example, when an exsequial Mass occurs on a suppressed feast." (18) The sufficiency of the cause is left to the judgment of the Ordinary. In practice there will be no difficulty, for in case the reason is doubtful, the Ordinary may give the dispensation or permission for the transference without further ado.

Another point that must be borne in mind in connection with the days on which this obligation is to be fulfilled, is that contained in canon 339, #2-#3. There we are told that, if the feast day on which the Missa pro populo is to be said, falls on a Sunday, the parish priest fulfills the obligation of both days by saying and applying one Mass for the people although he binates. Moreover, when a feast day is transferred to some other day but the obligation of hearing Mass and of abstaining from servile work is also transferred, then the Missa pro populo is not to be said on the feast day itself, but on the day to which the feast was transferred. Otherwise the Mass is to be said on the feast day itself, even if the Mass and the office be transferred to some other day. This, of course, will be of practical value only in so far as it regards the feasts of obligation on which the people are bound to abstain from work and must hear Mass. Accordingly, this part of the canon will apply to merely six days here in the U. S.

4. The obligation of applying the Missa pro Populo is a personal obligation, i. e. the pastor himself must celebrate the Mass and cannot have it said by another. The general rule, as laid down in the New Code, reads as follows:—1. The pastor is to apply the Mass "per se"; 2. when he is legitimately impeded he must have it applied by another; 3. when he cannot say it himself or have it applied by another on that day,

18. Kinane, J., J. C. D. apud Irish Eccl. Record. June 1919, p. 476.

he may transfer it to the following day if it can be said then. The gradation as can be noticed, stresses the personal obligation of the pastor. Only when he is legitimately hindered from applying it himself may he have another say it for him. What is to be meant by a "legitimate impediment" here? Are we to interpret this term according to the old law? It seems there is no other way possible. The term is of frequent occurence in the old law in connection with this point, and so it would seem but natural that the legislators meant to use it in the same signification as it had there. This is the more true since no further explanation has been given it in the new law itself. Father Noldin upholds this view in his "Summa Theologiae Moralis iuxta Codicem Iuris Canonici" when he follows the old interpretation in the explanation of this phrase. (19) According to this then the excuse sufficient to permit a priest to have someone else apply the Mass for the people must be quite grave. Such, according to Noldin would be — "infirmitas, obligatio celebrandi Missam conventualem, si parochus sit canonicus, vel aliud, quod prudenti iudicio vere grave existimetur. Causa gravia, quae parochum ab hac obligatione excusat, ex declaratione S. C. Concilii non est:—a) consuetudo contraria; b) exsequiae celebrandae; c) Missa pro sponsis dicenda; d) Missa pro certa die fundata, quae incidit in diem festum de praecepto; e) persuasio fidelium, qui putant missam parochialem semper pro se-ipsis applicari et ideo libenter ad eam audiendam confluunt." (20) From this it follows that a pastor cannot say the "Missa pro sponsis" or "pro defuncto, etiam praesente cadavere", on any of the days when the Holy Mass should be applied for the people. He must say the Mass for the people and have some other priest say the other Mass when necessary. In such cases it would be well for the pastor to apply to the Ordinary for permission to transfer the Missa pro populo to some other day so as to be able to say the Mass for the deceased or for the wedding couple. This would be sufficient cause for the transfer. (21)

5. Finally, the obligation of applying Mass for the people is a local one, i. e. the Mass should be offered in the parish church.

---

19. Noldin, H. l. c. vol. III. p. 211. 20. ibidem. 21. Kinane, l. c. p. 476.

The New Code says of this:—"Parochus Missam pro populo applicandam celebrat in ecclesia paroeciali, nisi rerum adjuncta alibi celebrandam exigant aut suadeant." C. 466 # 4. This ruling is not so strict as not to allow an exception whenever a reasonable cause intervenes. The gravity of the cause is left to the judgement of the pastor himself. Father Blat gives the following reasons as sufficient: "propter maiorem populi frequentiam in casu extraordinariae festivitatis, propter primam puerorum communionem in alique sanctuario paroeciae." (22) "The use of a winter chapel or school house, the repairing of the parish church, personal infirmity, the convenience of the people, etc." are causes sufficient according to Augustine. (23) An exception to the rule is also that of a vacation or any other leave of the parish priest. In that case the Mass may be applied in the place where he finds himself on such days, or it may be applied by the priest taking his place in the parish. C. 466 #5. This was the teaching also in the old law. (24)

The principal thing to be kept in mind by every pastor is this, that the application of the Mass is of grave obligation. It does not bind gravely on each particular occasion in regard to time, person or place. (25) For a grave sin frequent violations of the temporal, local and personal aspects of this duty are required. But the non-application of even one of these Masses is a grave fault. (26). Of course, all this is true when there is no aggravating circumstance which might make it grave, on a certain occasion, even when only the temporal, personal or local aspects are considered.

For whom is this Mass to be applied? For the parishioners only. Does this include the dead of the parish or is it to be restricted to the living members alone? The living are to be the only recipients of the fruits of this Mass and its application is not to be extended to the dead except under the condition "quatenus nempe sine praejudicio vivorum id fieri potest," because the

---

22. Blat, Alb. Comm. Textus Codicis. Iur. Can.' 2, p. 434.

23. Augustine l. c. vol. II. p. 551. 24. S. Congr. Concilii, 14 Dec. 1872.

25. Noldin, l. c. p 210; Lehmkuhl. Theol. Moralis, vol. II. p. 142; Kinane, H. l. c. June, 1919, p. 476.

26. Noldin, l. c. p. 210.

living members alone have the right to the whole fruits of the Mass. (27).

The Missa pro populo need not be a high Mass. The law simply states that a *"Mass"* is to be applied and does not make any distinction between a low and a high Mass. Consequently, a low Mass will suffice to fulfill the obligation as long as it is applied for the right intention.

The Missa pro populo must be applied in the same manner as a stipend Mass, i. e. "ex justitia". On this account no other stipend may be taken on such days even though the pastor binates. This is the general teaching of theologians and canonists. There is but one exception to this rule and that is Christmas Day when, saying three Masses, the pastor may take a stipend for each of the other two. C. 824 #2. The only sum of money allowed the pastor on the other days for the second Mass is some retribution "ex titulo extrinseco". A donation for the trouble in getting to the place would be such a compensation, i. e. it is not a stipend for the Mass but a sum not intrinsically connected with the Mass, one which does not oblige the pastor *"ex justitia"* to apply this Mass for any certain intention. (28) The second Mass may, however, be said for any intention as long as no stipend is taken for it.

Another point to be considered here is that referring to the kind of Mass that is to be said on the prescribed days. According to decision of the S. Congr. of Rites (on July the 8th, 1910 and on May the 27th, 1911), the Missa pro populo must, in churches having but one Mass on these days, be the Mass of the day. This holds good also on those Sundays to which some feast has been transferred "ex peculiaribus indultis". One could not, therefore, say the Mass of the feast on that Sunday, but must say the Mass of the Sunday. (30) Moreover, speaking of certain dioceses, where the priests were allowed to take a stipend for the second Mass as long as they sent it in to the diocesan treasury, the question was raised "utrum in ecclesiis paroecialibus, ubi unus

27. Noldin, l. c. p. 209.

28. Augustine, l. c. vol. II. p. 552.

29. S. Congr. Rituum. July 8, 1910. apud Acta Apost. Sedis. vol. II. May, 27, 1911, l. c. vol. III. p. 282-283.

tantum est sacerdos, dictis diebus, enunciata Missa necessario sit celebranda de die currente; an possit esse cum cantu de requie in die et pro die obitus sive depositionis, physice vel moraliter praesente cadavere"? The answer came back "Ad primam partem affirmative; negative ad secundam partem", i. e. the Mass must be of the day and not a requiem Mass even when the body is physically present.

How many Masses must be said by the pastor who has charge of two or more parishes, or when being pastor of one parish he is at the same time the administrator of another? One Mass offered for all the people of all the parishes in charge is sufficient. C. 466 #2.

The obligation of applying this Mass for the people starts as soon as the pastor takes possession of the parish. C. 339 #1. The manner of installation has been referred to in the preceding pages and follows the order of either the particular law or of legitimate custom, unless the Ordinary dispenses from all these rites, in which case the dispensation takes the place of the formal installation into the parish. C. 1444. Our manner is the latter.

Part III. THE PASTOR AS TEACHER.

Sect. 1. Catechising.

Among the many present-day dangers to Catholic education we find the indifference of parents one of the greatest. The parents hold a place of honor in the education of their child and also an obligation which they cannot shirk. C. 1113. To their exclusive care the child is left in its tenderest years. But when the child grows up and is ready for further instruction the parents must see to it that this be secured if they themselves are unable to give it. This is the case with most parents. They have neither time nor ability to give the child the necessary training in matters of the Catholic religion. At this point they must make a choice of another teacher and, sad to say, many make a choice of the non-catholic schools. The result very frequently is, that the child, being brought up amidst such surroundings, gradually forgets the church, to frequent the sacraments, etc., in short, falls away from little that he learned at home and before long ceases to go to the Catholic Church. Having no solid foundation on which to rely, he is easily led to believe various lies about his religion, his views are contorted and he follows the steps of those around him. How important then, is the proper religious instruction of our Catholic youth! But where is the Catholic child to secure this necessary instruction if the parents cannot give it?

The Good Mother, the Church, cares for all such matters and consequently, is ready to offer the child, which hungers, bread and not a stone. It has ordered certain of its members to supply this spiritual food to the young as well as to the old. Thus we read in the Council of Trent: —"Dominicis et aliis festis diebus pueros in singulis parochiis fidei rudimenta et obedientiam erga Deum et parentes diligenter ab iis, ad quos spectabit, doceri curabunt." (1).

But who are these "ad quos spectabit"? There are many who fall under this class, and it is not of practical value to enumerate them all. But among them we find those who are called pastors. Thus the New Code tells us:—"Debet parochus — — — — — — maximam curam adhibere in catholica puerorum institutione." C. 467, and again: "Proprium ac gravissimum officium, pastorum praesertim animarum, est catechicam populi christiani institutionem curare." C. 1329. There can be no doubt about this. If the pastor is to take care of the people, he must necessarily take good care of the youth of the parish. They are the future of the parish,—of the Church. If the children are left without religious training, the pastor is omitting one of the most important duties. But we cannot expect that each and every pastor will be able to take care of all the religious instruction himself. For this reason the common law expressly states:—"Parochus in religiosa puerorum institutione potest, imo, si legitime sit impeditus, debet operam adhibere clericorum, in paroeciae territorio degentium aut etiam, si necesse sit, piorum laicorum, potissimum illorum qui in pium sodalitium doctrinae christianae aliudve simile in parochia erectum adscripti sint." C. 1333 #1. Consequently, if the parish priest has an assistant, he also is to take up a part of the training in this regard according to the wishes of the pas-

1. Concilii Tridentini Acta et Decreta sess. XXIV, c. 4. de ref.

tor. The pastor has the right to demand this from his helpers. The Bishop may even go so far as to punish an assistant, who, without sufficient cause, would refuse to assist the pastor in the fulfillment of this obligation. C. 1333 #2. The same may be said of other clerics living within the parish and belonging thereto. When there are no clerics to help the pastor and the parish is unable to do all himself, he may call in members of the laity to help him. For this reason it is well to have in every parish that society called the society of Christian Doctrine.

The best medium through which Catholic doctrine can be imparted to the little ones is the Catholic school. It is the desire of the Church that such schools be erected wherever possible. C. 1379. The Third Council of Baltimore contained a like order for the pastors to erect parochial schools if possible:—"Quibus omnibus bene perpensis statuimus et decernimus:—I. Prope unam quamque ecclesiam ubi nondum existit, scholam parochialem intra duos annos a promulgatione hujus Concilii erigendam et in perpetum sustentandam esse, nisi Episcopus ob graviores difficultates dilationem consedendam judicet." (3). And certainly, a Catholic school is of the greatest importance even in such parishes as have a sufficient number of the clergy to attend to all the religious instruction of the Catholic children.

"Ten thousand, four hundred and sixty churches with resident pastors in the United States, and only five thousand, seven hundred and eighty-eight parochial schools. (1919). Allowing for the churches that are prevented by circumstances from having schools, the appaling fact still remains that there are very, very many parishes in which, without sufficient reason, the education of the young is left to the state. I have heard it time and again from the lips of priests, "I do not believe in parochial schools," or "we get along just as well without them." But the pastor who glories in the magnificence of his church building, who boastfully shows you about the well-appointed rooms of his rectory — — — should bow his head in shame if he cannot lead you through the class-rooms of a well-equipped parochial school." (4). The parish

3. Concilii Plenarii Baltimorensis III Acta et Decreta. #199 p. 104.

4. Schmidt, G. The American Priest, Chapt. VI. p. 44-45.

school should not be looked upon as a place to work in but as a force to work with. It means much time and labor for the pastor, but this is what the parish priest is there for. Moreover, it is one of the strongest bulwarks, which the Church has for its perpetuation and a hold on the future parish. Sunday schools cannot supplant the regular Catholic school. They may be of practical value when there is no other means at hand, but they are not able to give the child the complete training that is received in a good Catholic school and which is so necessary in order to enable the child to defend the Church, in later years, against the unjust attacks of Her opponents and to repel the influences bearing upon him in an attempt to rob him of his God and his religion. Surely the words of the III. Council of Baltimore are as true today as they were at the time when they were uttered:—"Si nullo umquam tempore, certo hac nostra aetate Ecclesia Dei et spiritus saeculi de educatione juventutis mirando quodam et acerrimo conflixere duello. Homines enim spiritu mundano penitus imbuti, jam multis ab annis, nullium non movent lapidem, ut Ecclesiae quod ipsa a Christo accepit (Math. XXVIII.—19: Marc. X.—14.) Catholicam juventutem docendi munus eripiant, et in manus societatis civilis tradant gubernii saecularis potestati." (5.) This is one of the many reasons why each and every pastor should strive, might and main, to have in his parish, if possible, a parochial school. We, here in America, can rightfully boast of our Catholic schools, but let us make their number greater as time goes on.

But what will the parochial school be, if the pastor rests satisfied with putting up a nice, large building and then cares no more about it? It will not produce the fruit of which it is capable unless the guiding spirit of the parish priest pervades its very walls. The good, hard-working sisters will, as a rule, do their part, but they will be working under a handicap if the pastor does not cooperate and labor with them. He must be the father of the school. His influence must be of aid both to teachers and to pupils. Only through the cooperation of all these three can full results be expected.

---

5. Conc. Plen. Balt. III. Acta et Decr. p. 99 #194.

In the first place it should be the parish priest's aim to see that all that pertains to the teaching of the catechism and sacred history be handled by himself. This ought not be left to the nuns or lay teachers, altogether. They may be allowed to see to parts of this instruction, if necessary, but otherwise it ought to be the boast of the pastor that he himself instructs the little ones in these subjects. The Council of Trent ordered the parish priest to impart this instruction himself and Pope Leo XIII., in his encyclical letter "Acerbo nimis" of April 15, 1905, says that:—"All parish priests, and in general all those entrusted with the care of souls, shall on every Sunday and feast day throughout the year, without exception, give the boys and girls an hour's instruction from the catechism on those things which every one must believe in order to be saved." Thereupon the Pontiff adds other particular instructions in this regard. The New Code introduces some mitigations as compared with this encyclical letter of the Holy Father. The New Law is as follows:—After stating that it pertains to the pastor, as a grave duty, to instruct the people in their religion, the law goes into detail in connection with the instruction of the young:—"Debet parochus:—1. Statis temporibus continenti per plures dies institutione, pueros ad sacramenta poenitentiae et confirmationis rite suscipienda singulis annis praeparare; 2. Peculiare omnino studio, praesertim, si nihil obsit, Quadragesimae tempore, pueros sic instituere ut sancte Sancta primum de altari libent." C. 1330. "Praeter puerorum institutionem de qua in can. 1330, parochus non omittat pueros, qui primam communionem recenter receperint, uberius ac perfectius catechismo excolere." C. 1331. Consequently, the new law does not demand the full hour's instruction on every Sunday and Holyday as was the case under former legislation. But what is stated in the New Code is certainly the minimum that can be demanded from the parish priest. As the Council of Baltimore says:—"Scholas suas sicut pupillas oculorum suorum diligant, eas frequenter, unamquamque partem earum semel saltem in hebdomada invisant et inspiciant, puerorum moribus invigilent, zelum eorum congruis mediis stimulent. Catechismum et historiam sacram ipsi per se doceant, aut certe ut a magistris sodalibus congregationum rite doceatur, efficiant." (6) From all this we can see that it is the desire of the Church that her pastors impart religious instruction to the young through their own efforts, if this can be done.

But the religious instruction of the children is not the only duty resting upon the pastor in reference to his parochial school. He must take an active interest in everything that pertains to that institution. Only through the cooperation of the pastor and teachers will the school produce the results so badly needed. Here again we may quote the words of the Council of Baltimore, wherein the parish priest is instructed as follows: "Ceteris studiis autem attentos oculos advertant, examinationibus publicis semel vel etiam bis in anno scholas notitiae fidelium subjiciant ac favori commendent. Operam dent ut in scholis adhibeantur semper libri a Catholicis scriptoribus concinnati. Sanctis motivis ducti haec omnis curent." (7.) Although the times have changed since these words were first uttered, we cannot deny that the pastor is to take an active part in the many tasks besides the teaching of the catechism. Although a new system of school administration and management has come into practice in many of our dioceses, none deny the pastor the right of inspecting the school for himself and of examining the children as before. Moreover, he has the right to be notified by the Superintendent of the schools, whenever such makes a call upon his parish school.

The pastor can make or unmake a school. "It is generally conceeded," says a resolution passed by the Catholic Educational Association, "that the most vital factor in the developement of the parish school is the priest, and as the growth of the Church in this country depends primarily on the success of the christian education, it is recommended that each pastor be urged to do his utmost in the matter of visitation, examination and sympathetic encouragement of the institutions under his care." (8.) The pastor must, therefore, bear the right attitude toward the school, the teachers and the pupils.

6. Conc. Plen. Balt. IIII. Acta et Decreta p. 105. #201.

7. Conc. Plen. Balt. III. p. 106 #201.

8. Catholic Ass. Bulletin XIII. No. 1. p. 221.

A few words may be said here of the relations between the pastor and the sisters teaching in his parish schools. Fundamentally, the attitude must be one of respect. We Americans acknowledge that every woman has a right to our reverence. How much more is this true of our teaching Sisters. As the Sacerdos writes in the American Eccl. Review:—"They are the chosen souls of the Most High, the spouses of Christ, the King; they have left all that is dear to the human heart to follow the call of the Heavenly Bridegroom. They have bound themselves by the strongest ties to a special union with Christ, and Him they are following in the godly work of leading the little ones to their Master. The zeal and the fervor with which they are striving after perfection and the fervor with which they are performing their arduous duties, may well compel the admiration of us priests and make us blush for our shortcomings. Ah! these wonderful nuns! the glorious vivandieres in the march of the army of Christ! No stars bedeck them, nor crosses; no pet sings of them; no trumpets blare round their rough and toilsome march and struggle; but some day the bede-roll will be called, and the King's right hand will pin on their breasts the cross of His Legion of Honor." (9.) Complying with this reverential attitude the pastor will always try to cooperate and help the teachers wherever possible. He will refrain from too much interference in their work, he will aid them and encourage them in all their labours. He will be solicitous not only for their bodily welfare but more so for their spiritual needs. It ought not be too much for any priest to rise somewhat earlier in the morning so that his teachers could get the opportunity of receiving Our Lord and still be able to take a bite to eat before the daily grind in the school-rooms begins. Even if this causes the pastor a little discomfort, he will see results growing in many different ways.

But what is the pastor to do if he is unable to have a parish school? In cases of this kind the parish is certainly at a disadvantage. The pastor will have to look for other means and ways of imparting religious instruction to the young. In most places the parish priest of such a parish conducts what is called

9. Amer. Eccl. Review. vol. 57. p. 13.

the "Sunday school". In this manner the children of the congregation are brought together, as often as the conditions of time and place allow, on certain days and catechism is taught them. It is not as efficient a system as the Catholic schools provide, but one must make the best of what is possible. No definite rules can be given as to how often these classes are to be conducted. This must be left to the pastor, who, knowing the circumstances of the place, can best select the time suited to most of the pupils. But he must instruct them at least as often as canons 1330-1331 order i. e. before their first confession and communion, after the reception of the first communion and again before they receive confirmation.

This much about the instruction of the young. But catechetical instruction is not to be restricted to them alone. It is but very little that a child can learn and comprehend during the short years of his parochial school life, and less in the Sunday school. The child's mind is not fully developed and many of the truths are but hazy notions in his mind. Besides, much of what was learned is soon forgotten. Consequently, if no further training follows, the child, when grown up into manhood, will have an insufficient idea of most of the things that were not already forgotten. Frequent repetition and more thorough explanations are necessary. How is this to be done? The pastor cannot expect the older people to come to school for these instructions. The New Code tells him how this may be done. "Diebus Dominicis aliisque festis de praecepto, ea hora quae suo iudicio magis apta sit ad populi frequentiam, debet insuper parochus catechismum fidelibus adultis, sermone ad eorum captum accomodato, explicare." C. 1312. In some places these instructions take place immediately before the regular sermon, in others during one of the Masses instead of the regular sermon. The Ordinary of the place has the right of determining, if he so chooses, anything that pertains to this duty and then all are bound to follow his instructions. The religious pastors are not exempt from such orders. C. 1336.

Nothing need be said here about the religious instruction that must be given to converts. The pastor will not fail to do all in his power to clear up the difficulties of the stray sheep and to teach them the truths of our religion. This is one of the most important offices of the parish priest and it should not be shirked. That pastor has a right to be proud, who can truthfully say, that he was the instrument of bringing others into the true fold of Jesus Christ.

Sect. 2. Preaching.

The pastor's duty in connection with the preaching of the word of God is expressly stated in canon 1344:—"Diebus dominicis ceterisque per annum festis de praecepto proprium cuiusque parochi officium est, consueta homilia, praesertim intra Missam in qua maior soleat esse populi frequentia, verbum Dei populo nuntiare." This is not a new law. The Fathers of the Council of Trent stated this obligation in very much the same words. (sec. V. c. 2.) And it stands to reason, that those, who are to care for souls, should teach them the truths of their religion. If they are to lead the congregation to the desired goal, they should announce to them all that is necessary or simply useful toward this end. This duty of preaching is not one that flows merely from the ecclesiastical law, but it comes, first of all, from the divine law. As Bouix remarks:—"Imo parochos ad praedicandum teneri iure divino, tradit eadem synodus, (Tridentinus) sessionis 23, capite 1, in hunc modum: "Cum praecepto divino mandatum sit omnibus, quibus cura animarum commissa est, suas oves agnoscere, pro his sacrificum offerre, verbique divini praedicatione — — pascere." Quamvis enim ibi de Episcopis loquatur synodus, paulo post tamen et de parochis haec eadem intelligit." (9.)

This obligation of preaching the word of God to the people is a personal obligation, i. e. it must be fulfilled by the pastor himself. The Code places this aspect of the duty before us in the second part of the same canon, saying:"Parochus huic obligationi nequit per alium habitualiter satisfacere, nisi ob justam causam ab Ordinario probatam." C. 1344 #2. Consequently, the parish priest is not at liberty to commit this office to anyone else habitually unless he has a good reason and this reason has re-

9. Bouix, D. l. c. p. 587.

ceived the approbation of the Ordinary of the place. A just cause here would be e. x. a failing memory, throat trouble, etc. But still, as Father Augustine says:—"Wherever it is customary for the pastors and curates or assistants to take turns at preaching, and the custom has been ratified by the Bishop, no breach of the law occurs." (10.) But we must always remember that this permission of the Ordinary is necessary for habitual transference only. If the pastor has a good reason for asking another to take his place on one or the other occasion, no permit need be secured. Of course, he should never commit this part of the parochial office to another unless he has some good cause for so doing.

How often must the pastor preach? The New Code answers this question in the following manner:—"Diebus dominicis ceterisque per annum festis de praecepto". C. 1344. Consequently, taking this duty from its temporal aspect, it all depends upon the number of the Holydays of obligation in the place. If all those mentioned in canon 1247 are days of obligation in the place where the pastor is situated, he will have to preach on all of them. If, as is the case here in the U. S., only six of these days besides Sundays are of obligation, the pastor will not have to preach on the other days. The suppressed feasts do not count in among the number mentioned in canon 1344.

But is the pastor never allowed to omit a sermon on one of the days prescribed? No, not without the permission of the Ordinary. . "Potest Ordinarius permittere ut solemnioribus quibusdam festis aut etiam, ex justa causa, aliquibus diebus dominicis concio omittatur." C. 1344 #3. But this does not mean that the parish priest has to ask permission separately for each time that he wishes to omit the duty of preaching. The Ordinary can give a general permit, for instance by a circular letter, or by a general statement at some occasion e. x. et a diocesan synod, "provided always", as Father Augustine says, "that no abuse creeps in and no contrary custom develops." (11.)

10. Augustine, l. c. vol. VI. p. 365.

11. Augustine, C. l. c. vol. VI. p. 366.

The pastor has not only the duty but also the right to preach in the parish church on the days mentioned. Wherefore, the Bishop should not send another to take his place if the parish priest himself is willing and able to announce the word of God. This is clear from a declaration of the Sacred Congregation of the Council:—"Si curatores animarum per se velint munus praedicationis obire, non debent impediri." (12.) But this right of the pastors does not hold good against the legislation of canon 1343 in which we are told that the Ordinary has the right of prohibiting others to preach in the same city and on the same day when he himself is to speak, or when he orders another to speak in his presence. C. 1343 #2. This right of the Bishop does not extend to the larger cities and, consequently, he should not prohibit all preaching in such places, even when he himself has a sermon in one of the churches.

As was stated the pastor is held to preach on all Sundays and days of obligation. But there are certain parts of the year when the Church desires more frequent talks to the people. This is the case during the holy seasons of Lent and Advent. C. 1346 #1. The frequency, the time, etc., are left to the prudent judgment of the Ordinary of the place.

Having stated when the pastors are to preach, we turn next to the qualifications of the preacher. Doctor Stang enumerates these in the following order:—"a vocation, a mission, a virtuous life, the necessary knowledge of language, philosophy, theology, canon law, church history, liturgy and the Fathers. "A special calling from God," says the learned Doctor, "is the first and fundamental requirement of the preacher, because preaching is a priestly function." (13.) With regard to the second qualification, it will be practical to quote here what the present Holy Father. Pope Benedict XV., has to say:—"Speaking of the fact that preaching is properly the duty of the Bishops, he says, that they, unable to take care of all, must have help from others, and then ads: "Wherefore it cannot be doubted that all those who in addition to the Bishops are thus engaged, are employed in the

12. Barbosa l. c. p. 122.

13. Stang. Pastoral Theology, p. 5.

performance of an episcopal duty. Let this then be the first law laid down: that no one on his own responsibility undertake the office of preaching. In order to fulfill that duty everyone must have a lawful mission, and that mission can be conferred by the Bishop alone. "How shall they preach, unless they be sent? (Rom. X. 15)." (14.) According to the New Code the word Bishop is changed to "Ordinarius loci" C. 1337. The New Code furthermore defines to what persons this mission can be given:— "Concionandi facultas solis sacerdotibus vel diaconis fiat, non vero ceteris clericis, nisi rationabili de causa iudicio Ordinarii et in casibus singularibus. 2. Concionari in ecclesia vetantur laici omnes, etsi religiosi." C. 1342.

If a pastor is approved as a preacher in one diocese he cannot, by that fact, use this faculty and preach in any other. A special permission and approbation must be secured from the Ordinary of the place in which he is to speak. C. 1337. For this reason the New Code demands, that those pastors, who ask priests from different dioceses to preach in their churches, should secure proper permission for them from the Ordinary of the place. Without this permit from the Ordinary no priest is to be admitted to the pulpit. Let the pastor see to it that he asks this permission in due time, "tempestive". C. 1341 #1. This term was declared to mean two months by the Sacred Congregation of the Council in 1729. But, as the means of communication have improved greatly since that time, it need not be interpreted so strictly. As long as the Ordinary is given time, sufficient to make an investigation if necessary, the spirit of the law will be fulfilled. I say "sufficient to make an investigation" for the reason, that unless the visiting priest is known to the Ordinary as one possessing the required qualification, the Ordinary may demand that testimony of the preachers learning, piety and morals be given him by the Ordinary of the one so invited. C 1341. The priest called need not be known personally to the Bishop of this diocese in which he is to speak. The Ordinary may take the word of another as guarantee of his fitness and thus dispense from the testimonial. But the Ordinary is not bound to do this and can demand a writ-

14. "Humani Generis" June 15, 1917.

ten testimony from the Bishop of that priest if he so chooses. Therefore, let the pastor ask this permission in time. Another qualification demanded in a preacher is a virtuous life. In fact, the Holy Father lays so much stress on this requirement that he says: "But if a priest is unequal to being both holy in life and rich in learning, holiness of life is, without question, to be preferred to mere learning. (16.) The last requisite mentioned above is that of sufficient knowledge. This, of course, is important, for how can the preacher hope to teach what he himself does not know?

The right and duty of ascertaining whether the priests possess these qualifications belong to the Ordinary of the place. He is to determine this point before he grants the faculty of preaching to the person concerned. C. 1340 #1. But his right and duty does not stop there. If, after this faculty has been granted, the Ordinary finds that the required qualities are wanting, he shall withdraw the permission. C. 1340 #2. If there is a doubt about the preachers knowledge, the Ordinary may even order another examination unless the doubt can be dispelled by other means. When a pastor has been deprived of this faculty of announcing the word of God by the Ordinary, he has the right of having recourse but "in devolutivo" only and not "in suspensivo", i. e. he can bring the matter before the competent higher superior but may not preach in the meantime. C. 1340 #3.

After determining the requisites in a preacher, we come to the subject matter of the sermon and the manner of delivering it. The subject matter of sermons is treated in canon 1347. There we are told that sermons are to explain those points of our religion which are necessary for the faithful to believe and do in order to be saved. This is evident. Before going into other topics, all of which may be very useful, the pastor must teach his spiritual children the things most necessary for their welfare. Only after this has been covered should he turn to the other subjects. This is the general rule. Now, since the matter of sermons is so extensive, it will not be in our power to state all that should be spoken of in the pulpit. But it will not be amiss to

16. "Humani Generis", June 15, 1917.

mention at least some of the points that are not to be mentioned in that holy place. In the first place money matters are not to be made the subject matter of sermons. Although it will be necessary to mention such things at times, this should be treated among the announcements and not in the sermon itself. 2. Never mention any names of persons in finding fault with them nor give any hints from which the identity of the persons concerned could be learned. This is a cowardly manner of acting, a priest hiding himself behind the sacredness of the pulpit when attacking an individual or individuals. 3. Do not bring your personal grievances into the pulpit. 4. Ridiculing people or nationalities or professions or making slurring remarks about them, have no place anywhere, much less in the Church. 5. Do not use irony, sarcasm or silly jokes in your sermons. 6. Do not speak of things which are not altogether true or according to the interpretation of the Church. Controverted questions, so as to suggest doubts, should never be made use of. 7. Moreover, as the New Code states, the preacher is to abstain from all profane arguments and those abstruse ones which are above the mental capacity of his hearer. C. 1347. Some of these matters, if brought into a sermon, may be not only useless, but also detrimental.

How is the pastor to preach? The common law answers this in the following manner:—"Evangelicum ministerium non in persuasibilibus humanae sapientiae verbis; non in profano inanis et ambitiosae eloquentiae apparatu et lenocino, sed in ostensione spiritus et virtutis exerceant, non semetipsos, sed Christum crucifixum praedicantes". C. 1347 #2. We are to preach Jesus Christ and Him crucified. And consequently, just as we are not to bring in anything that is not necessary or useful for this end, neither are we to employ a delivery which does not tend toward making this point clear and bringing the people closer to the bosom of Him, Whom we are preaching. "Non in persuasibilibus humanae sapientiae verbis. The Holy Father, Pope Benedict XV., uses the same words, taken from the I epistle of St. Paul to the Corinthians, chapter 2, verse 4, in his encyclical letter mentioned above. From the words of the sovereign Pontiff it is clear that the preacher is not to make his appeals, for the most part, from reason alone. "Unquestionably", says the Holy Father, "that is wrong, for the supernatural order, merely human resources are of no help whatever. But the objection may be urged: The people have no confidence in the preacher who insists on divinely revealed truths. Is that true? With non-Catholics,granted. However, when the Greeks sought the wisdom, forsooth of this world, the Apostle, nevertheless, preached to them Christ crucified. If we direct our attention, however, to Catholic people, even those among them who are unfriendly to us, generally keep in their hearts the roots of faith. Their intellects are blinded because their souls are corrupted. Lastly, what end did St. Paul have in his preaching? Not to please men, but Christ. "If I yet pleased men, I should not be the servant of Christ." Gal. I. 10." (17.) Again, the preacher is not to use a profane and an ambiguous manner of delivery in his preaching. The purpose of every pastor when preaching must be to lead the people to a fuller knowledge of God and to guide them to the haven of rest and happiness eternal. Unless this is the goal and the preacher aims toward it, the speaker is but an "idle declaimer". As the same encyclical letter remarks, some are lead by vain glory and, consequently, are ashamed to speak of ordinary subjects in an ordinary way. They express "high rather than practical thoughts". "They seem to have only one aim," says the Holy Father, "to please their hearers and curry favor with those whom St. Paul describes as "having itching ears". (II. Tim. IV. 3). Hence that unrestrained and undignified gesture such as may be seen on the stage or on the hustings, that effiminate lowering of the voice or those tragic outbursts; that diction peculiar to journalism; those frequent allusions to profane and non-catholic literature, but not to the Sacred Scriptures or the Holy Fathers; finally that volubility of utterance often affected by them, wherewith they strike the ears and gain the hearers' admiration, but give them no lesson to carry home. How sadly are those preachers deceived". Thereupon the Holy Father goes on to say that some of the preachers are even worse than this, forgetting what St. Gregory says:— "The priest does not preach that he may eat, but should eat that

17. "Humani Generis".

he may preach" and undertake this office for money's sake. They care not where they can do more good but only where they can get the most out of it in a financial way. Miserable is the man who would stoop down so low. Let all the preachers, be they pastors or not, take heed from these words of the chief visible Pastor and ever try to combine proper subject matter with good delivery and thus propound the truths necessary and useful to their people and preach Christ and Him alone. Say what is good and say it in the proper manner. Only when these two things are combined can the preacher hope to secure all the effects that are desired. High sounding terms and far flung gestures bring nothing but possible admiration from those who listen. This is not the end of the preacher. We preach Christ and Christ crucified. Unless the people are led to him all our words, all our manners of delivery, are in vain.

Naturally, every preacher must be on his guard against erroneous or heretical teaching. The law imposes heavy penalties upon such as would be guilty of these delinquencies. Excommunication "ipso facto" is the lot of heretics and schismatics. C: 2314. And if, after they have been been admonished, they still persevere in this state, they are to be deprived of their parish and whatever other office, dignity, pension, or function they may possess in the Church and declared 'infames'. Then, after another admonition has been given in vain, they are to be deposed. If a pastor is suspected of heretical teaching, i. e. becomes a "suspectus de haeresi" as the term is understood in the new law, and does not free himself from this suspicion after having been admonished, he should be barred from all the legitimate acts of the Church. And if, after a second admonition the suspicion is still unremoved, he should be suspended "a divinis". Thereupon, after six more months have elapsed and the pastor is still in the same way, he is to be considered a heretic and is subject to the penalties mentioned above. C 2315. Again, if the pastor teaches anything that is not exactly heretical, but nevertheless condemned by the Holy See, he shall be admonished to mend his ways. If after such warnings have been given, the pastor still continues to preach the same matter, he ought to be deprived of the faculty not only of preaching but also of hearing confessions and of teaching in any capacity. "Other penalties may be added in the sentence of condemnation, and the Ordinary may, after giving due warning, demand whatever he deems necessary to repair the scandal given by this pastor. C. 2317." (18.)

Missions should be given the people of the parish at least once in every ten years. C. 1349. Regulations laid down by the Ordinary in regard to the holding of these missions must be observed by all the pastors, whether religious or secular.

"Si parochus graviter neglexerit — — puerorum populique institutionem, concionem diebus dominicis ceterisque festis, — — ab Ordinario coerceatur ad norman can. 2182-2185." C. 2382. Here we see the penalties to be imposed upon those who seriously neglect this duty of catechising or preaching. The three canons referred to here contain the following instructions:—The first canon states that whenever a parish priest neglects "graviter" the obligations of catechising or preaching the word of God as demanded by the common law, he shall be admonished by the Bishop, reminding him of his strict obligation and of the penalties that fall upon such delinquents. C. 2182. If this does not help, the Bishop should punish him with some salutary punishment in proportion to the gravity of the negligence. The ordinary should not, however, put the penalty upon the contumacious pastor before he has given him an opportunity of defending himself and explaining the reason for his negligence. He should also, first consult two of the consultors. C. 2183. If after all this has been done and the punishment is of no avail, the Bishop may deprive the pastor of his parish at once, if he be a removable pastor. If the parish priest be an irremovable pastor, he may be deprived of a part or of all the fruits of his benefice according to the gravity of the transgressions. C. 2184. If, even after this privation has been made, the irremovable pastor does no better, the Bishop may also remove him from his parish. C. 2185.

---

18. Ayrinhac, Penal Legislation in the New Code. p. 200.

Part IV. SACRAMENTS.

Sect. 1. The Sacraments in General.

"Through the means of preaching and catechising the priest prepares souls for the Sacraments of the Church, and leads them to the union with Christ. The object of all his pastoral activity should consist, first, in teaching his people the necessity of the Sacraments, the dispositions required for worthy reception of them and the meaning of the various ceremonies that surround them: secondly, in communicating constantly and faithfully these means of grace to the souls committed to his care and in justifying, sanctifying them and making them pleasing of God. "Sic nos existimet homo ut ministros Christi: et dispensatores mysteriorum Dei." (I. Cor. IV. 12). (1)

In the new Code we are told that the pastor is bound to administer the sacraments as often as the people ask for them reasonably or legitimately. C. 467 #1. This is a duty which follows from the tacit contract or agreement, which the pastor assumes when he takes charge of the parish. It is, therefore, a matter of justice between the parish priest and the congregation over which he is placed. As Genicot says:—"Ad hoc enim se obligavit dum munus pastoris assumpsit; insuper intercedit contractus, vi cuius accipit stipendium, vel sustentationem, vel saltem honorem a subditis, sub onere praestandi ea quae sunt pastoris: inter quae reperitur administratio Sacramentorum. Sic iustitia obligantur, relate ad saeculares subditos, — — parochi.". Consequently, the pastor is not left to choose what he desires to do. Moreover, he is held to administer the sacraments personally unless he is legitimately hindered from doing so or when he can do so through another "sine incommodo et offensione petentium". (3.) The point concerning the reasonableness of request need not be taken up here. That will be found treated thoroughly in work on Moral Theology. The fact here remains that when

1. Stang, Wm. D. D. Pastoral Theology, Book II, #14, p. 65.

2. Genicot, Eduardus, S. J. Institutiones Theologiae Moralis, edit. 8a. vol. II, tract XI. cap. 2 p. 107.

3. Ferreres, J. B., S. J. Compendium Theol. Moralis, tomus II. cap. II., art. II. #135, p. 75.

the petition is reasonable the pastor is bound to respond. Care must be taken lest the matter be taken too lightly and requests, which are legitimate, be called unreasonable, just because the pastor may not feel disposed to minister when the person asks it. Of course, when such cases as those of scrupulous persons, who desire to confess daily and possibly several times a day, turn up, the pastor will not be bound to respond on each occasion, for, as Ferreres says:—"quum tam frequens confessio satis non expediat, nec ipsi jus strictum ad absolutionem tam frequentem habeant." (4.)

But while on the one hand the parish priest is held to administer to such as request the ministration reasonably, on the other hand he is also bound to deny these means of grace to those who are unworthy. "Denegare Sacramenta indignis minister Sacramentorum regulariter et sub gravi tenetur." (5.) This is demanded firstly by the natural law, since the natural law obliges the dispenser of the goods of the Lord to act in a faithful manner according to His will. But the will of Christ is that the pastor "give not that which is holy to dogs; neither cast ye your pearls before swine." (6.) The word "regulariter" is used above for the reason that there are cases when the pastor ought not deny the sacraments to the unworthy. Further treatment of this point will be taken up as we proceed with the various sacraments. However, a thorough discussion of such points is not to be looked for here.

Very important legislation, which should be kept in mind by every dispenser of the Sacraments is that found under canon 733 as follows:—"In sacramentis conficiendis, administradis ac suscipiendis accurate serventur ritus et ceremoniae quae in libris ritualibus ab Ecclesia probatis preacipiuntur. 2. Unusquisque autem ritum suum sequatur, salvo praescripto can. 851 #2; 866." The observance of the rites and ceremonies in the administration and reception of the sacraments was always insisted upon by the

4. Ferreres, J. B. l. c. tom. II. Tract. de Sacramentus in genere, cap. II. art. II p. 156.

5. Genicot,op . cit. vol. II. Tract. XI, cap. 2. p. 108.

6. St. Matthew, chapt. VII, verse 6.

Church. Consequently, every parish priest should provide himself with approved rituals and follow them as directed. Such books can be secured at any of the Catholic book stores. Perusal of these books from time to time is necessary in order to keep one from falling into a state of laxity. The law also demands that each is to keep his own rite, with due regard, however, to the canons mentioned. In these two canons we find the following legislation: " The priest shall distribute Holy Communion according to his own rite, either in unleavened or in leavened bread. But in a case of necessity, if no priest of the respective rite is present, a priest of the Oriental rite, who would otherwise use leavened bread, may administer the Holy Eucharist in unleavened bread, and, conversely, a priest of the Latin rite or Oriental rite, who would ordinarily use unleavened bread, may give Holy Communion in leavened bread: but each must observe the rubrics of his own rite." C. 851. (7.) Canon 866 treats of the rite of Holy Communion and says that all the faithful may receive the Holy Eucharist in the species consecrated in any Catholic rite, although they are to be advised to receive the species consecrated in their own rite when making their Easter duty. Holy Viaticum is also to be received by each of the faithful in his own rite, but in case of necessity it may be received in any Catholic rite.

The subject of the pastor's intention and attention in administering the Sacraments need not be taken up here.

Penalties for those, who neglect their duties in regard to the administration of the sacraments, are mentioned in canon 2382 as follows:—"Si parochus graviter neglexerit Sacramentorum administrationem — — Ordinario coercetur ad norman can. 2182-2185." Since the treatment of this subject was taken up under the heading of "The pastor as preacher and teacher" it will not be necessary for us to go over it again, for the legislation concerning the penalties is the same in both cases.

Sect. 2. Baptism.

"Minister ordinarius baptismi sollemnis est sacerdos: sed eius collatio reservatur parocho vel alii sacerdoti de eiusdem parochi vel Ordinarii loci licentia, quae in casu necessitatis legiti-

7. Augustine, op. cit. vol. IV. p. 222.

me praesumitur." C. 738 #1. "Functiones parocho reservatae sunt, nisi aliud iure caveatur:—1. Baptismum conferre solemniter." C. 462. From these two canons we can easily see that the solemn administration of the sacrament of baptism is reserved to the parish priest. It is one of his rights. Consequently, no one is allowed to confer this sacrament in that manner on any of the pastor's subjects without first securing the pastor's permission or the permission of the Ordinary of the place. One exception is made to this general rule, i. e. in case of necessity the permission of the pastor may be lawfully presumed. But even when such permission is legitimately presumed, the stole fee is to be handed to the proper pastor of the subjects. C. 463 #3. However, that part of the stole fee, which is over and above the regular stole fee of that place, may be kept by the one who administered the sacrament if it is evident that it was given for the sake of the person baptizing. Father Augustine says that this is generally understood that a larger stipend, given to one who is not the pastor, was intended for the personal service, and, may, therefore, be retained by the one acting in the case. (1.) The proper pastor should not, however, forget to give the one who so baptized, in a case of necessity, some recompense, for such a person has a right to it.

The New Code is so insistent upon this right of the pastor to baptize his own subjects solemnly, that it orders even the "peregrini", i. e. those who have a domicile or quasi-domicile in some parish, but are found outside of that place at present, to return to their proper parishes to be baptized solemnly by their own parish priest. C. 738 #2. An exception is made to this rule when the return cannot be made easily or without delay. In that case, the pastor of any parish may baptize the peregrinus solemnly within this, the officiating pastor's, parish. The vagi, i. e. those, who have no domicile or quasi-domicile anywhere, may be solemnly baptized by the pastor of the place in which they now actually stay, since such a pastor is their proper parish priest. C. 94 #3. Infants and minors have the same domicile as their parents or those to whose power they are subject, although

1. Augustine op. cit. vol. II., p. 543.

minors who are seven years of age or more and who are not insane, can secure their own quasi-domicile. C. 93 #2. A wife who is not lawfully separated from her husband, retains the domicile of her husband but can obtain a quasi-domicile in another parish. If she is legitimately separated, she can also secure a proper domicile of her own. C. 93. An insane person has the same domicile as the one in whose charge he is placed. C. 93. When one and the same person has a domicile in two different parishes either of the pastors may baptize him solemnly within his proper parish limits. If the same person has a domicile in one parish and a quasi-domicile in another, he can probably receive baptism solemnly also from either pastor. This is the opinion of Genicot, while Ferreres does away with the "probabilius" and says that it is certain that either of the two parish priests may do so, basing his argument on St. Alphonsus. (2.) With Father Augustine I agree in saying that: "The pastor of one's domicile has no preponderance over the pastor of one's quasi-domicile in the administration of the Sacraments." (3.) And this, I think, is the teaching of the Church. The law simply states that "sive per domicilium sive per quasi-domicilium suum quisque parochum et Ordinarium sortitur." C. 94 #1. It does not say that the proper pastor is secured only through a domicile but expressly enumerates both as the sources for securing a proper parish priest. Consequently, the pastor of one's quasi-domicile need not ask the domicilian pastor for permission if he wishes to baptize such a person solemnly within his own parish limits. This, however, must always be remembered, that a pastor is not allowed to act solemnly in any baptism outside of his own parish, whether it be for his own subjects or others. The next canon makes this point clear, saying:—"In alieno territorio nemini licet, sine debita licentia, baptimum sollemnem confere ne sui quidem loci incolis." C. 739.

Thus far we have been treating of solemn baptism only, for that is the usual manner in which the pastor is held to confer it. C. 755. Private baptism may be made use of only in certain cases.

2. Genicot, op. cit. l. c. p. 125; Ferreres, op. cit. p. 125.

3. Augustine, op. cit. vol. II. p. 18.

Firstly, in danger of death, when the pastor should first make use of the ceremonies necessary for the validity of baptism and then, if there is time, he should also use the ceremonies which follow baptism. C. 739 #1. Ferreres says:—"unde in baptismo domi conferendo in casu necessitatis, omnia sunt omittenda quae baptismum praecedunt, quaeque postmodum supplenda sunt in ecclesia ad quam praesentandus est puer quum convalescit; possunt tamen adhiberi si minister sit sacerdos aut diaconus illae ceremoniae quae baptismum subsequuntur." (4.) The Code is more insistent upon the use of the ceremonies that follow baptism than this quotation of Ferreres. The Code says: "serventur" and not "possunt adhiberi." Another case in which private baptism is allowed is that of the conditional baptism of an adult heretic. For this, however, the permission of the Ordinary of the place is required. 759 #2. In no other case may the Ordinary permit private baptism. Whenever private baptism had been conferred the ceremonies that were omitted should be supplied as soon as possible in the parish Church. The supplying of ceremonies need not be carried out in the case of a conditional baptism of an adult heretic. When this sacrament is conferred only conditionally the ceremonies, that were not used in the first place must be used here, except in the case mentioned above regarding the conditional baptism of adult heretics. When all the ceremonies were made use of in the first instance, they may be repeated or left out in the conditional baptism. C. 760.

The Ordinary may also allow that solemn baptism be conferred in private houses in individual cases. C. 775. "In domibus autem privatis baptismus sollemnis administrari non debet, nisi hisce adiunctis: 1. Si baptizandi sint filii aut nepotes eorum qui supremum actu tenet populorum principatum, vel ius habent succedendi in thronum, quoties isti rite poposcerint; 2. Si loci Ordinarius, pro suo prudenti arbitrio et conscientia, iusta ac rationabili de causa, in casu aliquo extraordinario id concedendum censuerit." C. 776. But, even when permission has been received to confer baptism in this manner in private houses, it should always take place in the chapel of the house or, if that is wanting,

4. Ferreres, op. cit. l. c. p. 186.

in some decent room, and the priest is to use "aqua baptismali de more benedicta".

Outside of these exceptional cases, solemn baptism is to be conferred in the baptistery of a church, or public oratory. Every parish church should have a baptismal font. C. 774 # 1. This is demanded by the common law notwithstanding any contrary customs, privileges or statutes. The law adds:—"salvo iure cumulativo aliis ecclesiis iam quaesito." This means that if any church or churches have a right, received in some legitimate manner, of solemnly baptising the people belonging to the parish church, this right is to be respected. Thus Ferreres gives an example of such cumulative rights:—"Sic cathedrales Barcinonensis, Caesaraugustana (del Pilar) etc., jus habent baptismus conferendi infantibus sive propriae civitatis, sive dioecesis, qui a propriis parentibus illic deferantur, quin ad hoc requiratur licentia proprii parochi, neque huic emolumentum aliquod sit solvendum." (5.) Those cathedrals had a cumulative right with all the other churches situated within that territory, of solemnly baptizing any child from within the whole city or diocese, as long as the parents brought the child to these cathedrals. No permission was necessary from the proper pastor of the child so baptized nor was the stole fee to be handed over to such a parish priest. The second part of this canon 774 says, that the Ordinary may also for the sake of the convenience of the people, allow or even order another baptismal font to be erected in some church or public oratory other than those in possession of such fonts. He cannot, however, allow such fonts to be placed in semi-public or private oratories.

As was already stated, every solemn baptism is to be conferred in a church or public oratory which has a baptismal font, the two cases excepted. There is also another exception to this general rule, i. e. whenever the distance is so great, the child so weak or some other cause is present, which makes it gravely inconvenient or dangerous to take the child to the parish church or to some other church or public oratory within the parish limits enjoying the right of a font, the pastor may administer this sacra-

5. Ferreres, op. cit. l. c. p. 189

ment solemnly in the church or public oratory nearest the child's home, even though it has no baptismal font, as long as this place of worship is located within the parochial territory. C. 775.

The New Code desires that all intended baptisms of adults i. e. those having use of reason, be reported to the Ordinary of the place so that, if he so wishes, he may administer the sacrament to them himself or have it conferred by someone delegated by him. C. 744. This notification is, however, not of strict obligation. It is more of a wish than an order. But, no matter who confers this solemn baptism upon the adult, the formula prescribed for adults should be made use of, unless the Ordinary allows him to use the form "pro baptismo infantium." The Ordinary can give this permission in cases of grave and reasonable necessity. C. 755 #2. Moreover, adults ought to be baptized "si fieri commode queat" on Holy Saturday or on the day before Pentecost Sunday. C. 772. The Church desires to preserve the ancient rites of the Church in this regard, which were used especially in metropolitan churches and cathedrals. The minister of such solemn baptisms of adults is to fast. C. 753. But this is not of strict obligation for the pastor. Rules regarding the profession of faith, abjuration of heresy, etc., should be known by the minister in all such cases and also in those of conditional baptism. Instruction and penitence are necessary on the part of the adult as well as the will to receive this sacrament. C. 745 #2. When the adult is in danger of death and there is no time to instruct him carefully in the principal mysteries of our Faith, the sacrament may be conferred as long as he shows, in some manner, that he assents to them and promises seriously to observe the precepts of the Catholic religion. C. 732 #2. This presupposes that the person is able to show his intention of receiving the sacrament. But it may happen that the party is found in such a state that he cannot even ask for this means of grace. What is to be done then? The last part of this canon answers that. If the person is, for example, in a state of unconsciousness at present and consequently, cannot ask that baptism be administered to him, the pastor may baptize him conditionally as long as he has shown this intention in the past at least in "aliquo probabili modo." If the person so baptized recovers afterwards and there remains a doubt about the validity of the first conditional baptism, he is to be baptized again *"sub conditione"*. C. 752 # 3. If, however, it should be ascertained by the investigation that follows that there was no intention at all in the first case, baptism must be conferred absolutely if the person then desires to receive it. The pastor must take care to determine such points, lest it happens, in some cases, that the signs taken for an intention were mistaken.

The insane and maniacs, if they have been so from their birth or from a time before they came to the use of reason, should be baptized like infants. If they became insane, etc. after the age of reason, they cannot be baptized unless they wish it during lucid intervals. Then baptism must also be conferred during these moments in which they enjoy the use of their mental faculties. All those who are suffering from "lethargia vel phrenesis" are to be baptized only during their waking hours and if they desire the sacrament. "Lethargia" is a sleeping sickness prevalent in some parts of the world, e. x. Africa, around Lake George, etc. "Phrenesis" is a sort of brain fever, a wild delirium. Of course, when a person suffering from any of these four diseases is in danger of death, he may be baptized conditionally whether he is in a lucid interval or not, or whether he is in a sleeping state or not, as long as he has previously shown a desire to receive this sacrament, as was stated above for those in an unconscious condition. C. 754.

Every pastor should see to it that all his people and especially those coming in frequent contact with such cases, know how to administer the sacrament of baptism correctly in a case of necessity. Midwives and doctors should receive special instructions in this regard. C. 743. This is of the greatest importance, for it is of no unfrequent occurence that an infant cannot be reached by the pastor in time to baptize him before death. And sad indeed, would be the state of a parish if the people knew not how to administer this sacrament in such times of need. Instructions concerning this subject should be given during catechetical instructions mentioned in a previous subdivision, or in special talks on that point. He should mention what matter is to be used, teach them the formula and explain with what intention all is to be done, so that, when they are called upon to confer this sacrament, they may do as the Church prescribes. Midwives and doctors can be given more thorough information in private talks and by means of pamphlets or books. Canons 746-748 inclusive treat of some of the matter which the pastor, the doctor and the midwife ought to be acquainted with.

Canons 749-751 take up the baptism of foundlings and of the children of infidels and of non-catholics. Whenever a foundling is brought to the pastor for baptism he must first of all inquire whether there is any information concerning any previous baptism. If the fact of it's baptism cannot be ascertained after careful investigation, the child is to be baptized conditionally. C. 749. The children of infidels may never be baptized without a guarantee of their Catholic education and the consent of at least one of the parents, guardians or grandparents, as the case may be. If none of these are among the living or if they all loose the right to keep the infant or, again, if they are unable to exercise this right, then the child may be baptized as long as it's Catholic education is assured. However, it is understood, that when a child of infidel parents is in danger of death and there is little if any hope of his recovery and reaching the age of reason, it may be baptized even contrary to the will of the child's parents. C. 750. What was said here about the baptism of children of infidels may be repeated about the conferring of this sacrament upon children of two heretics or schismatics or of two Catholics who fell into heresy or schism. C. 751.

When the parents of the child belong to different Catholic rites, the baptism of the child is to take place according to the rite of the father, unless some special law rules otherwise. The same principal is held in legislation regarding Ruthenians in the U. S. (5.a) Naturally, if one of the parents is a non-catholic, the child is baptized in the Catholic rite of the Catholic parent. C. 756.

The pastor shall also take care that all the children of his parish receive christian names. Although there is no law, which

5a. S. Congr. de Prop. Fide. "Cum Episcopo" Aug. 17, 1914. Apud. Acta. Apos. Sed. vol. VI. p. 458.

binds under sin, that the name of some saint be given, the church says that parish priests should try to persuade all to select some christian name. If his arguments fail the pastor himself is to add a christian name to the one chosen by the parents. A profane name of some impious man should never be given, but as Noldin says:—"si tamen impedire non potest, quominus nomen impii alicuius imponatur, ideo baptismus negandus vel differendus non est, sed puer baptizandus est addito submissa voce nomine alicuius Sancti." (6.) In making the entry of the baptism in the baptismal records of the parish both names are to be entered therein. C. 761.

The Church further orders that sponsors be used at every solemn baptism if they can possibly be secured. C. 762. One sponsor of either sex is necessary and sufficient, but two may be allowed, but then of different sexes. C. 764. If it can be done without difficulty, sponsors are to be called in also for private baptisms. In such a case the same sponsor is to be used later when the ceremonies are supplied. When no sponsor was present at the private baptism, one ought to be on hand when the ceremonies are supplied, but in this case the sponsor, who acts only in the second instance, does not contract any spiritual affinity with the child. C. 762 #2. This is also true when different sponsors are used respectively for the private baptism and the conditional baptism later. Neither contracts this affinity with the child. In the latter case the same sponsor should be called if possible. If the same one is used, he contracts spiritual affinity like any sponsor at a valid baptism. When there was no sponsor at the private doubtful baptism or at the first doubtful, solemn baptism, or when the one who served in these first baptisms is dead or cannot be called without great inconvenience, etc., no sponsor is necessary at the repetition of the baptism. C. 763. Rules regarding sponsors are contained in canons 765-767. There the pastor will find who may act validly and licitly in such a position.

One of the changes that have been introduced in the New Code is that found in canon 768, i. e. that spiritual affinity is

6. Noldin, op. cit. vol. III, p. 95.

now contracted only between the sponsor and the child and between the minister and the child. There is no spiritual affinity between the sponsor and the parents of the child baptized as was the case heretofore under the old legislation.

The duty and the responsibilities of the sponsors should be explained to the people on certain occasions. As Father Woywood remarks: "Sponsors have by the very office which they took upon themselves the duty to take an interest in their God-child and to watch carefully over its training, in order that the person for whom they stood as sponsors may, throughout his or her whole life, behave in such a maner as to bear out the promises made to the Church by the sponsor in the name of the child." (7).

People should be made to understand that it is their important duty to have their children baptized as soon as possible. C. 770. The practice of putting off this sacrament for a long time, until probably the mother can also go to church to receive the churching at the same time, is to be done away with. The term as used in the common law it "quamprimum" and this is interpreted to mean within three or at most eight days after birth. (8.) Moreover, if there is a particular law of the diocese giving the time within which this sacrament is to be received, it would be a grave omission to defer the reception of it without just cause for a long time. Where the particular law is not found, a notable postponement of this sacrament would not necessarily be a grave sin as long as there is a serious intention of not neglecting baptism and there is at the same time no danger of death. (9.) The Church allows baptism to be conferred on any day and desires that the people do not put it off too long. C. 772.

As soon as the sacrament has been conferred the Pastor is to make a record of it in the parochial baptismal register. C. 777. The data that this entry must embrace follows:—1. the name of the person baptized; 2. names of the parents of the child; 3. names of the sponsors; 4. name of the officiating minister; 5. the place

---

7. Woywood, S. apud Homiletic and Pastoral Review, vol. XXI, No. 1. Oct. 1920, p. 24. Canon 769.

8. S. Congr. de Prop. Fid. Sept 11, 1841. apud Collectanea S. C. de Prop. Fid. #939, vol. I. p. 523.

9. Noldin, op. cit. vol. III. p. 87. Genicot, op. cit. p. 130.

of baptism; 6. the date of baptism, containing the day, month and year. When the child is an illegitimate one the case is somewhat different. All the entries are made as usual with the following exceptions; the name of the mother is not set down unless her maternity is publicly known or unless she freely requests it to be entered. This request must be made either in writing or before two witnesses. The father's name is not put into the register unless he willingly asks it to be entered or unless the fact that he is the father of the child is known from some authentic public document. The request here, when made by the father, must also be made either in writing or before two witnesses. In other cases the names of the parents are not entered and the child is simply registered as the son or daughter of unknown parents or if only one of them e. gr. the mother's name is entered, then as the son or daughter of an unknown father. C. 777 #2. All records are to be made without delay, lest the notice be lost.

Whenever the pastor baptizes a child that does not belong to his parish, he shall notify the proper pastor of the child of this fact. C. 778. The reason for this is that the Church wants every pastor to enter the baptisms of his own subjects in the records of that parish. This is of great importance on account of the authentic testimony which it is able to furnish later on.

Sect. 3. Confirmation.

Although, as the New Code states in Can. 787, confirmation is not necessary "necessitate medii ad salutem", nevertheless, the pastor is to see to it that all members of his congregation receive this sacrament at the proper time. But, we may ask, what is the proper time at which it should be received? The answer is given in the next canon:—"Licet sacramenti confirmationis administratio convenienter in Ecclesia Latina differatur ad septimum circiter aetatis annum, nihilominus etiam antea conferri potest, si infans in mortis periculo sit constitutus, vel ministro id expedire ob justas et graves causas videatur." C. 788 Ordinarily, therefore, this sacrament is to be conferred upon the child at the age of seven or thereabouts, i. e. after the child comes to the use of reason. It should be administered to it thereafter as soon as possible and it will be the obligation of the pastor to see that it is received. An exception to this general rule of the age of seven is danger of death. In such a case this sacrament may be administered to a child of more tender years. This holds good also whenever the minister of the sacrament deems it expedient to confer confirmation upon a child, who has not reached the age of reason. For this, however, a grave and just reason is required. Father Noldin gives the following as sufficient reasons for confirming one at that age:—"si Episcopus occasionem recipiendi hocce sacramentum raro tantum praebere possit; si alicubi existat consuetudo confirmandi infantes." (1.) Such customs are found for instance in South America, in Spain, in the Pillipines and among the Greeks, etc.

Those who are perpetually insane from their birth, may be validly and licitly confirmed. Those, who had the use of reason for some time after the age of reason and were baptized, if they become insane later, may be confirmed as long as they can be presumed to be in the state of grace: "etenim censendi sunt habere intentionem habitualem implicitam huius sacramenti percipiendi." (2). Neophytes, who were baptized for some reason while they were "plane rudes" should not be confirmed unless they can be instructed sufficiently so that they could elicit the intention of receiving this sacrament. (3.)

Before any person, who enjoys the use of reason, is allowed to receive this means of grace, he should be in the state of grace and possess sufficient knowledge. C. 786. Consequently, the parish priest will take care that all go to confession before the sacrament is conferred upon them. Although only those, who are conscious of mortal sin, are bound to confess, still it is well for all to go and prepare their soul better for the reception of the sacrament that is to follow. Instruction should be given the children by the pastor as the law demands:—"Debet parochus: 1. Statis temporibus, continenti per plures dies institutiones, pueros ad sacramenta poenitentiae et confirmationis rite suscipienda

1. Noldin, op. cit. vol. III. p. 107.
2. Genicot, op. cit. vol. II. p. 145.
3. Noldin, op. cit. vol. III. p. 107.

singulis annis praeparare." C. 1330 #. 1. When he cannot give this instruction himself he should have someone else take his place. It is not necessary to mention here that baptism must precede the reception of confirmation and that an intention is also necessary.

Each person to be confirmed must have a sponsor and no one is allowed to have more than one. C. 793 #2. The common law moreover, allows that the same sponsor be used for at most two persons, unless the minister decides otherwise on account of some just reason. C. 794 #1. The custom of employing one male sponsor for all the boys and one woman for all the girls is to be done away with. Noldin says:—"Plane interdicitur, ut unus patrinus omnes pueros et una matrina omnes puelas teneat, nisi adsit indultum apostolicum.. (4.) Father Augustine moreover, remarks:—"The Roman court will not, — — except for reasons of strict necessity (praecisa necessitate) — — tolerate the custom that one man stands for all the confirmandi, and one woman for all the confirmandae." (5.)

Rules concerning sponsors are to be found in canons 795—796. There we are told who can act validly and licitly as sponsor at Confirmation. The parish priest must make himself acquainted with these regulations so that he may know whom he may admit to such offices.

The change in the New Code regarding spiritual affinity arising from sponsorship in confirmation must also be taken into consideration. Although this office brings upon the sponsor certain responsibilities and produces spiritual affinity between the sponsor and the child confirmed, C. 797, there is no longer any impediment to marriage between the two as of yore. Formerly, the sponsor could not marry either the child confirmed or the parent of the child without a dispensation. But this is done away with in the new legislation and no impediment whatever exists between the sponsor and the parents and between him and the child. C. 1079. This should be kept in mind for it will become of great importance when a case of this kind turns up in marriage.

4. Noldin, op. cit. vol. III. p. 111.

5. Augustine, op. cit. vol. IV. p. 119.

Finally, the pastor must make the proper entries into the confirmation register of the parish. He should enter the name of the child or adult confirmed, the names of the parents, the name of the minister of the sacrament, of the sponsors together with the date and place of confirmation. C. 470 #1, and C. 798. If the proper pastor of the one confirmed is not present at the ceremony, the minister of the sacrament should notify him of the fact that these subjects were confirmed. This can be done by the minister himself or through another by his orders. C. 799. The pastor of the place where the confirmatus was baptized should also make a note of this confirmation in the baptismal record, aside the person's name. C. 798 and C. 470 #2.

Sect. 4. The Most Holy Eucharist.

A. The Mass.

"Omnis pontifex ex hominibus assumptus, pro hominibus constituitur in iis, quae sunt Deum, ut offerat dona et sacrificia pro peccatis." (1.) "This," says Father Stang, "is the priestly function par excellence, ut offerat sacrificia." (2.) And Thomas a Kempis exclaims:—"O how great and honorable is the office of the priests, to whom it is given to consecrate with sacred words the Lord of Majesty; to bless Him with their lips, to hold Him with their hands, to receive Him with their mouths and to administer Him to others." (3.) With what purity of heart, then, ought these priests of the Most High perform this sacred function. If in the old law God wanted that the priests should be perfect, how much more is this demanded in the New Law. Is it any wonder then, that the New Code legislates regarding this very point and demands that the priest, before he ascends to the altar, be free from at least the stain of mortal sin? If the Church asks the people to be in the state of grace when they approach the communion railing, is it not to be required of the priest? "Sacerdos sibi conscious peccati mortalis, quantumvis se contritum existimet, sine praemissa sacramentali confessione Missam celebrare ne audeat; quod si, deficiente copia confessarii et urgente necessitate,

1. Heb, Chap. V, verse 1.
2. Stang, Wm. D. D. Pastoral Theology, Chap. III, #24, p. 120.
3. Thos. a Kempis, Following of Christ, book IV, Chap. II, #6.

elicito tamen perfectae contritionis actu celebraverit, quamprimum confiteatur." C. 807. The Church demands that every priest who is conscious of any mortal sin, not as yet confessed and remitted, should first approach the sacred tribunal of penance before he ascends the steps of the altar. An act of perfect contrition is not enough, the Church orders that he confess, unless there be no opportunity. And if, on account of a want of confessors, the pastor celebrates Mass, which is demanded by urgent necessity, before he makes his confession, he should confess as soon as possible. This is the minimum that the Church requires of its priests. The priest should, moreover be a man of virtue, an "alter Christus". But more of this in other works.

Before the pastor approaches the altar he should prepare himself well by pious prayers. C. 814-815-817. During Mass all rubrics must be observed with scrupulous accuracy. C. 818. Let every parish priest remember, that these rubrics prescribed for the Mass are not only directive but preceptive. Nor is the priest allowed to make any new ceremonies or add other prayers therein. Moreover, each parish priest is to use the rite proper to him when he celebrates Mass and should be assisted by a male server. A female server may be employed only "deficiente viro, justa de causa" and then she is not to be admitted into the sanctuary but is to give the responses from afar off. C. 813. A priest cannot make use of another priest as server when this is done only for the sake of greater solemnity or honor. C. 812.

How often is the pastor to celebrate Mass? The general rule for all priests is, that they must offer up Holy Sacrifice "pluries in annum". C. 805. But the law also tells the Ordinary to see to it that they would celebrate at least on Sundays and Holydays of obligation. For pastors there is a special canon regarding this point. These ministers are to offer up Mass not only on all Sundays and Holidays of obligation but also on those feast days, which were once of obligation but are now suppressed. This Mass is the Missa pro populo which every pastor, excepting the habitual pastor, is held in conscience to offer up on these days. C. 339 # 1; C. 466 #1. This is a personal obligation for the pastor. But, besides this obligation, arising from the parochial office and the quasi-contract made by the pastor when assuming charge of the parish, the parish priest is held to offer a Mass for every stipend that he accepts. Apart from these considerations, the pastor is held to say Mass as often as his people are bound to attend, unless he makes other provisions for the people.

Legislation as to time and place of Holy Mass must also be observed. As canon 820 states, the Holy Sacrifice of the Mass may be celebrated on any day except those excluded by the rite of the priest. The Latin rite excludes only the following days:—1. Holy Thursday. On this day only a solemn Mass may be said and that only in those churches which keep the Blessed Sacrament and in which the functions of the 'tridui sacri" are carried out at least according to the form of the small ritual. Private Masses are forbidden on Holy Thursday, but the Bishop may allow them to be said, for the convenience of the people, also in those parish churches in which the liturgical functions cannot be carried out. This Mass should then be said before the solemn Mass celebrated in the cathedral or in the mother church. The permission to say private Mass in such parish churches must be renewed every year. (5.) In those parish churches where the sacred functions of the "triduum" are carried out, private Mass before the solemn Mass may be allowed by the Bishop so that the infirm, who could not assist at the solemn Mass, might have the opportunity of hearing Mass on that day. If it should happen that a feast day, on which the people are held to hear Mass, falls on Holy Thursday, the Bishop should see to it, that as many Masses are said as will be necessary to give all the people the opportunity of satisfying their obligation. (6.) — 2. Good Friday. No Mass is allowed on this day, be it a low or high Mass, except in case of necessity. But in those parochial churches in which the holy functions of Holy Week were performed on Maundy Thursday, the "Missa Praesanctificatorum" ought to be said. A case of necessity which would allow Mass on this day would be to consecrate in order that Holy Viaticum could be given

5. S. Rit. Congr. July 31, 1821. apud Collectanea S. C. P. F. #761, p. 442.

6. Noldin, H. S. J. op. cit. vol. III, lib. III, cap. 2, quaestio 6, art. I. p. 236.

to one who might otherwise die without it. The Mass should then be that "de passione Domini". If the feast of the Annunciation of the B.V.M. should fall on Good Friday, the office and Mass of the feast (together with the duty of attending Mass and abstaining from servile work, in places where this is a day of obligation) are transferred to the Monday after the first Sunday after Easter. (7.) If another feast of obligation falls on Good Friday the office and the Mass are transferred to the next non-impeded day but the obligation of abstaining from servile work binds on Good Friday itself. The obligation of hearing Mass ceases on Good Friday since private Masses are not allowed and the Mass of the presanctified is not sufficient for the satisfying of this precept. (8.) — 3. Holy Saturday. Low Mass cannot be said anywhere on this day unless the pastor has an apostolic indult, which is very rarely given. Of course, a private Mass could be said if it was necessitated by the need of Sacred Hosts for the Viaticum. Solemn Mass may be said on this day in those churches in which the liturgical functions of the "tridui sacri" have been carried out. Lehmkuhl also thinks that, when this parochial Mass cannot be sung on account of want of chanters a low Mass may be said instead. In such cases he says:—"non videtur reputari debere pro Missa privata, quae sit prohibita". (9.)

The pastor is never allowed to say Mass more than once each day, with the exception of Christmas Day and All Souls day, unless he has an Apostolic Indult or the faculty of binating from the Ordinary. C. 806 #1. Moreover, when this privilege of saying two Masses on the same day is secured by the parish priest, he is not allowed to take more than one stipend on that day. "Quoties autem plures in die celebrat, si unam Missam ex titulo justitiae applicet, sacerdos, praeterquam in die Nativitatis Domini, pro alia eleemosynam recipere nequit, excepta aliqua retributione ex titulo extrinseco." C. 824 #2. Here we notice but one exception to the general rule quoted above, i. e., that the pas-

7. S. Rit. Congr. Feb. 11, 1690 apud Decreta Authentica Congr. Sacrorum Rituum etc., vol. 1. #1822, p. 393.

8. S. Rit. Congr. March 20, 1706, apud Decr. Auth. Congr. S. Rit. vol. II. #2164 p. 1.

9 Lehmkull, Aug. S. J. Theologia Moralis, pars. II, lib. I. Tract. IV. cap. 3, art. I. p. 155.

tor can take stipends for more than one Mass on Christmas Day. As was proven before, the pastor must say the Missa pro populo on all Sundays and holydays, even those suppressed. This is a duty binding in justice and consequently, when the pastor says this Mass he cannot take a stipend for the other Mass. All that could be taken is something "ex titulo extrinseco." On Christmas day he is allowed to take a stipend for the two Masses when three are said. On All Souls day only one Mass stipend may be taken, although no Mass need be applied for the people on that day. The other two Masses must be applied according to the intentions prescribed, i. e., the one "pro omnibus fidelibus defunctis" the other "ad mentem s. Pontificis." (10.) If the pastor says only one Mass on this day he can take a stipend for that Mass and apply it for the intention desired by the donor. But he cannot take any compensation whatever, even from an extrinsic title, for the other two Masses when he says all three, nor is he allowed to transfer the intentions of the other two Masses to another day and take stipends for all three Masses on All Souls day. Offenders of this kind can be punished by the Ordinary even to the extent of suspension and deprivation of the stipends received. (11.) —

Regulations, whether of common law or of diocesan statutes, regarding Mass stipends must be carefully observed. All trafficing in stipends should be strictly avoided. C. 827. The amount prescribed by the Ordinary of the diocese is to be the regular norm, nor is the parish priest allowed to demand more, nor, if it be prohibited by the Ordinary, less. C. 831-832. If the donor of the stipends is willing to offer more of his own accord, this may be taken. Care should also be taken as to the entering of Mass stipends. Every pastor ought to have a special book for this purpose and mark down with each stipend an intention as soon as possible after its reception. C. 843-844. When he has Mass intentions that may be given to others, he must always hand over the whole stipend as received, unless the donor expressly allows

10. Benedict XV. Const. "Incruentùm Altaris". Aug. 10, 1915.

11. S. Congr. Concilii, Oct. 15, 1915, apud Acta Apost. Sedis, vol. VIII, p. 480.

the pastor to keep some part of it or unless it is evident that the sum over and above the regular diocesan stipend was given "intuitu personae". C. 840. This has reference only to manual stipends. In the transference of the quasi-manual stipends, when the large stipend takes the place of the partial endowment of the benefice or pious institution, the general rule is just the opposite. In such cases it is sufficient to hand over the regular diocesan stipend and whatever is over and above this may be retained. Of course, if the founder's will evidently forbids such a retention, the whole "pinguis eleemosyna" must be given to the one who is to say the Mass. C. 840 #2. Mass stipends are not to be given to any priest unless the pastor knows him to be absolutely reliable. If the priest is not known he must have some proper papers from his Ordinary to recommend him. C. 838. The obligation of saying the Masses which are transferred to another ceases only after notice is received of their reception and acceptance. C. 839. Consequently, if the stipends are lost on the way, the pastor must suffer the loss and is still bound in justice to offer these Masses. The rules regarding the acceptance of only as many Masses as can be said within the year and of transferring to the Ordinary those, that remain unsaid when the year elapses, still remain in force. C. 835 and C. 841.

A few words may be inserted here about the time when Mass is to be said. The general rule is that no Mass is to be started before one hour before the aurora and no later than one hour after noon. C. 281 #1. This is a practical change from the old law according to which Mass could not be started before the aurora nor later than noon. (12.) Where the aurora does not appear at all, as is the case in some of the polar regions during certain seasons of the year, the Mass may be started at the time in the usual, moral and civil life when the people rise for work according to the approved custom of the region. (13.) When the aurora remains for the whole night, there does not seem to be anything to prohibit the celebration of Mass, "servato decoro" from mid-night

---

12. Sabbetti-Barrett, edit. 22. Compendium Theol. Moralis. Pars. II, tract. XIV, cap. IV. #713, p. 619.

13. Genicot, op. cit. vol. II. tract. XIIV. sect. 2, cap. III, # 236, p. 208-209. Noldin, H. op. cit. vol. III, Lib. IV. cap. 2, quaes. 6, art. I, p. 238.

on. This is the opinion of Genicot, but Noldin remarks:—"attamen ne id sine justa causa fiat, decentia prohibet." On Christmas night only one Mass can be said at midnight in the parochial churches and that one should be the parochial Mass. No other Mass can be said then without an Apostolic Indult. C. 821 #2. This Mass is not to be started before the mid-night hour. The abuse of starting this Mass sooner, so that the pastor would be at the *Gloria* or even at the elevation when the bells chime out the mid-night hour, was ordered abolished by the sacred Congr. of Rites, and besides, the canon itself expressly states "inchoari media nocte." The observation of the rules concerning the time when Mass is to be started is of importance and it is of grave obligation not to start too soon or too late. What length of time is required before it becomes a mortal sin is a controverted point. Ferreres says that, according to the more common opinion it would not be considered a grave matter unless Mass was begun a whole hour before or after the time prescribed by law. (15.) Noldin has the following to say about it:—"Qui ergo sine justa causa notabiliter ante vel post tempus ab ecclesia statutum, i. e. integris duabus horis ante auroram vel post meridiem celebrat, grave peccatum committit, nisi particularia adiuncta excusent." (16.) Genicot holds the same as the latter. Sabbeti-Barrett agrees with them and bases his statement on St. Alphonse. Consequently. we can take this as the rule that if any one starts Mass an hour before the time prescribed i. e. two hours before the aurora, he commits a mortal sin unless he has some good reason to excuse him. The same can be said about starting Mass after the regular time set down by law. Causes which may excuse one when he says Mass before or after the prescribed time are such as 1. the necessity of celebrating in order to be able to administer the Viaticum; 2. the custom of saying Mass outside of the regular time so that laborers and servants could hear Mass, even if this be on week days; 3. in case the High Mass lasts till after one o'clock and there is a large part of the people, who come for the private Mass,

14. Genicot, op. cit. l. c. p. 208; Noldin, op. cit. l. c. p. 238.

15. Ferreres, J. B. Compendium Theol. Moralis, vol. II, Tract. De Eucharistia, pars, II, cap. IV, art. I, #486, p. 282.

16. Noldin, op. cit. l. c. p. 239.

which is customarily celebrated after the High Mass, and who would otherwise not fulfill the obligation of the day on days of obligation; 4. when the pastor wishes to make a journey and cannot celebrate during the regular time; 5. and also, as Noldin says: —"in funere magni principis, occasione contionis, publicae supplicationis, collationis ordinum, matrimonii, etc." (17.)

As to the place where Mass is to be celebrated much need not be said here. It will suffice to say that, when a pastor desires to celebrate outside of a church or oratory as mentioned in canon 822 #1, he must always have the permission of the Ordinary, unless he has the privilege of a portable altar. C. 822 #2-3-4. Moreover, if the parish priest should be in a place where no altar of his own rite can be found, he may celebrate on an altar consecrated according to any other Catholic rite, except on the Greek *antemension*. C. 823. He may never celebrate on a papal altar unless he has an Apostolic Indult. C. 283 #3. Churches of heretics and schismatics cannot be used as places for the celebration of Mass, although such churches were formerly blessed or consecrated according to a Catholic rite. C. 823 #1.

The pastor has the right to demand a celebret from any priest that comes to the parish and wishes to say Mass in the parish church. This must, "per se" be demanded. The celebret must be signed by the Ordinary and should possess his seal if the priest be a diocesan priest, or be signed by the Superior, if the priest be a religious. If the priest belongs to the Oriental Church he must have authentic papers from the S. Congr. for the Oriental Church. C. 804 #1. When a priest has not these documents the pastor need not admit him to the celebration of Mass in his church. But the pastor may allow such a priest to say Mass there if he knows him to be in good standing. If unknown to the pastor, he may still allow him to celebrate once or twice as long as the stranger is clothed in the ecclesiastical garb, enters his name, his diocese and the office, which he holds, in the special book kept for that purpose and accepts nothing for saying Mass from the church in which he celebrates. C. 804 #2. If the pastor knows that the visiting priest is under some censure, ir-

17. Noldin, H. op. cit. l. c. p. 240.

regularity or suspension, he cannot allow such a one to ascend to the altar even when he has a celebret. It need not be mentioned that when this is known from the confessional no prohibition can be made. Whenever the Ordinary of the diocese makes some other rules regarding the admittance of strangers to the celebration of Mass in the churches of the diocese, these regulations must be followed by all even by the religious, who are exempt. The Ordinary cannot, however, make any ruling contrary to the general law of the Church nor for the admittance of religious to the celebration of Mass in churches of their own order. C. 804 #3. According to Doctor Augustine, Ruthenian priests in the U. S. and Canada may be admitted to the altar without any other papers but the celebret from their respective Ordinary or Ruthenian Bishop. (18.)

B. Holy Communion.

A pastor is bound to administer Holy Communion to his faithful as often as they reasonably ask for it. C. 467 #1. This was the common teaching of Doctors and theologians even before the New Code came into effect. It is a duty which binds the pastor in justice. And surely, as Barbosa remarks:—"nec par est, ut parvuli petant panem, et non sit, qui eum illis frangit". (19.) But no pastor with the true spirit will need to be told of this obligation. If he is to be a Father to those entrusted to his care, he will not be averse to feed them with the Food so necessary for their spiritual welfare. No command is necessary for the zealous parish priest. He will not only give this Bread of Life to those who seek it, unless they be unworthy, but he will also exhort them and encourage them all to receive as often as possible.

Holy Communion may be administered on any day of the year excepting Good Friday. On this day it may be given only as Holy Viaticum. C. 867 #2. On Holy Saturday, Holy Communion may be distributed before Mass or immediately after Mass. It may not be distributed before Mass on this day nor after the priest has left the altar. Within the Mass, it must be given after the Communion of the priest and at no other time.

18. Augustine, op. cit. vol. IV. p. 130.

19. Barbosa Aug. De Officio et Potestate Parochi, c. XX. n. 15, p. 201.

(20.) After Mass it cannot be administered except "continuo ac statim, ita ut distributio Eucharistiae sit veluti moralis continuatio Missae". (21.) On all other days Communion may be given at any time when Mass may be said, and, for a reasonable cause, even outside of the hours prescribed for the celebration of Mass. C. 867 #4. Judging from this canon alone we would say that the old law, about not distributing Holy Communion during the midnight Mass on Christmas, is done away with. This is the opinion of Blat, although Noldin holds the contrary. (22.)

The pastor is bound to admit each and every one of his faithful, *"servatis regulis de indignis"*, to the Holy Table. C. 853. He must also exhort his people to receive as often as possible, even daily. C. 863. Moreover, the people should be advised to receive their Paschal Communion in the parish church. C. 859 #3. This law is not of strict command for the people. But if they receive Paschal Communion in some other church, they are to notify the pastor of the fact. Finally, the parish priest should give proper instructions to the people regarding the utility and necessity of this sacrament, the proper dispositions with which it should be received, etc.

In distributing Holy Communion in the church, the pastor is never to go so far or to such parts of the building so as to lose sight of the altar. C. 868.

The most work in connection with this sacrament will be that of preparing children for their first Holy Communion. The following rules and regulations are to be followed. Before the child is admitted to First Holy Communion "plenior congnitio doctrinae et accuratior praeparatio merito requiritur." C. 854 #3. What this fuller knowledge and preparation is to consist in is told us in various places in the Code. Before the new law came into effect the pastors were governed by the decree of the S. Congr. of the Sacraments, given on the 8th of August, 1910. In order to give a birds-eye view of the old and new regulations,

---

20. Ferreres, J. B. op. cit. tom. II. tract. de Eucharistia, pars. I. cap. III, art. III, #394, p. 225.

21. Ferreres, op. cit. l. c. p. 225.

22. Blat, l. c. lib. III., De Rebus, p. 202. Noldin, op. cit. vol. III. cap. 1, quaest. 4, art. 2, p. 146.

I shall place them side by side, so that all changes may be easily noticed. The decree will be quoted in its english translation while the Code will be given in its official latin language:—

1. "The age of discretion both for Confession and for Communion is the time when the child begins to reason, that is about the seventh year, more or less. From this time on the precept of both Confession and Communion begins." — "Omnes utrisque sexus fidelis, postquam ad annos discretionis, id est ad rationis usum pervenerit, debet semel in anno, saltem in Paschate, Eucharistiae sacramentum recipere." C. 859 #1.

2. "Both for Confession and Communion a complete and perfect knowledge of Christian Doctrine is not necessary. The child will, however, be obliged to gradually learn the whole catechism according to its ability.

3. "The knowledge of Christian Doctrine required in children in order to be properly prepared for First Holy Communion is that they understand according to their capacity those mysteries of Faith which are necessary as a means of salvation, that they be able to distinguish the Eucharist from common material bread, and also approach the sacred Table with the devotion becoming their age". "Extra mortis periculum plenior doctrinae christianae et praeparatio merito exigitur, ea scilicet, qua ipsi fidei saltem mysteria necessaria necessitate medii ad salutem pro suo captu percipiant, ea devote pro suae aetatis modulo ad sanctissimam Eucharistiam accedant." C. 854 #3.

4. "The obligation of the precept of Confession and Communion which rests upon the child, falls back principally on those in whose care the little ones are, that is, parents, confessors, teachers and their pastors. It belongs to the Father, however, or to the person taking his place, as also the confessor, according to the Roman Catechism, to admit the child to First Holy Communion." "Obligatio praecepti communionis summendae, quae impuberes gravat, in eos quoque ac praecipue recidit, qui ipsorum curam habere debent, id est in parentes, tutores, confessarium, institutores et parochum.." C. 860. "De sufficienti puerorum dispositionis ad primam Communionem iudicium esto sacerdoti a

confessionibus eorumque parentibus aut iis qui loco parentum sunt. Parocho autem est officium advigilandi, etiam per examen, si opportunum prudenter iudicaverit, ne pueri ad sacram Synaxim accedant ante adeptum usum rationis vel sine sufficienti dispositione; itemque curandi ut usum rationis assecuti et sufficienter dispositi quamprimum hoc cibo reficiantur." — C. 854 #4-5. (23.)

The question of age has consequently been definitely settled. The old custom of not admitting children to First Holy Communion until the age of twelve must be altogether done away with and the New Code followed. The child is to be admitted as soon as sufficient knowledge and the proper dispositions are found in him. The admittance to First Holy Communion is not, as can be noticed, a strict parochial right and all contrary rulings, whether of Provincial Councils or of diocesan statutes are abolished hereby. C. 6 #1. The New law mentions the confessor as the first of those, who are to judge of the child's disposition for the reception of the Lord, placing the parents or those, who take the place of the parents, next in order. It leaves to the pastor only the office of watching over all, lest those, who are not disposed, be admitted and those, sufficiently prepared, be barred. Of course, where the pastor is also the confessor he will be the first and, as a rule, the only judge. The parents generally leave all this to the pastor himself. But if the pastor is not the child's confessor his office comes in only when he prudently suspects that the confessor or parents are acting imprudently in repelling or admitting a child. Doctor Kinane says of this point: "Is the confessor to be judge in the internal forum, and the pastor in the external? Or is the parish priest's decision to prevail in both? Or in neither? Does the new clause effect a substantial change in the arrangements of the "Quam Singulari"? Until we have some further indication of the mind of the legislator, we shall find it difficult to reconcile the privileges granted to parish priest and the confessor respectively." (24.) The pastors duties

---

23. Quam Singulari, S. C. Conc. apud Schulze, F. Pastoral Theol. supplement, p. 465 sqq.

24. Kinane, Irish Eccl. Record, vol. II, p. 115.

are not completed after the first reception of Holy Communion. He must use all diligence that those, who received for the first time, receive regularly and as often as possible, even daily. Further instruction is also to follow now. Moreover, according to the decree "Quam Singulari" the pastor is to "announce and distribute General Communion once or several times a year to the children" and on such occasions he shall admit not only First Communicants, but also those who have been admitted privately since the last general Communion.. (23.)

Another duty in regard to this sacrament is that of administering Holy Communion to the infirm. This communion should always be carried publicly. C. 847. Only a just and sufficient cause can excuse from this. The right to carry it in this manner within the parish is one of the rights of the pastor. C. 462 #2. This holds good even when carried to those infirm who are not subjects of the parish priest. C. 848 #2. In a case of necessity other priests may also carry the Lord publicly to the infirm. So also in those cases when the permission of the pastor can be presumed. C. 848 #2. "Publicly" here means the manner in which it used to be carried and is still so carried in some countries, i. e. in procession, composed of the pastor, a cleric or the sexton and the people that go along. Here in the U. S., Holy Communion is generally carried privately. When this is the case, it is no more a reserved function of the pastor, since the law expressly states:—"Communionem privatim ad infirmos quilibet sacerdos deferre potest, de venia saltem praesumpta sacerdotis, cui custodia sanctissimi commissa est." C. 849 #1.

"Infirmi tamen qui iam a mense decumbunt sine certa spe ut cito convalescant, de prudenti confessarii consilio sanctissimam Eucharistiam sumere possunt semel aut bis in hebdomada, etsi aliquam medicinam vel aliquid per modum potus antea sumpserint." C. 858 #2. But what is meant here by the term "decumbunt"? It certainly does not mean that the sick person would have to be in bed continually for the last month. There are some illnesses when the infirm cannot stay in bed at all, and certainly if all the other requirements are present the Church will not ex-

25. "Quam Singulari" apud Schulze, op. cit. loco cit. p. 466.

clude these from such a privilege. The S. Congregation of the Council tells us that this privilege could be used by such as can get out of bed occasionally for a time. (26.) But this privilege cannot be made use of by such as are habitually out of bed and walking around (even making a trip to church, etc.,) but cannot fast. (27.) In the last case mentioned H. Communion should be given the sick person early in the morning if they can observe the fast up to that time or else a dispensation from the sacramental fast is to be asked for from the S. Congregation of the Sacraments. Besides, the person is to receive "de prudenti confessarii consilio" and not of his own accord and judgment, nor according to the pastor unless he be the confessor. By liquid food is meant coffee, broth, wheat-meal, ground toast etc., as long as the mixture retains the nature of a liquid food. (28.) In every case the sick person should receive fasting if that can be done. But when the privilege granted in canon 858 #2 is allowed, he can make use of this privilege on the two days even when he is able to receive while fasting on the other five days of the week. This concession would not be taken from him just because he could observe the fast on the other five days of the week. (29.) A priest cannot make use of this concession for the celebration of Mass, but he could if he receives Holy Communion instead of saying Mass. Thus also, if the priest were found in the condition mentioned in Canon 585 #2 and were allowed to receive Holy Communion twice a week while not fasting, he could still celebrate Mass on the other five days if he is able to fast then.

Another of the rights of the parish priest is the carrying of Holy Viaticum publicly or privately to the sick of his parish. C. 466 #3; C. 850 # 1. This means to any person situated within the parish limits, be he a subject of the pastor or not. In case of necessity any priest may bring this Consolation to the infirm. So also in other cases when the permission of the pastor or of the Ordinary of the place can be presumed. To this reserved func-

26. S. Congr. Conc. March 6, 1907.

27. Noldin, H. op. cit. vol. III. lib. IV. cap. I, quaes. 5, art. 4, p. 174.

28. S. Congr of the Holy Office, 7th of Sept 1897. apud Collectanea S. Congr. de prop. Fide #1983, vol. II, p. 363.

29. Noldin, H. op. cit. l. c. p. 174; Augustine, op. cit. vol. IV. p. 236.

tion of the pastor only two exceptions are made by the general law. The one is that the dignitaries and canons of the chapter have the right to administer Holy Viaticum to the Bishop whether he be found within the pastor's parish limits or not. C. 397 #3. But if these are wanting the pastor has the right next in order. The second exception is made in canon 514 # 1—3. This canon states that:—"In omni religione clericali ius et officium Superioribus est per se vel per alium aegrotis professis, novitiis, aliisve in religiosa domo diu nocteque degentibus causa famulatus aut educationis aut hospitii aut infirmae valetudinis, Eucharisticum Viaticum — — — — ministrandi. 2. In monialium domo idem ius et officium habet ordinarius confessarius vel qui eius vices gerit. 3. In alia religione laicali hoc ius et officium spectat ad parochum loci vel ad cappellanum quem Ordinarius parocho suffecerit ad normam can, 464 #2." C. 514.

The bringing of the Holy Viaticum to those in need is not only a right but also the duty of the parish priest. If the Catholic, who is in danger of death is bound to receive Our Lord (C. 864 #1.) it certainly follows that the pastor must be ready to administer Holy Viaticum to him. The parishioner has the right and duty of asking for this means of grace without delay and accordingly, the parish priest is to supply it with readiness. C. 865. There can be no doubt about this. Canon 467 tells us that the parish priest is held to administer the Sacraments to the faithful as often as they reasonably ask for them, while, the following canon furthermore binds him to take special care of the infirm, especially when they are near death's door. C. 468 #1.

Holy Viaticum need not and should not be postponed too long. The people should be instructed to call the priest in time, so that the sick could be reached while they still possess the use of reason. C. 865. It matters not what time of the day or night the pastor is called, this means of grace may be administered at any time. (C. 867 #5.) and even when the sick person has already received Holy Communion on that day. C. 864 #2. If the confessor deems it prudent, Holy Viaticum may be administered on several days in succession, while the danger of death lasts. C. 864 #3.

At times pastors may refuse Holy Viaticum to a child who has the use of reason, just because they consider the child an infant. This is an abuse which was condemned by the decree "Quam Singulari" as follows:—"It is an utterly detestable abuse not to administer Viaticum and Extreme Unction to children having attained the use of reason and to bury them according to the manner of infants." (30.)

The New Code lays down severe penalties for those pastors who are negligent in their duties regarding the administration of Holy Communion, whether to the infirm or others. The Bishop may even go so far as to deprive a pastor of his parish or to remove an irremovable pastor in the manner stated above in regard to pastors negligent in the duty of preaching and catechising. C. 2382; C. 2181-2185.

Every parish priest should make it a practice to visit the sick at certain intervals, and as often as his duties will allow. The habit of administering the last sacraments and then never visiting the sick is an abuse which the Church wishes to eradicate. The time of sickness is a time of trial and the kind visits and consoling words of the pastor will help immeasurably on such occasions. Besides, how can the pastor tell whether he will be needed again or not before the death of the infirm party? May it not happen that this ministration may again be required? If the priest makes short visits often, questioning the patient whether he needs anything in the spiritual line, encouraging him in his sufferings and consoling him in his trials, he will be able to rest, satisfied that he is doing all in his power. He should also tell the people to call him when the end is near if he is not there at that time. The mother watches over her child to the last; shall the spiritual father do less? "Sedula cura et effusa caritate debet parochus aegrotos in sua paroecia, maxime vero morti proximos, adiuvare, eos sollicite Sacramentis reficiendo eorumque animas Deo commendando". C. 468 #1. And when the end is near, the pastor will impart to the departing soul the Apostolic Benediction, according to the formula prescribed in the ritual, and commend the soul to the Mercy of God. C. 468 #2.

---

30. "Quam Singulari", apud Schulze op. cit. l. c. p. 466.

Sect. 5. Penance.

"Receive ye the Holy Ghost. Whose sins you shall forgive, they are forgiven them; and whose sins you shall retain, they are retained." (1.) With these words Christ instituted the sacrament of Penance and made men dispensers of this divine mercy. No limits, but the barriers of sinful obstinacy were put upon this power. . "If your sins be as scarlet, they shall be made as white as snow; and if they be red as crimson, they shall be white as wool." (2.) Consequently, how important that the faithful be well instructed regarding the nature, the efficacy, the need of this means of grace and forgiveness, as well as about the proper dispositions for it's reception. This the pastor is to teach them. Aye, and more. He must also give them the opportunity of receiving this sacrament by being willing at all times to administer it to them whenever they reasonably ask for it. This is demanded by the New Code in the following terms: "Parochi — — — — gravi justitiae obligatione tenentur audiendi sive per se sive per alium confessiones fidelium sibi commissorum, quoties ii audiri rationabiliter petant." C. 892 #1. The necessity of the proper fulfillment of this obligation is clearly seen when we consider on the one hand, the great amount of good it brings and, on the other, the immeasurable harm which its neglect produces. Sacramental absolution is necessary for all who had the misfortune of falling into mortal sin after baptism. "Qui post baptismum mortalia perpetravit, quae nondum per claves Ecclesiae directe remissa sunt, debet omnia quorum post diligentem sui discussionem conscientiae habeat, confiteri et circumstantias in confessione explicare, quae speciem peccati mutent." C. 901. If this is a binding duty upon the faithful, the pastor must give them the opportunity of fulfilling it. He should not be averse to hearing confessions often, but should try to make it easy for all to go to the sacred tribunal. "No sacrament has such an eminently pastoral character as the sacrament of penance, for it represents to us the priest as *"Pastor Ovium"*, as the shepherd who goes in search of the lost sheep and who, after having found it among the

1. St. John, Chapter 20, verses 22-23.
2. Isaias, Chap. 1, verse 18.

thorns or in the desert, places it on his shoulders and carries it back to the fold." (3.) The importance of this pastoral duty cannot be over-estimated. The wise and prudent administration of this sacrament will be of benefit not merely to the individual penitent but to the whole community. The Fathers of the II. Council of Baltimore saw the harm in the neglectful attitude of the confessor and therefore included in their legislation the instruction that every confessor should always show himself prompt and ready to enter the confessional. (4.). Besides being prompt and willing to hear confessions at all times the pastor must also be kind and patient. Impatience, harshness, etc., must be left outside the door of the sacred tribunal. Even if the case should demand the refusal of absolution, there is no reason for acting in a gruff, hard manner. That will not aid in bringing the penitent back to right ways, but may serve to repel him forever. The kindness of a Father is necessary, for harsh, unkind words or rebukes "may destroy the efforts which divine grace is making to bring forth the secrets of iniquity." (5.) There is no doubt that the fulfillment of this parochial duty is often difficult and tiresome, but the parish priest must be willing to bear this, to aid the sheep entrusted to him on their way Home. Besides the virtues of kindness and patience, other qualities are also required in a good confessor, e. gr. knowledge, so that he could teach and judge, prudence, in order that he might diagnose correctly and apply the right remedies, etc. These are important requisites and without them the confessor cannot hope for fruits which would otherwise be forthcoming from his ministration.

Before any priest can hear confessions in any place, he must have jurisdiction there. The pastor receives this jurisdiction by the very grant of the parochial office. His is ordinary jurisdiction "*within the parochial limits*". C. 873 #1. Consequently, he can also exercise it in favor of his subjects in any part of the world. C. 881. #8. Still, he cannot delegate it to anyone even for the hearing of confessions of his own subjects in the parish church. C. 874. Nor can he hear the confessions of religious

3. Schulze, F. Pastoral Theology, p. 134.
4. Conc. Plen. Balt. II Acta et Decr. #280, p. 150.
5. Stang, Pastoral Theol. Chap. IV. #26, p. 144.

and novices in their own houses, even when such are located within the parish. For this a special jurisdiction is necessary. C. 876. But if such i. e. religious and novices, come to the parish church to confession he may hear them there. C. 522. The same holds true if they come to some public or semi-public oratory within the parish, where he is hearing confessions. In all such places the pastor can hear the confessions of each and anyone that comes to him, be he subject, peregrinus, vagus or even a subject of some Catholic Oriental rite. C. 881 #1. For the hearing of confessions of others than his subjects outside of his parish limits, the pastor needs special power which he receives in the faculties from the Ordinary.

A pastor, who is approved by the Ordinary to hear confessions may, when he is on a sea voyage, hear the confessions of any and all the passengers on the boat with him. And if this boat makes any stops on the way, he may also absolve all those who come aboard or if he himself makes a landing during these short stops, he can also absolve all who may incidentally approach him. There he can also absolve from the cases reserved in that place by the Ordinary of that port. C. 883. This faculty of the traveling pastor holds good even in the presence of priests approved in that place where the short stop was made.

Canon 885 tells us that not all the prayers, prescribed for the administration of the sacrament of penance, are of necessity for the validity of the formula, still all should be made use of unless a just cause excuses. For the omission of the prayers that precede the absolution itself, i. e. the "Misereatur" and the "Indulgentiam", lack of time on the part of the confessor or of the penitent or a great multitude of people will be sufficient to excuse. (6.) The prayer following the absolution itself, i. e. the "Passio" may be omitted in the more frequent confessions. (7.) According to Noldin this last prayer may probably be left out licitly in all confessions. (8.) But this does not agrée with the New Code, which states that these prayers which are not necessary for the validity should not be omitted "sine justa causa".

6. Noldin, op. cit. vol. III. lib. V. cap. 1. quaestio 3, #237, p. 278.
7. Rituale Romanorum, tit. III, c 2, p. 73.
8 Noldin, op. cit. l. c. p. 279.

Moreover, it behooves that this prayer be seldom omitted, since, according to a probable opinion, it elevates the good works of the penitent.

When the confessor cannot doubt the dispositions of the penitent before him, he cannot deny or postpóne the absolution. C. 886. A salutary penance is also to be imposed and the seal of confession always kept inviolable. C. 887; C. 889. The practice of speaking in general terms about things of the confessional must be avoided.

The place for hearing confessions is any church, public or semi-public oratory. C. 908. The confessional for the hearing of confessions of women should be placed in an open and conspicuous place, "Et generatim in ecclesía, vel oratoris publica aut semipublico mulieribus destinato." C. 909. Such a confessional must be immovable and have a screen with small perforations between the confessor and the penitent. C. 909 #2. This screen is necessary not only in the confessionals for women but also in those for men as was decided by the "Pontifical Commission for the authentic Interpretation of the New Code. (8a.) The confessions of women may never be heard outside of the confessional, except this be necessitated by infirmity or some other cause of real necessity. C. 910. And even in the cases when the confessions of women may be heard outside of the confessional, the pastor is to make use of all the precautions prescribed by the Ordinary of the diocese ex. gr. "crates"., etc. In some diocese the absolution of women outside of the confessional, except in case of necessity, is invalid, in others the confessor incurs ipso facto suspension. The confessions of men may be heard also outside of the church and even in private houses. C. 910 #2.

It will be necessary to say a few words here about the faculties given to parish priests by common law. In the first place canon 899 #3 says, that pastors may, during the time within which people are held to make their Easter duty, absolve from any and all reserved cases which are reserved by the Ordinary. Moreover, every reservation of the Ordinary ceases for those who are so sick that they are unable to leave the house, as well as for

8a. A. A. S. vol. XII. p. 576.

those who come to confession in preparation for marriage. C. 900 #1. Such reservations also cease in case the lawful superior refuses the faculty of absolving in a certain instance. So also when the confessor prudently judges that "the power to absolve cannot be obtained without grave inconvenience on the part of the penitent, or when there is danger of violating the seal of confession." (9.) Moreover, a confessor of one diocese can absolve from cases reserved in another diocese as long as the same case is not reserved in this diocese, and it is not a "censura ab homine". This can be done even when the penitent comes to the parish from the other diocese for the very purpose of receiving absolution from such a reserved case. C. 900, #3; C. 2247 #2.

Now what about absolution from censures? In danger of death any priest can absolve from any censure or sin. C. 882. "In periculo mortis omnes sacerdotes, licet ad confessiones non approbati, valide et licite absolvunt quoslibet poenitentes a quibusvis peccatis aut censuris quatumvis reservatis et notoriis, etiamsi praesens sit sacerdos approbatus, salvo praescipto. Can. 884, 2252." Therefore, it is not even necessary that the priest be one approved for confessions in that diocese. Any simple priest, without any approbation, can do this in such cases. We find similar legislation already in the Council of Trent:—"It has been piously held by the Church of God that there is no reservation in regard to those who are in danger of death. In order that none may perish, every priest can absolve penitents from any sins and censures." (10.) There is, however, one instance when absolution imparted in danger of death is illicit except in case of necessity i. e. the absolution of an accomplice 'in peccato turpi." Although such an absolution, given by the partner in the crime, is valid in danger of death it remains illicit unless it be a case of necessity. C. 884. Moreover, any accomplice who absolves or "fingens absolvere complicem in peccato turpi incurrit ipso facto in excommunicationem specialissimo modo Sedi Apostolicae reservatam; idque etiam in mortis articulo, si alius sacerdos, licet non appro-

---

9. Kubelbeck, Wm. The Sacred Penitentiaria etc., Chap. VII. p. 78. C. 900 #2.

10. Conc. Trid. ses. 14, c. 7.

batus ad confessiones, sine gravi aliqua exoritura infamia et scandalo, possit excipere morientis confessionem, excepto casu quo moribundus recuset alii confiteri." C. 2367. Canon 2252 moreover tells us that when a penitent in danger of death has been absolved from a censure "ab homine" or from any one of those censures reserved to the Holy See "specialissimo modo" by a confessor wanting in the special faculty of absolving in such cases, he must, after his recovery and under pain of falling back into the same censure, have recourse to the person, who inflicted the censure (if it be a censura ab homine) or to the S. Penitentiaria, the Bishop or any other person having the special faculty of absolving from these censures (when the censure is "a iure"). This recourse must be made according to canon 2254 #1, i. e. "saltem per epistolam et per confessarium" within one month after the penitent has become well, that is, as Creusen-Vermeersch say:—"intra mensem postquam, periculo remoto, vires satis recuperaverit ut facile ipse negotium perficere possit." (11.) The name of the penitent, however, is to be kept secret. When the person, who inflicted the censure, or the S. Penitentiary, or the Bishop or confessor having the special faculty of absolving give the decision after the recourse was made, the penitent must abide by the instructions. This recourse is to be made at all times as long as it can be done "sine gravi incommodo. C. 2254 #1. When, however, this is morally impossible the confessor can impart the absolution even from such censures without imposing upon the penitent any obligation of recourse, excepting in the case of the censure incurred by absolving or *"fingens absolvere"* an accomplice *"in peccato turpi"*. C. 2254, #3. The confessor should, however, enjoin all that the law requires, impose a salutary penance and satisfaction for the censure, warning the penitent that unless he performs this penance and satisfaction before a certain date he will again fall back into the same censure from which he has just been absolved. These same powers are granted to all confessors in case of urgent necessity. Any confessor can absolve from reserved cases in the sacramental forum under these

---

11. Creusen-Vermeersch. Summa Novi Iuris Canonici, lib. V. tit. VIII, c. I, p. 199.

conditions: 1. that the case be urgent; 2. that the censures latae sententiae cannot be endured without grave scandal, infamy or that it be difficult for the penitent to remain in the state of mortal sin until provision could be made by the competent superior for his absolution. The obligation of recourse is to be imposed as above excepting when it becomes morally impossible to do so. In that case the action explained previously is to be followed. C. 2254. Of course, if the confessor has the special faculty of absolving from these cases, then he absolves without imposing any obligation of recourse, but gives his commands which the penitent must follow. C. 2254, #2. But if a penitent who has been absolved and ordered to have recourse to a higher superior, goes, after making this recourse to a confessor, who has the faculty of absolving from such cases, confesses his crime and censure and receives absolution from the latter, then he will have to follow the orders of this last confessor and need not heed those which will come later from the higher superior to whom the recourse was made in the first place. C. 2284. #2. Canon 2290, moreover, gives the confessor similar faculties in "casibus urgentioribus, si ex observatione *poenae vindicativae latae sententiae*, reus se proderat cum infamia et scandalo." In such instances, the confessor can suspend the observance of the vindicative penalty (as found under title IX. of the 5th book of the New Code) imposing upon him the obligation of a recourse as stated above to the S. Penitentiary or to the Bishop having the faculty of dispensing from the penalty. C. 2290, #1. In case this recourse is impossible the confessor himself grants the dispensation from the vindicative punishment according to canon 2254, #3 explained above. C. 2290, #2.

If a confessor absolves from a censure and sin without knowing that such is reserved, the absolution is valid as long as the censure is not one inflicted by man ("ab homine") or one that is reserved to the Holy See in a most special manner ("specialissimo modo reservata"). C. 2247, #3.

Every confessor has in the more urgent cases, the faculty of dispensing from any irregularity arising from an occult crime (excepting 1. those persons, who commit voluntary homicide, or 2.

those, who procure abortion, when the effect followed, as well as all the cooperators in this crime and finally, 3. those cases that have been brought before the judicial forum) if the case be an occult one and recourse cannot be had to the ordinary and there is danger of serious harm or infamy for the penitent if he remains in this state. This dispensation can, however, be given only for the exercise of orders already received and not for the reception of orders. C. 990, #2.

The confessor should study the Code so that he would have a good working knowledge of the law. This will often aid him out of tight places in which he might not know how to act without this knowledge. Familiarity with the new legislation should be the aim of every pastor, for although cases of censures are not of frequent occurence, this is the greater reason for being on the guard lest we forget how to act when they do turn up. Besides this common law the pastor should also study his faculties in order that he would know whether his powers were extended or restricted by the Ordinary.

It may be of practical value to add a few words here about the place and manner of seeking dispensations and absolutions. This may save the parish priest much time and labor. The S. Penitentiaria is the Tribunal which has jurisdiction over all things pertaining to the forum internum even non-sacramental. All absolutions, commutations, sanations and condonations in the internal forum must be petitioned from this S. Tribunal "reticito nomine poenitentis" if the matter must be sent to Rome at all. C. 238. Absolution from a censure "ab homine" is to be sought from the person who inflicted the censure or passed the sentence, or from his superior, successor or delegate. C. 2253 and 2245. Absolution from a censure reserved by law must be sought from him who constituted the censure or from him to whom it is reserved, their competent superiors, successors and delegates. C. 2253. From a censure reserved to the Holy See absolution must be sought from the Holy See, i.e. S. Penitentiaria, or from those who were given the special faculty of absolving in those cases. Care must always be taken that the seal of confession is not violated and that all that is necessary be expressed clearly without violating this seal. If there are more censures in one and the same case, all of them will have to be mentioned, otherwise the absolution holds good only for those expressed in the petition. But if the absolution is general, i. e. "pro omnibus casibus concessa" even though the petition was made for only a certain censure, the absolution is good for all censures in the case, except those reserved to the Holy See 'specialissimo modo", as long as the censures omitted in the petition were omitted in good faith. If they were left out "mala fide", those omitted are not absolved. C. 2249, #2. The formulas for absolutions, commutations, condonations are found in many authors, and need not be mentioned specifically here.

The general rule in reference to the place where the *supplica* is to be sent by the pastor is this. If the case is one that belongs to the external forum and is not such as will bring defamation, etc., upon the parties it ought to be sent to the Ordinary of the diocese. Otherwise directly to the S. Congregation at Rome. For matters pertaining to the internal forum the supplica is to be sent directly to Rome to the S. Penitentiaria.

The supplica when sent to the S. Penitentiaria may be written in any modern language, but the Latin characters are to be made use of. If the confessor employs an agent at Rome, when writing to the S. Penitentiaria, he should follow the following instruction of that S. Tribunal:—"Ceterum si opera alicujus procuratoris in alma Urbe uti velint, litteras obsignatas praelaudato Cardinali Poenitentiario Maiori tradendas supressis nominibus ad ipsum procuratorem transmittere quidem poterunt, aut memoratos casus S. Penitentiariae proponendos nunquam aut nullimodo narrare seu manifestare audeant." (13.)

Sect. 6. Holy Orders.

The duties of the pastor in connection with the sacrament of Holy Orders are not very numerous. In the first place the New Code imposes upon the pastors the obligation of watching over the candidates for the priesthood, who live within the parish.

13. Apud. Acta S. Sedis, vol. VII. p. 208.

They are to give an account of their conduct whenever this is demanded by the Ordinary or the rector of the Seminary which the candidates are frequenting. The testimonial thus given to the student at the request of the Ordinary or at the end of the summer vacation should be a faithful exposition of the candidate's morals during the time spent in that parish. As Father Stang remarks:—"A greater service is rendered to the Church in America by keeping one student from becoming a bad priest than by assisting ten young men to become good priests." (1.) At times the pastor may also be asked to make an investigation into the life of some student. C. 1000, #1. When this is asked of the parish priest, he should fulfill the office conscientiously and make a truthful report to the episcopal curia.

According to the new law, the pastor is also to announce from the pulpit the names of those students of his parish, who are about to be promoted to sacred orders. This does not hold with regard to those students who are religious with perpetual vows. C. 998. This proclamation is to be made publicly in the parish church unless the Ordinary dispenses therefrom or orders that another form of announcing these names be introduced, e. g. a written announcement to be affixed to the doors of the church for several days, including at least one feast day. If the oral form is to be used, the proclamation is to be made on a Sunday or feast day of obligation during the parochial Mass or during any other divine service, which is frequented by a large part of the people. C. 998, #2. If the ordination of the student does not take place within six months after this announcement has taken place the proclamation must be made anew, unless the Ordinary decides otherwise. C. 998, #3.

Whenever a person baptized in the parish receives subdeaconship, a note of this fact is to be made aside his name in the baptismal record. C. 1101 and C. 470, #2.

The pastor should also tell his people that they are bound to reveal each and any impediment that may be known to them and which would bar the candidate from the reception of the Orders about to be conferred upon him. C. 999.

1. Stang. Pastoral Theology, p. 190.

Not only is the pastor to watch over the conduct of the students, who have entered upon studies leading to the sacred Priesthood, but he is also to guard carefully those children, who show some signs of a vocation to the ecclesiastical life. He should shield them from the harmful influences of the world, nourish and foster within them this seed of a vocation and instruct them in the ways of piety, and, also, if needs be, in the necessary elements of the studies toward that end. C. 1353. But if the pastor does nothing positive, he should not, at least, by his language and example, tear down the high ideals which the child may have of the priesthood.

A wholesome practice is that found with some parish priests of having their people pray for the candidates to the priesthood. This should be done at all times, but especially at the times when sacred orders are being conferred. A word or two on the part of a good pastor will bring this about. The people think much of their priests and students to the priesthood and will gladly offer up prayers in their behalf, if they are but reminded of this occasionally.

Sect. 7. Matrimony.

When we look over the legislation contained in the New Code of Canon Law, we notice that, more space has been devoted to the treatment of the subject of Matrimony than to that of any other Sacrament. The subject is a very extensive one, embracing many details. The Church wishes to define matters pertaining thereto very minutely in order that Her mind may be made clear. Accordingly, it is of the greatest importance for all such as will come into contact with matrimonial affairs, to have a good working knowledge of this law. It will, of necessity, entail much time and labor to secure this knowledge, but the proper fulfillment of one's duties demands that this time and labor be spent.

Among those, who will be called upon most frequently to deal with such matters, are the parish priests. Consequently, it will be necessary for them to study the general law of the Church and it's interpretation in this regard before they attempt to handle such affairs. This can be done by devoting oneself to works on this subject. The New Code has introduced some changes from the old law and these will have to be taken into consideration and therefore, books, which treat this subject according to the New Code will have to be consulted. It is my aim and hope to be able to help the pastors in this regard, although it is not my intention to treat in detail all the legislation referring to matrimony. I hope to give a general exposition of the rights and duties of the parish priests in this regard.

Before touching upon the parochial rights and duties connected with any particular marriage, it may be well to say a few words in regard to the duty of a pastor concerning the instruction of his people about this sacrament. The parish priest must use prudence in teaching his parishioners the doctrine of the Church concerning the nature, the properties, the effects, etc. of this sacrament, and give them a good idea of the impediments and other obstacles to its proper reception. C. 1018. This duty is his as teacher of his people, for upon him devolves the obligation of instilling into their minds knowledge necessary for the worthy reception of the sacraments. The law says that he is to teach them *"prudently."* Consequently, anything that would be of no service and might only be used to evade the law, should not be mentioned. The same holds true in regard to points which might only give scandal. Besides instructing the people in regard to the sacrament of matrimony, the parish priest is also bound to discourage mixed marriages. The parochus should explain to them that the Church prohibits these marriages most severely. C. 1060; C. 1102. The II. and III. Councils of Baltimore also admonished the pastors of the U. S. in this regard The former stated that the pastor was to give such an instruction at least once a year especially during Lent or Advent, while the latter advises that talks of this sort be given frequently. If the pastor cannot deter the faithful from entering into such undesirable unions, he should, at least, do all in his power to prevent them from celebrating the marriage contrary to the laws of God and His Church. C. 1064 #2. But this is not all that is

1. Conc. Plen. Balt. II, # 336, p. 175.
2. Conc. Plen. Balt. III, #133, p. 67.

demanded from him. He must also watch over such people after their marriage and see to it that they fulfill the promises made before the wedding. This obligation is a grave one as the S. Congregation of the Propagation of the Faith notes in an instruction to the Archbishop of Baltimore:- "Post celebratas mixtas nuptias, parochi gravi conscientiae onere se gravari sciant invigilandi ut promissae a coniugibus conditiones observentur, et effectum sortiantur." (3.) Moreover, the pastor must also try to keep his people from entering into matrimonial unions with such as have notoriously renounced their Faith even though they have not joined a non-catholic sect. C. 1065 #I. This same duty binds the parish priest with reference to marriages with those, who belong to societies condemned by the Catholic Church. He may not assist at any such marriages before notifying the Ordinary and abiding by his instructions. C. 1067 #2. According to the laws of the Church a boy can marry validly at the age of sixteen, a girl at the age of fourteen. C. 1067 #1. But what is allowed for validity is not always expedient and best. Circumstances and conditions e. g. climatic conditions of the place, the physical developement of the contracting parties, etc. must be taken into consideration. As Noldin says:—"Qui adepti sunt annos pubertatis, nondum ubique matrimonium licite inire possunt. Etenim non in omnibus regionibus cum annis pubertatis incipit potestas generandi; sed antequam adsit aptitudo generandi, per se non licet inire matrimonium." (4.) And Wernz remarks:- "Pubertas naturalis multum differre potest a pubertate legali; etenim citius adest in civitate quam in ruri, in hominibus studiis deditis quam in operariis laboribus corporalibus occupatis, in regionibus meridionalibus quam in septentrionalibus. V. g. media aetas pubertatis naturalis in Laplandia sunt 18. anni. Hafniae in Dania 16. anni et 9. menses, Monachii in Bavaria 16. anni et 5. menses, Viennae 15. anni et 8. menses, in insula (Corcyrensi (Corfu) 14. anni, in civitate Calcuttensi 12. anni et 6. menses, in Aegypto 10.

---

3. Instr. S. C. de Prop. Fide, June 25, 1884, apud Collectanea S. C. de P. F. vol. II #1621, p. 201.

4. Noldin H. op. cit. editio X. p. 661.

anni." (5.) The customary time observed in the region in which the pastor is situated should be observed. C. 1067 #2. On the other hand marriages should not be put off too long, since the Church considers the age of 25 in a woman as an "aetas superadulta" and sufficient cause for asking a dispensation from a matrimonial impediment in certain cases.

When the parties present themselves at the rectory to make known their intention of a future marriage, the pastor must first determine whether he can assist validly and licitly at their marriage. For, although C. 462 #6 says that the assistance at marriages is a parochial right of the pastor, this does not mean that each and every pastor may assist at each and any marriage. What then is necessary in order that the parish priest might assist validly and licitly? In the first place, as C. 1095 tells us, a parish priest can assist validly at any marriage within his territory only after he has taken canonical possession of his parish, (according to C. 1444 #1) or has begun to exercise his office and is not deprived of his jurisdiction and right by any condemnatory or declaratory sentence of excommunication, interdict or suspension from office (a change from the old law), and as long as he asks for and receives the consent of the parties without being forced to do so by violence or grave fear. C. 1095 #1. Under these conditions he can assist validly at any marriage within his territory, whether the parties be his subjects or not. As was said the pastor cannot assist validly when he is excommunicated, suspended from office or interdicted by a *condemnatory or declaratory sentence.* Consequently, if the parish priest incurs some secret or even public excommunication which is merely *"latae sententiae"*, he is not disqualified in reference to valid assistence at marriages within his territory. The same would be true in case he commits a crime having attached to it an "ipso facto suspension or interdict." A condemnatory or declaratory sentence must be passed. According to C. 1874 it would then be necessary that the pastor be nominally excommunicated, interdicted or suspended from office, before it would dis-

5. Wernz, F. X. Ius Decretalium, tom. IV. tit. XII. #311, nota 6. p. 106.

qualify him from acting validly at marriages within his parochial territory. Of course, if a pastor is transferred, removed or deprived of his parochial office or when he resigns and his resignation has been accepted, or, again, when he is reduced to the lay state, his jurisdiction and right cease thereby. Furthermore, the Code demands that the pastor ask for and receive the consent of the two parties, without being constrained to it by force or grave fear. This is a change from the Law of Trent. According to the latter a marriage would be valid even if the pastor was forced to assist. Today the presence of force or grave fear would make the marriage contract invalid. According to the decree "Ne Temere" the pastor had to be asked and invited to attend. The interpretation of that law was extended to an interpretative or implicit invitation, so that there is not so much difference between that and the present legislation.

Any pastor, who can assist validly at a marriage can also give another priest permission to assist validly at that marriage within the parochial limits. C. 1095 #2. The following notes how this permission is to be given. The New Code introduces another change here. In former years a pastor could give universal delegation, but today this is forbidden. As the Code says this delegation must be given:- 1. expressly, 2. to a certain priest, 3. for a determinate marriage. Firstly, it must be express delegation. This may be done orally or in writing. It may also be given by signs if they are sufficiently clear to signify the delegation. Tacit, presumed or an interpretative delegation is not sufficient. Although free *assistance* is necessary for the validity of the marriage, a *delegation* extorted by force or grave fear would be a valid delegation, so that were one, who extorted this delegation in that manner, to act freely at the marriage ceremony, the marriage would be valid, presuming of course that all other requirements are present. (6.) Secondly, the delegation must be made to a certain priest who is not excommunicated, interdicted or suspended from office by a condemnatory or declaratory sentence. This part of the canon is of the greatest importance. The name of the delegated priest need not be expressed

6. Noldin, A. op. cit. lib. 8. quaestio 8, art. 2. p. 720.

as long as such terms are used as would designate the person, so that he could not be confused with others. Thus if the pastor says:- "I delegate the pastor of the parish of Our Lady of Lourdes, Cleveland, Ohio" or "I delegate the first assistant of the parish of St. Wenceslaus, Cleveland, Ohio" this is sufficient to determine the person as long as other circumstances do not cause confusion and render this determinate delegation indeterminate. The best and safest manner of making these delegations is to name the person desired and then no mistake need be feared. The determinate delegation may extend to more than one. Thus the pastor may say:- "I delegate the pastor and assistants of the Church of St. Wenceslaus" or " the parochial clergy of the parish of St. Martin." But he could not make a valid delegation in this manner:- "I delegate any priest for this marriage of John N. and Anna N. whom they may choose." This is not a determined person and the delegation is invalid. The pastor delegating may also give the priest delegated by him for this determined marriage the faculty of subdelegating. As Noldin remarks:- "eiusmodi enim delegatio non censetur indeterminata, dummodo delegatus sibi non substituat (non subdeleget) nisi personam determinatam." (7.) i. e. the delegate must also then observe the law and make a determinate subdelegation. Thirdly, the delegation must be made for a determinate marriage. A delegation made for all the marriages within the parish is not valid for any of them. Even the Bishop cannot now delegate a priest to assist at all the marriages within the diocese. It is necessary that the marriage at which the determined priest is to assist be specified. In order to make certain that all will be legitimately performed, it is best and most practical for the pastor, when delegating another, to name the parties, who are to be married. The only persons that may be given a general delegation are the assistants of the parish and this in the sense that they will be able to assist at all the marriages that may be celebrated within that parish. C. 1096 #1. These assistant priests are the ones mentioned in C. 476, i. e. those given to a pastor be-

---

7. Noldin, H. op. cit. 1. c. p. 721.

cause he cannot take care of the people on account of their great number or for some other reason.

Now that we have treated of the valid assistance at mariages and the valid delegation of this jurisdiction to others, let us turn to the requirements for the liceity of the pastor's assistance at marriages within his territory. Canon 1097 tells us that before the parish priest can assist licitly at any marriage, even within his parochial boundaries, it is necessary for him to ascertain whether the parties are free to marry, i. e. free from all impediments, whether public or occult. The process to be followed in this examination and investigation will be explained later. Secondly, the pastor may not assist at a marriage unless at least one of the parties belongs to his parish, i. e. has a domicile, quasi-domicile or a month's residence in that parish. If this condition is wanting the pastor will have to tell them that they should be married by their proper pastor, or, if they insist upon being married here, he must secure the permission of their proper pastor or Ordinary. In cases of grave necessity this permission will not have to be asked for. Vagi, who are actually staying in the parish at present or are actually moving through the parochial territory, may be married by the pastor in his parish as long as he obtains permission of the Ordinary or the priest appointed for such affairs. C. 1032. Besides, the general rule is that the marriage is to take place before the pastor of the bride when the two contracting parties have different proper parish priests. But any reasonable cause will excuse from this law and allow the pastor of the bride-groom to marry the couple. Catholics belonging to different catholic rites are to be married by the pastor of the bride-groom and according to that rite. Particular laws may effect a change in this regard.

If the pastor assists at a marriage to which he has no right and asks no permission, he is held to return the stole fee to the proper pastor of the parties. C. 1097 #3.

These are the general rules. Now as to their practical aplonging to different Catholic rites are to be married by the pastor proceeds to take up the affairs of the future marriage he is to find out whether they or one of them belongs to his parish, i.

e. is his subject. Only such are his subjects in reference to matrimony as have either a domicile, a quasi-domicile or a month's residence in his parish. C. 1097. At other marriages he cannot assist licitly unless he first secures the proper permission of the pastor of the parties or of at least one of them, or if they are vagi, the permission of the Ordinary or the priest, appointed to give this permission, must be obtained. C. 1032. Cases of necessity excuse from seeking this permission. He may, however, also assist licitly at the marriages of such as have only a diocesan domicile or quasi-domicile. C. 94 #3.

Since the notions of domicile, quasi-domicile and monthly residence are of such great importance here, it will not be out of place to repeat what was said about the first two in a previous chapter and to add an interpretation of the third. What then is a domicile? a quasi-domicile? a month's residence? According to Canon 92 #1. a domicile is that legal habitat acquired by an actual residence in the parish with the intention of remaining there permanently unless something unforeseen should call one away. If no intention is present, an actual stay of ten complete years in the parish also secures the domicile. A quasi-domicile is acquired by an actual stay of six complete months in the parish or by a stay of shorter length combined with an intention to remain there for the greater part of the year, i. e. at least six months. This was the interpretation given to the term "greater part of the year" by the S. Congr. of the Holy Office. (8.) A month's stay is interpreted to mean thirty complete days, morally continuous. But this need not be an altogether uninterrupted stay. Thus, if a person is absent from the parish for a day or two during these thirty days, he is still said to have a month's residence there. This would hold true even if the person left the parish with the intention of not returning and then changed his mind and came back within a day or two. Noldin moreover, holds that, when a person comes to stay in a parish, but is obliged to leave the place for a day or two every week on account of

8. Litt. Ency. S. C. S. Off. June 7, 1867. "Ad Episcopos Angliae et Stat. Foeder. Amer. Sept." apud Collectanea S. C. de Prop. Fide. vol. II. #1305. p. 2.

business, he is still said to possess a month's residence there when the thirty days are up. (9.)

But we must also bear in mind that, while a person has a domicile in one parish, he may also at the same time, have a domicile or quasi-domicile in another. Thus John's permanent home is in parish A, and he intends to retain his home there forever, unless something unforseen calls him away. But John only stays in that parish during the summer, spending the cold months in another climate. He also intends to keep that second place as his constant winter home. Thus his intention is directed equally between them. John then has a domicile in each place. So also, while John intends to keep a certain parish for his permanent home he may actually stay in another parish for six months and thus acquire a quasi-domicile in that place at the same time. Again while one has a domicile in one parish he may have a month's residence in another.

Furthermore, a person may have no *parochial* domicile or quasi-domicile and still possess a *diocesan* domicile or quasi-domicile. For instance, John roams through a diocese for the space of six months, without any intention of staying there longer. He stays at no parish for more than a week or two nor does he intend, at any time, to remain there longer. In this case John has no domicile or quasi-domicile in any parish because the actual stay and the intention are both wanting. But he has a diocesan quasi-domicile. So also in case a person were wandering through a diocese in this way for ten years, he would then have a diocesan domicile.

A vagus is one who has no domicile or quasi-domicile in any place. C.91. This is the definition generally used. But here in connection with matrimony we would have to make a change by adding to it thus: a vagus is he who has neither a domicile, nor a quasi-domicile, nor even a month's stay in any place.

Having explained these different terms, we may conclude that a pastor may assist validly and licitly, the other requisites present, at the marriage of those parties, who are living within

9 Noldin, H. op. cit. vol. III, 1. c. p. 718.

10. S. Congr. Concilii, "Romana et Aliarum" #4, March 28, 1908.

his parish for at least a month, as well as of those, who actually stay there no matter if only for a day, with the intention of remaining for at least six months. However he cannot assist at any marriages not even of his own subjects outside of his own parish without first securing the proper delegation. The pastor may also marry such as have no parochial domicile, quasi-domicile or month's residence but only a diocesan quasi-domicile or domicile, as long as they actually stay in the parish at the time. For the licit assistance at all other marriages within his parish he will have to secure the proper permission from the pastor of the parties or of at least one of them, unless grave necessity excuse him from seeking this permit. C. 1097 #1-3; C. 1032.

Now all would be very clear and followed without much difficulty if both parties had the same domicile, quasi-domicile or month's residence. But complications may arise in the minds of pastors when the parties to be married belong to different parishes or, worse still, when each of them has more than one domicile, or, again, besides a domocile also a quasi-domicile, etc. What is the pastor's right in such cases? The law states that a parish priest has the right to marry licitly any person, whom he can claim by reason of domicile, quasi-domicile or month's residence, as long as he assists within his own parochial territory. C. 1097, #1-2. Consequently the pastor of any of the domiciles or quasi-domiciles or month's stay of either of the parties may do this. There is one exception to this rule however, i. e. that the marriage should take place before the pastor of the bride, whether this be the pastor of the bride's domicile, quasi-domicile or month's residence. Any one of these has preference to the pastor of the domicile of the bride-groom. But, as was said, any reasonable cause is sufficient to allow the parish priest of the bride-groom to assist at that marriage, as long as he does so within his own parish. If neither of the parties has a domicile, quasi-domicile or month's residence but one at least has a diocesan domicile or quasi-domicile, they may be married by that pastor within whose parish in that diocese they are actually staying. No permission need be asked of the Ordinary in this case. If both parties are vagi, they may be married by the parish priest of the place in which they are actually staying or through which they are actually passing, as long as the permission of the Ordinary or of the priest appointed to give such permits is secured.

If the parties belong to different rites the pastor of the bride-groom has the first right. C. 1097 #2. A particular law may make a change in regard to these marriages.

This, then, is the ruling of the New Code. Unless the pastor can claim the parties in any of the ways mentioned in this canon 1097 he may not assist at the wedding ceremonies without proper permission. If he does he is in justice bound to turn over the stole fee to the proper pastor of the parties. C. 1097 #3. The marriage will, of course, be valid as long as it took place in the officiating pastor's parish and all the other requirements for this validity of the marriage contract were present. The stole fee that must be restored does not include the Mass stipend that might have been received at the occasion. Nor is the stole fee to be restored to the pastor of the parties if the marriage was celebrated without permission in a case of grave necessity, which excuses from securing it. If the pastor of the bride-groom should assist without any cause to excuse him, the stole fee need not be handed over. The same holds true when one of the parties is a vagus and the pastor sought no permission from the Ordinary or from the priest delegated to grant it in such cases. It may be well to say here, that a permission of this kind must be asked when only one of the parties is a vagus while the other has a domicile in the parish.

For practical reference it will be useful to quote certain cases in which the pastor of parish A may assist validly and licitly at marriages within his own parish:- When

1. John and Anna both have a domicile in parish A.
2. John and Anna both have a quasi-domicile in parish A.
3. John and Anna both have a month's residence in parish A.
4. Anna has a domicile, quasi-domicile or month's residence in parish A, while John has a domicile, quasi-domicile or month's residence in parish B.

5. John has a domicile, quasi-domicile or month's residence in parish A, while Anna is a vaga. Proper permission has been secured from the Ordinary or the priest appointed to give such permits. Or in a case of grave necessity, the marriage was celebrated without this permission.

6. John has a domicile, quasi-domicile or month's residence in parish A, while Anna has a domicile, quasi-domicile or month's residence in parish B, but a reasonable cause excuses them from not celebrating their marriage in parish B.

7. John and Anna both have a domicile, quasi-domicile or month's residence in parish B but marry in parish A and a grave necessity excuses the pastor of parish A from asking permission of the pastor of parish B.

8. John and Anna both have a domicile, quasi-domicile or month's residence in parish B but the pastor of A has secured the proper permission of the pastor of B or of the Ordinary of the diocese.

9. John belongs to parish B while Anna belongs to parish C. But the pastor of parish A secures permission to marry them from either of the parish priests of parishes B or C or from the Ordinary of the place.

10. John and Anna do not belong to parish A at all. John belongs to parish B while Anna is the subject of the parish priest of C. The pastor of C refused to grant the pastor of A the permit to marry them and consequently, the pastor of A asks for and receives permission from the pastor of B or from the Ordinary of the diocese.

11. John is a vagus while Anna has a domicile in parish B. The pastor of A secured permission to assist at this marriage from the Ordinary or the priest appointed to grant such permits, or the marriage was celebrated with no permission because a case of grave necessity excused the pastor of A from seeking this permission.

12. John and Anna are both vagi and permission to assist has been secured from the Ordinary or from the priest delegated to give these permits, or a grave necessity excused from seeking this permission.

13. John belongs to parish A while Anna belongs to parish B. But John is a member of the Latin Catholic rite while Anna belongs to the Oriental rite, and there is no particular law changing this general law.

Outside of his own parish, the pastor of parish A cannot marry anyone, not even his own subjects, validly. Proper delegation must be received from the pastor of the place in which the marriage takes place and, if the parties were not subjects of this parish, the permission of the proper pastor of at least the bride must be secured. This permit can also be given by the Ordinary of the place. Grave necessity will excuse from asking for this permission, but the delegation can never be dispensed from. This must be given by the pastor or the Ordinary of the place and in the manner mentioned above. This is necessary for the validity of the marriage.

After the pastor ascertains that they are his subjects and that he may assist at the marriage he will proceed to determine their free state, i. e. whether there is some obstacle to the marriage or not. C. 1097 —1. This duty is also emphasized in C. 1019, #1:- "antequam matrimonium celebretur, constare debet nihil eius validae ac licitae celebrationi obsistere." This careful regard for the reverence due the sacrament as well as for the interests of family and society has been marked throughout time, even during the first centuries. At first the Bishop, to whom all marriages had to be reported, made all the investigations in reference to the state of the contracting parties. But when the number of Catholics grew large and parishes began to spring up in greater numbers, this obligation fell upon the clergy of these parishes. This investigation must always be made in time and rules of the Ordinary, if there are any, should be carefully observed. C. 1020 #1 & 3. This duty belongs to the pastor of the parties even when he is not to assist at the marriage, i. e. if he delegates another to assist. If the parties belong to different parishes, either of the proper pastors is competent to make the investigation, but it is the duty of the one in whose parish the marriage will be celebrated. This obligation is "per se" a grave one and should not be dispensed with, even when the pastor feels certain that both of the parties are free. (11). The procedure to be followed is indicated in this and the following canons. The pastor is to question each of the parties separately and cautiously whether they are conscious of any impediment, whether they consent freely to the marriage, (this question is to be put especially to the bride) and whether they are sufficiently instructed in the Catholic religion. C. 1020 #2. The last question may be omitted if the pastor knows that the parties have sufficient instruction. If the pastor has any doubt as to the free state of the contracting parties even after questioning them he may ask them to provide two witnesses. These witnesses must be known by the person who receives their deposition, and should, if possible, be close relatives of the parties. (12). The parish priest may first ask the parties about such impediments as those of consanguinity, affinity and other public impediments which do not bring disgrace upon them. All other questions but especially those regarding occult impediments or those public ones, which would bring disgrace upon either or both of the parties, should be put to them privately and separately. So also the question regarding free consent. However, the parties are to be admonished to inform their confessor, when approaching the sacred Tribunal of Penance that they are about to be married, so that the confessor could ask them the necessary questions, etc. (13).

If the pastor finds that one or both of the parties are not sufficiently instructed in christian doctrine, he must teach them. But if they are so dull that they cannot learn all that they should know, or when they can hardly learn anything by heart and retain

11. Gasparri, P. Tractatus Canonicus de Matrimonio. vol. I. cap. II. #188, p. 119.

12. Gasparri, P. op. cit. vol. I. cap.II, #175, p. 112.

13. Avrinhac, Marriage Legislation in the New Code, p. 47.

it, they "are not to be kept indefinitely from marriage, which was instituted for the requirements of nature, and which consequently must not to be forbidden anyone except for his own fault." (14.) The points to be known by one about to marry are the following:- Matters regarding the sanctity, unity and indissolubility of the sacrament of marriage, the primary and secondary ends of matrimony, the obligations of husband and wife, the obligations of parents towards their children as well as all those things which are to be believed explicitly "necessitate medii et praecepti." (15.) When the Pontifical Commission for the authentic interpretation of the New Code was asked whether it would be advisable to postpone the marriage in case the parties were grossly ignorant, the answer came back stating that the "pastor should rather teach them the elementary points of Christian doctrine" and proceed with the marriage. (16.) Further instruction should be given later.

The pastor must also ask the parties to bring their respective baptismal certificates. At times it may be necessary for the parish priest himself to send for these. C. 1021 #1. This must be demanded at every occasion as long as the parties were not baptized in that parish, even if this same pastor baptized them in another parish. Nor is the baptized non-catholic free from this. He also must produce an authentic testimonial of the fact of his baptism. Again, if the parties were not confirmed, the pastor should try to have them receive that sacrament before marriage if that can be done without grave inconvenience. C. 1021 #2.

The method to be followed in all the investigations is not treated in detail in the New Code. The law leaves much of this to be determined by the Ordinary of the place. C. 1020 #3. Particular rules of the Ordinary must then be abided by. If the pastor sees any reason for it, he ought also take other means be-

---

14. Benedict XIV, De Syn. Dioc. l. VIII. c. 14.
15. Wernz. op. cit. Tom. IV. Pars. I. tit. III #131. p. 175-176.
16. Pont. Commissio ad Co. Can auth. Interp. June 1918.

sides those prescribed in order to get at the truth. General investigation will also be made by him.

If another priest than the one assisting at the marriage makes the investigations, he should inform the latter of this fact by an authentic testimonial. C. 1029.

When, during the examination, a positive doubt arises about the free state of the parties and an impediment is suspected, the parochus must look into the case more carefully . C. 1031 #I. n. I. If the case is such as will not bring disgrace upon the parties concerned, he shall ask at least two witnesses, who are reliable, to testify under oath. When no witnesses can be had or when the impediment in question is such as would bring disgrace upon the young people if witnesses were to be questioned about it, the parties themselves must make statement under oath concerning the doubt. The banns, however, need not be put off until all is cleared up, but may be commenced at once. C. 1031 #I. n. I. If doubt remains until the end the Ordinary is to be consulted before the marriage takes place.

If a certain impediment is found to exist, the case is different. If it be a public one, i. e. one that can be proved in the external forum, the banns should not be started until after the impediment is removed "ad externum". But if the banns were started before the impediment has been discovered the pastor may continue to announce them all, and refer the matter to the Ordinary C. 1031 #2. n. 2. If the impediment is occult, i. e. one that cannot be proved in the external forum, the pastor may commence or continue the proclamation of the banns, since there is no external reason for refraining. In such cases it will be necessary to send the matter to the Ordinary without, however, revealing the identity of the persons concerned. C. 1031 #2, n. I. Canons 1043-1044 and 1045 must be kept in mind here.

When the pastor finds no impediment, and there are no prudent doubts, the pastor, after having proclaimed the banns, must admit the parties to the celebration of marriage. C. 1031 #3.

The banns must be proclaimed. Before any marriage can take place between Catholics, the banns must be publicly proclaimed. C. 1022. These are to be published by the proper pastor of the parties on three successive Sundays or Holidays of Obligation, during Mass or during any other divine service, provided it is attended by a large gathering of the faithful. C. 1024. Notice, the term "between Catholics"; for if the marriage is a mixed marriage or one contracted between a Catholic and an infidel, even after a dispensation has been secured, no banns are published. C. 1026. The Ordinary may make an exception to this rule if an apostolic dispensation had been received. But even then no mention is to be made of the religion of the non-catholic party. If either of the contracting parties lived in other parishes for at least six months since the time when they reached puberty, i. e. 12 for female and 14 for male, the pastor must notify the Ordinary of this matter and let him decide as to what is to be done in those parishes, i. e. whether the banns should also be proclaimed there or whether another form of investigation should take their place. C. 1923. The same should be done when the pastor suspects that an impediment may have been contracted in a place where the parties or one of them lived for a shorter period of time than six months. C. 1023 #3.

It matters not whether the three Sundays or Holidays of Obligation on which the proclamations are to made, come in succession or not. Thus if two Holidays of Obligation follow on Monday and Tuesday, the pastor will satisfy the obligation by announcing the banns on these three successive days. Still, it is recommended that a longer interval be allowed between the three publications.

The proclamations are to be made during Mass or during any other divine service at which many people attend. The parochial Mass is the service at which they should generally be made, but not necessarily, for the law expressly allows otherwise. The end of the law is to acquaint the people of the fact that the parties are about to enter the matrimonial state and to give the people an opportunity of revealing any impediment or other obstacle to the coming marriage. This, however, is brought about sufficiently when the banns are proclaimed at the other divine services when a large concourse of people is present. Consequently, if this last condition is fulfilled, the parish priest can announce the banns at vespers or evening services on Sundays.

The church is the proper place for making these annoucements, but when more expedient, they may be made in any other place where parochial services are being carried on.

Besides the oral form of proclaiming the banns, the Church allows another manner of announcing them. But before any other form than the oral may be used the permission of the Ordinary must be received. Thus, the Bishop may allow that, in those churches, where a large number of banns is to be proclaimed every Sunday and Holyday of Obligation, the oral form may be superceeded by the posting of the names of the parties to be married and of other requisities for proper publication on the door of the church for at least eight days before the marriage. These eight days must include at least two days of obligation, i. e. two Sundays or a Sunday and a Holyday of Obligation. C. 1025.

The banns must always be proclaimed unless a dispensation from them has been received. It may be necessary to celebrate the marriage in a shorter time than that including three feasts of obligation. In such a case the pastor must ask for a dispensation from as many as is necessary. The Ordinary can dispense from these proclamations. C. 1028. In some diocese the pastors also receive the faculty of dispensing from some of the banns. The cause for dispensing must be just but not grave, "dummodo" as Noldin says," finis legis obtineatur." Some causes are of such a nature as merely allow of a dispensation, while others are such that a dispensation should be given. Noldin enumerates some of the latter as follows:- "a. si periculum est, ne matrimonium malitiose impediatur; b. si periculum est, ne sponsus derelinquat puellam a se violatam; c. si ex dilatione matrimonii infamia contrahentium sequatur; d. si propter necessitatem itineris matrimonium differri nequeat; e. si sponsi propter senium vel propter condicionem plane dissimilem ludibrio exponantur; f. si civili matrimonio iam contracto maritus velit quidem

17. Noldin, H. op. Cit. vol. III lib. VIII. quaest. 4, art. 2. p. 613.

ritum ecclesiasticum peragi, nolit autem proclamationes fieri." (18.) Moreover, as Gasparri remarks, if it is morally certain that there is no impediment in this case, the wish of the parties may be sufficient cause for a dispensation. (19.) When the pastor asks for the dispensation he should mention the cause and also whether there is any suspicion or doubt about the free state of the parties. The Bishop has the right, as guardian of the law, of proceeding against the pastor, who would carelessly omit the publications without a dispensation.

The proper Ordinary has also the right of dispensing his subjects from the banns that would have to be published in another diocese. C. 1028. If the parties belong to two different dioceses and contract marriage in a third, the Ordinary of any of these three dioceses is competent to dispense from the publications in the other dioceses also. C. 1028 #2. If the marriage does not take place within six months after the announcements have been made, the banns will have to be published anew, unless the Ordinary decides otherwise. C. 1030 #2.

The marriage is not to take place until after three days have elapsed from the time of the last publication. C. 1030 #I. However, any good reason is sufficient to allow the ceremony to be held sooner, e. g. if the parties desire it. The Bishop may enforce this rule more strictly if he deems it expedient in his diocese.

Before the marriage takes place, the parties are to be exhorted to make a good confession and receive Holy Communion. C. 1033. Confession is not a requisite "sine qua non" even when the pastor knows that one or both of the persons are in the state of mortal sin. Although this state of the parties would make the reception of the sacrament sacrilegious, it would not render the marital contract invalid. If the persons cannot be persuaded to confess, the parish priest should try to have them make at least an act of perfect contrition. If one of the parties is a public sinner or is under public censure and refuses to confess and be reconciled to the Church, the pastor should not assist, un-

18 Noldin, H. op. cit. l. c. p. 613.
19. Gasparri, P. op. cit. vol. I. cap. II. #231. p. 144.

less there be a grave cause for his doing so. And even in that case, as in the first, he is to inform the Ordinary if time remain. C. 1066. Nor is the pastor allowed to assist at the marriage of those, who have notoriously given up their Faith (even though they did not join a non-catholic sect), without first consulting the Ordinary, who will advise whether assistance is advisable or not. C. 1065.

The same holds true in cases of minors, i. e. those under 21, (C. 88) who attempt to marry without the knowledge or against the wishes of their parents. C. 1034. Although parental consent is not necessary for the validity of the contract nor is it's absence even an impedient impediment, still the Church demands that the children show some respect and love for their parents. Moreover, this also serves as a barrier against hasty and imprudent marriages of young people. While the Church gives every one the right of free choice, it, nevertheless points out to children their duty toward their parents. Of course, if the objections of the parents are unreasonable, the child need not heed them. But if the objections are good, the child commits sin by persisting in the resolution of acting against their will. Gasparri speaks of this point in the following manner:- "Parentes non possunt filios cogere aut obligare ad contrahendum matrimonium, aut ad contrahendum cum his vel illis. Tantum permissum est filios invitare ob aliquam justam causam, e. g. ad tollendam gravia dissidia, vel ad sublevandam gravem necessitatem parentum, familiam propagandam, facultates ampliandas, nobilitatem augendam; nec filii tenentur obedire ratione praecepti parentum, sed ad summum ratione pietatis aut charitatis vi ipsius causae", and again," Mens Ecclesiae est filios familias matrimonium regulariter contrahere debere, de consilio et consensu parentum; idque ex praecepto morali potius quam legali. Si parentes sunt inviti ex rationabili causa, hoc matrimonium esse jure naturae illicitum, omnes admittunt, etsi filius pubes sit, nisi ius praevalens filio assistat: e. g. si ex matrimonio familiae dedecus, aut scandala, aut dissentiones, aut aliud grave damnum oriturum est. — E contrario, matrimonium licitum est undequaque,si parentes inviti sunt, quia vel nolunt filium (aut filliam) nuptias inire vel volunt ei uxorem indignam, aegram, durae cervicis contra ejus voluntate dare; vel si filius a parentibus injuste opprimetur." (20.)

Marriage may be contracted at any time of the year; the solemn nuptial blessing alone is forbidden during certain seasons of the year. C. 1108 #I. The solemn nuptial blessing may not be given from the first Sunday in Advent until Christmas Day inclusive, and from Ash Wednesday until Easter Sunday inclusive. C. 1108 #2. But when there is a just reason for contracting marriage during this '"closed" time the Bishop may permit the blessing to be given, "salvis legibus liturgicis," but the parties are to be warned to abstain from boisterous and wordly feasting. C. 1108 #3.

Now, if the Ordinary can grant this permission during the closed seasons, the question arises whether and how the commemoration pro sponsis is to be said if the nuptial blessing is allowed by the Bishop on Christmas or on Easter Sunday. The answer is that the oration is to be added under one conclusion to the oration of the day. 2. To the question as to whether the votive Mass pro sponsis can be said during the closed season of Advent and Lent, the answer was given, that if the Ordinary for a good reason allows the solemn nuptial blessing, the votive Mass can be said except on Sundays, feast of precept, feast of the I. and II. class, privileged octaves of the I. and II. order, privileged ferias and the vigil of Christmas. 3. To the question as to whether the votive Mass pro sponsis can be said on the privileged vigils of Pentecost and the Epiphany, the answer came that on neither vigil can this Mass be said. ' (21.)

The place where the marriage ceremony is to take place is the parochial church. The Ordinary and the pastor may grant permission to have it solemnized in some other church, public or semi-public oratory. C. 1109. The pastor cannot, however, grant permission to celebrate it in a private house. The Ordinary alone can give such a permission if there is sufficient reason for doing so and then in particular cases only. C. 1109 #2.

20. Gasparri, P. op. cit. vol. I. cap. III. p. 371.

21. Decisions of the Pontifical Commission for the authentic interpretation of the New Code as found in the Acta Apost. Sdeis. vol. X, p. 332.

During the marriage ceremony all the liturgical laws prescribed by the approved rituals or received by praiseworthy customs are to be observed, unless a case of necessity curtails them. C. 1100; C. 733. The pastor should also see to it that the nuptial blessing be given whenever this is allowed. It may be given to parties married for a long time if it was not imparted at the time of their marriage. The nuptial blessing cannot be given outside of Mass. C. 1101.

If the parties desire to contract marriage with the aid of an interpreter or procurator the parish priest must first see if there is a good reason for it, whether the mandate is authentic, and whether the procurator is a reliable, truthful man. Besides, if there is time the Ordinary is to be consulted. C. 1091.

Now let us suppose that everything is ready for the marriage and then an impediment is discovered. What is the pastor to do, supposing the parties do not reveal the impediment until after they are in church ready for the wedding ceremony? This used to be a "casus perplexus" under the old law. But the new law takes cognizance of this difficulty and grants very liberal faculties to the Ordinary and the pastor in such cases. Thus, canon 1045 tells us that when an impediment is discovered only after everything has been prepared for the marriage, the Ordinary can dispense from any and all ecclesiastical impediments, be they occult or public or even manifold in the same person, except from the impediments arising from Holy Priesthood and affinity in the direct line from a consummated marriage, as long as the marriage cannot be put off without probable danger of a grave evil until a dispensation could be gotten from the Holy See. Moreover, scandal must be removed and if the marriage is a mixed marriage, the usual prescribed guarantees must be given beforehand. This faculty of the Ordinary extends to all his subjects wherever they may be as well as to all persons actually living within the diocese. This faculty may also be used for the validation of an invalidly contracted marriage as long as the danger exists in delay and there is no time for recourse to the Holy See. C. 1045 # 2. Moreover, and this is the important part for pastors, under the same circumstances and in occult cases, this same faculty is given to pastors and those priests who assist at a marriage according to canon 1098 #2, as well as to the confessor (but to the last named only for the internal forum and in sacramental confession) when there is no time for recourse even to the Ordinary of the diocese or, if there is time, when it cannot be done without danger of breaking the seal of confession. C. 1045 #3.

Let us examine this case more closely, for it may be of great practical value for the pastor at some time or other. In the first place the canon says:- "cum omnia parata sunt ad nuptias". This does not mean that the parties have to be in church ready to be married within a few minutes. If the invitations have been sent out and arrangements for the wedding are all made, this will be sufficient to satisfy the law even if the impediment is discovered a day or two before as long as there is not enough time to have recourse to the Bishop on account of poor connections, distance, etc., or if the Bishop cannot be requested to grant the dispensation because of the danger to the seal of confession. The following solution of a doubt to this canon was recently given by the Pontifical Commission for the authentic interpretation of the New Code:- "Utrum ad normam can. 1045, #I, clausula" quoties impedimentum detegatur cum iam omnia sunt parata ad nuptias", intelligi debeat stricto sensu, scilicet quod impedimentum antea omnino ignotum fuerit et tum resciatur, an potius eo sensu quod quamvis antea cognitum, tunc solum tamen ad notitiam Parochi aut Ordinarii sit delatum. Resp.: Negative ad I am Partem, affirmative ad 2am. Romae, I Martii 1921. apud Acta Apost. Sedis. Vol. XIII. No. 4. Mar. 11, 1921 p. 178. Secondly, the canon says that the pastor can then dispense from all impediments of the ecclesiastical law except those arising from the priesthood and from affinity in the direct line from a consummated marriage. It makes no difference whether the other impediments are public or occult, impedient or diriment or even multiple in the same case. The pastor must ascertain what these impediments are for he cannot dispense from the impediments of the divine law, e. gr. he cannot dispense from impotency, previous valid marriage, with the former partner still among the living, etc. nor can the parish priest dispense from the form of marriage. Thirdly, the case in which the pastor can dispense must be an occult one. Here I would suggest a distinction between "case" and "impediment". According to my idea a case may be occult while the impediment is public or, again, the impediment may be occult as well as the case. An impediment is public as soon as it can be proven in the external forum; otherwise it is occult. C. 1037. In the past the S. Pentitentiaria considered the impediment occult or public according to the size of the place and to the number and disposition of the persons who knew of the impediment. Today this is changed and an impediment is considered a public one as soon as it can be proved in the external forum. The rules formerly used in judging an impediment as public or occult may probably be used in determining the occultness or the publicity of the case. Accordingly, if John and Anna were related in a forbidden degree but only two other persons are aware of the presence of that impediment, the impediment is a public one since it can be proved in court with the aid of these two witnesses, but the case is an occult one especially if all this takes place in a large city. In such a case the pastor could dispense if all the other requirements are present. This however is a mere suggestion and until a correct interpretation is secured from Rome, I would advise the use of the safer side i. e. giving case the same meaning as impediment in this canon.

As to the probable danger of grave evil, we might say that this will be present in almost every case when everything is ready for the ceremony as explained above and the marriage would have to be delayed. The faculty would hold good even if the parties hid the impediment "in mala fide" until the last moment. If this danger exists and the other requisites are present this faculty of the pastor can also be used for revalidating contracted marriages.

Scandal must also be removed. The duty of seeing to this devolves upon the one who is to give the dispensation. Various means should be suggested. But if it becomes impossible to remove all the scandal, it's partial removal, combined with the promise or desire or willingness of the parties concerned to do more, will be sufficient to satisfy the person granting the dispensation.

Finally, even in these cases where the pastor grants the dispensation, the usual promises must be given by the parties affected. if the marriage is a mixed marriage, i. e. one contracted with a dispensation from mixed religion or disparity of cult.

It may be well to mention in this connection that a similar faculty is enjoyed by pastors in cases of urgent danger of death. C. 1043 states that when an urgent danger of death necessitates the adjustment of matters of conscience or the legitimation of offspring, the Ordinary can dispense from all the impediments of the ecclesiastical law, be they public or occult or manifold, except from the impediments of Holy Priesthood and of affinity in the direct line from a consummated marriage. This faculty can be used by him in favor of all persons actually residing within the diocese and for all his subjects wherever these latter may be. But before the dispensation is granted all scandal must be removed as was stated before and if the dispensation is from the impediments of mixed religion or disparity of worship, the usual guarantees must be given . Under like circumstances and conditions the Ordinary can also dispense from the form of matrimony.

This extensive faculty is also granted to pastors by the following canon, 1044. Under the same circumstances and conditions quoted in the preceding paragraph, the parish priest can use this power when no recourse can be had to the Ordinary for a dispensation. Confessors also have this faculty under the circumstances and conditions mentioned but they can use it only in actual sacramental confession and it holds good only for the internal forum. Priests, who assist at a marriage according to canon 1098 #2 also possess this faculty in the manner in which it is held by pastors. C. 1044. When a pastor conceeds a dispensation in the external forum, in the case here mentioned, he must record it in the matrimonial register and notify the Ordinary of the diocese of his action. C. 1046.

After the marriage has taken place the pastor is to make proper entry of the fact in the "Liber Matrimoniorum." This must be done as soon as possible. C. 1103. #1. The data which this entry must embrace is:- 1. The names of the contracting parties; 2. names of the witnesses; 3. date of marriage; 4. place of marriage; 5. name of officiating priest; 6. all other data required by the rituals and the orders of the Ordinary of the place. A note of the marriage must also be made aside the names of the contracting parties in the baptismal records. If the parties were baptized in some other parish than the one where they were married, the parish priest of the place of marriage must inform the pastor of the place of their baptism of the marriage, so that the latter could make the proper entry in the baptismal records. C. 1103. #2. This notification may be made by the officiating pastor directly or through the episcopal curia of his diocese.

All dispensations granted in the external forum are to be noted in the matrimonial register. Dispensations granted in the internal, non-sacramental forum, from an occult impediment, are to be noted in the secret archives of the diocese unless the S. Penitentiaria decides otherwise in the rescript. And, even if such an occult impediment becomes public in the course of time, no new dispensation need be obtained for the external forum. But if the dispensation was granted only in the internal, sacramental forum no entry is made of it anywhere but a new dispensation for the external forum will be necessary if the occult impediment becomes public later on. C. 1047.

Mixed Marriage.

The Catholic Church fully realizes the evils that so often come from mixed marriages and therefore condemns them in no uncertain terms. As to marriages contracted by Catholics with baptized non-catholics the following words are used: "Severissime Ecclesia ubique prohibet ne matrimonium ineatur inter duas personas baptizatas, quarum altera sit catholica, altera vero sectae hereticae seu schismaticae adscripta; quod si adsit perversionis periculum coniugis catholici et prolis, conjugium ipsa etiam lege divina vetatur." C. 1060. It is for this reason that the law orders the pastor to do all in his power to deter the faithful from contracting such mixed marriages. C. 1064. And only after he fails in these attempts, should the parish priest use his influence in preventing such persons from contracting contrary to the law of God and of His Church.

The impediment of mixed religion is only an impedient impediment. But the Church is very strict in demanding certain promises called "cautiones". These are to be given before a dispensation is granted. Besides, moral certitude that these promises will be kept must be present. Moreover, a just and grave cause is demanded for granting such a dispensation. C. 1061 #1-2. The promises that are to be made should consist of the folloing matter:- The non-catholic party promises that he or she will remove all danger of perversion from the Catholic party. 2. both the contracting parties promise that all the children coming from this marriage will be baptized and educated in the Catholic Faith. C. 1061 #2. These guarantees must as a rule be made in writing. C. 1061 #3. The Catholic party must, moreover, strive to convert the other. This obligation binding the Catholic is one of charity, and the fact that faith is a free gift of God must be kept in mind and consequently, no force or threats should be made use of in attempting such a conversion. The law says "prudenter". C. 1062.

A mixed marriage of this kind is not to be solemnized in the church. This is clear from an instruction of the Holy Office given on the 3rd of January, 1871 as follows:- "ut mixta coniugia extra ecclesiam — celebrari debeant." (22.) Cardinal Gasparri does not think that this term "ecclesia" embraces the sacristy or the private chapel. (23.) Moreover, all the sacred rites used in Catholic marriages are prohibited. All that the pastor is to do is to ask for and receive the consent of both parties according to C. 1095 #1 n. 3. But if the omission of the rites would bring about greater evil, the Ordinary can allow some of the customary ceremonies to be used, but never the celebration of Mass. C. 1102 #2.

But, if this is all true about marriages between a Catholic and a baptized non-catholic it is the more true of unions between Catholics and infidels. C. 1071. These latter marriages, if con-

---

22. Instr. of the Holy Office, Jan. 3, 1871 #3. apud Collectanea S. C. de Prop. Fide, vol. II. # 1362, p. 42.

23. Gasparri, P. Tract. De Matr. vol. I. p. 350.

tracted without a dispensation would also be invalid since the impediment of disparity of worship is not an impedient impediment as that of mixed religion but a diriment impediment. C. 1070.

If the pastor knows that the parties in any one of the two above-mentioned cases have gone or will go to a non-catholic minister in order to give or renew their consent, he may not assist even when the dispensation has been secured from the impediment, unless the gravest cause demand it and all scandal be removed. And then only after he has consulted with the Ordinary. C. 1063 #1-2. But if the civil law demands that all parties marrying appear before a non-catholic minister, who holds a civil government office, for the sake of fulfilling a civil act and securing civil effects for their marriage, the parties are not forbidden to appear before such a magistrate nor is the pastor forbidden to assist at their marriage. C. 1063 #3. The parties should be told, however, beforehand, that they do not go there to give or renew any matrimonial consent but merely to fulfill a civil ceremony demanded by the State.

As was stated before, the parish priest has the duty of watching over all marriages contracted with a dispensation from mixed religion or disparity of worship and of seeing to it that the promises given to the Church are carried out. This is an obligation of not only the officiating pastor but of every pastor, within whose parish any such married couples are living.

Marriages of Consience

A marriage of conscience is a marriage contracted with the permission of the Ordinary according to the proper form but without any proclamation of the banns and with the obligation of secrecy, which binds all concerned, i. e. the parties contracting, the witnesses, the officiating minister and the Ordinary. Such marriages are not allowed except for a very grave and urgent reason, and the Ordinary alone, to the exclusion of the Vicar General, can grant the permission. C. 1104. The Vicar General needs a special mandate from the Ordinary before he can give this permission.

Father Augustine enumerates the following reasons as sufficient for allowing a marriage of conscience:- "If two live together unsuspectedly as married, though they were never married; if the civil law imposes conditions injurious to the freedom of marriage, if the civil power interferes with the liberty, e. g. of soldiers, or if disgrace and discord would be likely to follow from iniquitous laws impeding marriage" and then adds:- "There may be, as Benedict XIV. says, other reasons, but whatever they are, they must be very grave and serious in order to outweigh the great evils resulting from secret marriages. These evils are:- easy divorce, danger of concubinage and polygamy, spiritual and temporal ruin of the offspring." (24.)

The obligation of keeping the secret is a grave one and binds all those who assist, i. e. the parties, the witnesses, the pastor and Ordinary as well as the successors of the last named. C. 1105. But there is an exception to this general rule. The Ordinary is not held to this secret, if keeping it would cause scandal or grave injury to the sanctity of marriage or if the parties do not see to it that their offspring is baptized or, if baptized, then under false names, (because, in the last case, the legitimacy of the children and their right to inherit the property of their parents would be jeopardized) (25.) unless they send notice to the Ordinary within thirty days after the baptism has taken place, stating that the child is their legitimate offspring and was baptized. C. 1106. This same holds true if the parties do not have their children reared in the Catholic Faith. C. 1106.

The mode of registering these marriages of conscience differs from the ordinary manner. These marriages are not to be recorded in the "liber matrimoniorum" or the baptismal register of the parish, but are to be entered into a special book, prepared for such matters in the secret archives of the diocesan curia. C. 370 and 1107.

Dispensations.

Before any marriage, which is hindered by a matrimonial impediment, may be celebrated a proper dispensation must be secured. A dispensation is a relaxation of the law in a particular case made by competent authority in favor of one or the other

24. Augustine, op. cit. vol. V. p. 316-317.
25. Augustine, op. cit. vol. V. p. 317.

person, while the obligation of the law remains for others. C. 80. (26.) No Ordinary below the Roman Pontiff is competent to dispense from a general law of the Church, not even in a particular case, unless this power has been expressly or implicitly conceded to him, or unless it be difficult to take recourse to the Holy See and there be danger of great harm in delay. Moreover, the case must be one from which the Holy See ordinarily grants a dispensation. C. 81. Consequently, the Bishops cannot dispense from the matrimonial impediments unless they were given the faculty by the Holy See or unless it be a case as mentioned above. Nor could they dispense even in the last named case when the impediment is one from which a dispensation is generally not granted by the Holy See. The pastors have no power at all over the general laws of the Church unless they have been expressly authorized for this. The same holds good in reference to particular laws. C. 83.

Before a dispensation from any ecclesiastical law is granted a just and reasonable cause is necessary. This cause must be proportionate to the gravity of the law from which the dispensation is desired. C. 84 #1. If such a cause is not present, the dispensation, if given by an inferior, is not only illicit but also invalid. In doubt as to the sufficiency of the cause, the dispensation may be asked and given both licitly and validly. C. 84 #2. Rescripts granting faculties of dispensing to inferiors are to be interpreted strictly. C. 85.

Since the matter of dispensation plays such an important role in the parochial office, it ought to be each pastor's ambition to make himself acquainted with the new law on this point. Thus it will be of practical value for him to note, who can receive a dispensation, where it is to be sought, how it is to be asked for and how and what effects follow. Although it is not my intention to treat all of these points here, I will speak of the manner of asking for dispensation and the place where they are to be sought, adding to this some of the causes necessary for granting dispensations.

26. Bargilliat, M. Praelectiones Juris Canonici, vol. I, p. 61.

We have treated of the powers of pastors and confessors in cases of 1. urgent danger of death and 2. when everything is ready for the marriage before the impediment is discovered. Here we shall speak of the other cases. The rule today is that the parties themselves may have recourse to Rome if they so desire. But this is very, very seldom done here in the States. As a matter of fact, it is practically always the duty of the pastor to ask for the dispensations. Consequently, it is of the greatest importance that he know how to go about this. The first thing that the parish priest will have to do is to ascertain the nature of the impediment in question and the causes present for asking the dispensation. If the impediment is such as can be revealed to the Ordinary without defamation of the parties concerned or without danger of breaking the seal of confession, the pastor should send the petition to him "reticitis nominibus" so that he might dispense or send it on to Rome. The pastor should not make applications directly to Rome unless as in the cases stated, he is forced to do so. The Holy See generally receives petitions and grants dispensations through the Ordinary. For the internal forum the confessor will have to take direct recourse to the Holy See.

If, then, the nature of the case and the circumstances demand that the pastor write directly to Rome, he must know which Congregation is competent to deal with the matter. He must write to the S. Congr. of the Holy Office for all dispensations from the impediments of mixed religion and disparity of worship as well as for all instructions regarding these impediments either directly or indirectly. The same Congregation has also to do with the Pauline Privilege. C. 247. The Sacred Congr. of the Sacraments dispenses from all the other impediments in the external forum and also grants the "sanario in radice" for the whole world, except, the Oriental Church. C. 249. The Sacred Congr. for the Oriental Church dispenses from all the impediments those contracting parties one of whom at least is a member of the Oriental Church. The impediments from which the Holy Office dispenses do not come under the competency of this Congregation even when the parties are both members of the Oriental Church. C. 257. The Sacred Congregation for Regulars dispenses from the vow of chastity taken in religion. C. 251. The Sacred Congr. for the Propagation of the Faith receives all petitions for the external forum from her subjects. The Sacred Tribunal of the Penitentiaria dispenses from all occult impediments, in the internal forum, whether this be in the sacramental or extra-sacramental forum. C. 258. To one of these the pastor will then send the petition.

If it should happen that the Ordinary refuses to grant a dispensation from a certain impediment although he has the faculty of dispensing in such cases, the pastor may write directly to Rome and need make no mention of the refusal on the part of the Ordinary. But the contrary cannot be done, i. e. if a dispensation has been denied by the Holy See it cannot be given by the Ordinary, unless the Holy See consents. Nor can one Congregation grant a dispensation which was denied by another Congregation unless the first one petitioned gives it's consent. There is one exception to this rule, i. e. the Sacred Penitentiary can grant a dispensation even after one of the Congregations refused to do so. C. 43.

When a dispensation had been refused by one Ordinary it should not be asked of another Ordinary without making mention of the fact of the first refusal.. The second Ordinary is also instructed not to grant this dispensation before he finds out the reasons for the refusal on the part of the first Ordinary. C. 44. If the Vicar General denies a dispensation, the mention of this fact is necessary for the validity when the same dispensation is petitioned from the Bishop. And if the Bishop denies the parties a dispensation, the Vicar General cannot grant it validly thereafter even if the fact of the first refusal is mentioned. C. 44 #2.

In drawing up the petiton for Rome the following languages may be made use of:- Latin, English, Italian, French, Spanish, German and Portuguese. When petitioning the S. Penitentiaria any modern language can be used. The Latin language, being the official language of the Church, is preferred, if the petitioner has a necessary knowledge of it to make his mind perfectly clear. Otherwise it is beeter to use the modern language which he knows best. The latin characters are always to be made use of. (27.)

The supplica is to be made out in the names of the persons concerned. In the names of both if they are both Catholics, in the name of the Catholic, if the other is a non-catholic. If the impediment affects only one of them, the petition is drawn up in the name of this one. So also if the impediment affects both but was brought about by the delinquency of one of them. (28.) If the dispensation is sought for the external forum, the names of the parties are expressly mentioned, if for the internal forum, fictitious names are used.

Telegraphy should not be made use of in asking a dispensation from the Ordinary or from Rome, unless urgent necessity demands it. (29.)

Moreover, the petition is said to be "in forma ordinaria" when the petitioners are able to pay the taxes, and "in forma pauperum" when this cannot be done. In the same way, the dispensation is said to be conceded "in forma ordinaria" or "in forma pauperum" when the taxes are requested or when no taxes or only trifling amounts are asked. (30.)

Now what must the supplica contain? The manner of drawing up these petitions varies in different places but there are certain matters which must be contained for the validity of the dispensation. These essentials are enumerated in an instruction of the S. Congr. de Prop. Fide, (May 9, 1877) as follows:-

1. The name and the cognomen of the petitioners, distinctly and clearly, without any abbreviations. To this should be added the age of the parties. When giving the age it is required

---

27. Litt. Enc. S. C. de Prop. Fide. Sept. 29, 1868. apud Collectanea S. C. P. F. vol. II, #1335, p 18.

28. Wernz, F. X. op. cit. vol. IV. #632, n. 160, p. 520.

29. Litt. Encycl. Secret. Stat. Dec. 10, 1891, apud Collectanea S. C. P. F. vol. II. #1775, p. 267.

..uldin, H. op. cit. p. 685.

that either the number be given or the year, month and day of the parties' births. The age is not necessary for validity unless it be the cause for the dispensation. In petitions for dispensations for the internal forum the names given here are fictitious ones.

2. The diocese of origin or of actual domicile or quasi-domicile. If the parties have a domicile outside of the place of their birth, they may have the dispensation sent to the Ordinary of that diocese. In seeking a dispensation for the internal forum the name of the diocese is not given but only the place where the dispensation is to be sent to.

3. Impediment or impediments "in infima specie sua" i. e. the exact species of the impediments must be revealed; whether it is an impediment of consanguinity, or affinity, public honesty, etc. or again, if it is an impediment of crime, one must state whether it arose from conjugicide with a. promise of marriage or conjugicide with adultery or from adultery with a promise of marriage; etc.

4. The grade of the impediment, whether simple or mixed. remote or proximate, and in what line; also whether the parties are bound by a double bond of consanguinity e. gr. both from the mother's and father's sides.

5. The number of the impediments, not only of different kinds, but of the same species as well. Besides the diriment impediments, the impedient impediments must also be put down even if the Ordinary has the faculty of dispensing from them or has already dispensed from such.

6. Various circumstances, which affect the granting of the dispensation e. g. whether the parties have already contracted the marriage or whether it is to be contracted; if contracted, was it done so in good faith, at least on the side of one of the parties, or was it contracted after the banns were proclaimed and according to the proper form; was the marriage consummated with a hope of thereby securing the dispensation more easily; is the

marriage consummated; if so, was it done in good or bad faith; did bad faith exist on both sides or on one side, etc. (31.)

7. The cause for seeking the dispensation. This is of the greatest importance, for the expression and the verification of the causes belong to the substance of the dispensation. Although here we must remember, that even if the only cause given, in asking for a dispensation from a *"minor impediment"*, be false, the dispensation is still valid. C. 1054. It is not necessary to put down all the causes if there are many, but it is better to do so. Besides the canonical causes also others can be put down. At times a dispensation is said to be given without a cause. This means, that, the dispensation was granted without any canonical cause or without a cause expressly mentioned in the petition. (32).

8. The state of the parties in reference to wordly goods is also to be mentioned in the supplicio for a dispensation. This in order that the S. Congr. could determine the tax or grant the dispensation without any tax. If one of the parties is a non-catholic, his standing in this regard is not mentioned. Dispensations for the internal forum are conceeded gratis.

9. Finally, the request for the dispensation is to be included.

Now let us say a few words about the effects of a dispensation in case an error is made in the petition. If there be an error

31. Instruction of the S. Congr. P. Fid. May 9, 1877, apud Collectanea S. C. de P. F. vol. II. #1470, p. 106. "Olim ex variis decretis et instructionibus Romanarum congregationum ad validitatem dispesationis exprimi debebat copula incestuosa habita inter sponsos ante dispensationis executionem, etiamsi ipsa copula incestuosa non fuerit causa dispensandi. Nunc vero abrogatis hisce statutis per decretum s. Officii 25 june, 1885 dispensatio valida est, etsi reticita fuerit copula incestuosa inter sponsos habita. Quin etiam hoc eodem decreto, quo abrogatur obligatio exprimendi incestum commissum, abrogatur etiam obligatio exprimendi intentionem, si adfuerit, per illum facilius obtinendi dispensationem. (S. Officium, Mart. 18. 1891). Ideo sponsi consanguinei in examine sponsorum de incestu inter se habito et de intentione per eum facilius obtinendi dispensationem interrogandi non sunt; quodsi incestus inter ipsos habitus evaserit publicus vel si sponte ab eis aperiatur, haec circumstantia in libello supplici indicari vel etiam omitti potest. Ex aliis tamen rationibus necessarium esse potest ut in libello supplici declaretur incestus a sponsis commissus, e g. ad legitimandam prolem ex incestu susceptam". Noldin, H. op. cit. vol. III. p. 687.

32. Noldin, H. op. cit. vol. III. p. 687

in the names or surnames, the dispensation is valid as long as the error in the petition was merely accidental i. e. if one or the other letter was changed or if one of the names was left out when the person has two or more names, as long as the identity of the person is evident. (33.) If there were any error in regard to the impediment, the folowing rules are to be considered:- A dispensation granted for a certain degree of consanguinity or affinity is valid although another impediment of the same species which is of a lower or of the same degree, had been concealed. C. 1052. This holds good also when such an error would be made in the concession. When, in the petition, an impediment is given as doubtful and it is certain, the dispensation is illicit although valid, because the tacit condition "if there be an impediment" is always understood. When giving the degree of the impediment if instead of the nearer degree one mentions only the more remote, the impediment is invalid. When a dispensation has been granted from a marriage that is validly contracted between two baptized persons but not consummated or when permission is given, on account of the presumed death of the partner, to enter a new marriage, such dispensations or permissions always bring with them a dispensation from an impediment, which might have arisen from adultery with a promise of marriage or from adultery with an attempt at mariage, if these dispensations are necessary in such cases. But they do not bring a dispensation from the impediment arising from adultery and conjugicide or merely from conjugicide. C. 1075 #2-3; C. 1053.

When there is an error in regard to the causes the following rules must be kept in mind. In the first place we will have to distinguish between the different causes. As Father Augustine says: "A motive may be either final, which alone determines and moves the grantor to grant the favor; or it may be an impelling cause, i. e. one that helps to move the grantor. One final cause(causa motiva) is sufficient for obtaining a dispensation. But sometimes one impelling causa (causa impulsiva) is insufficient; whereas several of the same kind amount to a final

33. Noldin, H. op. cit. vol. III. p. 689.

cause." (34.) Now we can proceed to give the rules:- If the motive cause is a false one, the dispensation will be invalid although the impulsive cause may be true. If only one motive cause be given and that one be true the dispensation is valid although all the impelling causes may be false. If there are many motive causes and to this are added some impelling causes, the dispensation is valid as long as one of the motive causes is true. A slight exaggeration of a cause that is otherwise true does not invalidate the dispensation. Obreption and subreption in the petition do not invalidate dispensations from minor impediments (C. 1042 #2) even if the only motive cause given is false. C. 1054.

Error regarding the condition of the parties concerned does not invalidate the dispensation. (35.)

Causes are divided again into Canonical and non-canonical causes. "Canonicae causae vocantur, quae ex stilo curiae romanae tamquam admissae pro dispensationibus matrimonialibus expresse referuntur; non-canonicae vocantur omnes aliae, quae inter causas ex stilo romanae expresse non referuntur. Etiam causas non-canonicas in dispensationibus matrimonialibus admitti certum est; immo quandoque ex solis causis non-canonicis dispensatio conceditur." (36.)

The canonical causes are enumerated in the instruction of the S. C. of the Propagation of the Faith of the 9th of May, 1877 and as follows:-

"1. Angustia loci; 2. Aetas feminae superdulta; 3. Deficientia aut incompetentia dotis; 4. Lites super successione bonorum iam exortae, vel earundum grave aut imminens periculum; 5. Paupertas viduae; 6. Bonum pacis; 7. Nimia, suspecta, periculosa familiaritas nec non cohabitatio sub eodem tecto, quae facile impediri non possit; 8. Copula cum consanguinea, vel affini vel alia persona impedimento laborante praehabita, et praegnantia, ideoque legitimatio prolis, ut nempe consulatur

34. Augustine, op. cit. vol. V. p. 125.

35. Sapienti Consilio. Pii X. June 29, 1908.

36. Noldin, H. op. cit. vol. III. p. 680.

bono prolis ipsius, et honori mulieris, quae secus innupta maneret. 9. infamia mulieris; 10. Revalidatio matrimonii; 11. Periculum matrimonii mixti, vel coram acatholico ministro celebrandi. 12. Periculum incestuosi concubinatus. 13. Periculum matrimonii civilis. 14. Remotio gravium scandalum. 15. Cessatio publici concubinatus; 16. Excellentia meritorum." (37.) The interpretation of these causes will have to be sought in the works on moral theology and Canon Law.

Now when the pastor or confessor has the petition all drawn up according to rules prescribed, he sends it directly to the Bishop or to Rome as the case may be. When it must be sent to Rome he may send it directly to the respective competent Congregation or to an agent, if there is such there, through whom it can be sent to the Congregation. But in such cases, when the petition is addressed to the S. Penitentiaria, the following admonition of that Tribunal, which was quoted once before, must be strictly observed:- "Ceterum si opera alicujus procuratoris in alma Urbe uti velint, litteras obsignatas praelaudato Cardinali Poenitentiario Maiori tradendas suppressis nominibus ad ipsum procuratorem transmittere quidem poterunt, ast memoratos casus Sacrae Poenitentiariae proponendos nunquam aut nullimodo narrare seu manifestare audeant." (38.)

The procedure in seeking a dispensation from two impediments, the one public, the other occult follows the same rules, i. e. the public impediment is to be dispensed from by the S. Congr. of the Sacraments or one of the other Congregations competent in the public impediments, while the occult impediment must be dispensed by the S. Penitentiaria. For this reason two separate petitions must be drawn up and sent, the petition for a dispensation from the public impediment to the Congregation competent in this regard, the supplica for a dispensation from the occult to the S. Penitentiaria. In the petition for a dispensation from the public impediment only this impediment is mentioned with its particulars while the occult impediment is not

37. Instructio S. C. de. Prop. F. 9 Maii 1877, apud Collectanea S. C. P. F. vol. II. #1470, p. 104-105.

38. Wernz, F. X. tom. IV. vol. II. #632 n. 163. p. 521.

made known here at all. But in the other petition, concerned with the occult impediment, both the public and occult impediments are expressed and the fact that a dispensation was also asked for the public impediment is to be mentioned. According to some authors a petition can be sent first to the Penitentiaria and later to the other Congregation competent in the public impediment, but in such cases they say, the dispensation from the occult impediment does not take place until the public impediment has been removed. Giovine denies this and says that the S. Penitentiaria never dispenses from an occult impediment before a dispensation has been asked also from the impediment that is public. Cardinal Gasparri has the following to say regarding this assertion of Giovine: "Sed sententia communis certa est imprimis ex praxi s. Poenitentiariae; haec enim passim dispensat super occulto etiam ante dispensationem a Dataria super publico; proinde in facto errat Giovine. Praetera si attendamus verba a s. Poenitentiaria adhibita in hac dispensatione, omnis evanescit difficultas." (39.) Gasparri speaks here of the Datary because he wrote under the old law and, at that time, the Datary granted most of the dispensations in the external forum from public impediments.

The pastor must moreover be acquainted with the manner of interpreting the rescript granting the dispensation. Information that a dispensation had been granted is not sufficient, the dispensation must be in hand, unless the information comes from the Holy See itself. C. 53. The clauses contained in the rescript must be carefully studied and observed to the letter. The authenticity and integrity of the same must also be evident. C. 53. If the pastor has been delegated to grant the dispensation, he is to do so in writing and make express mention of the pontifical indult, and of the impediment from which the dispensation is granted. C. 1057. Writing is necessary only in the execution of rescipts pertaining to the external forum. C.56. If the executor makes any kind of an error in the execution of the rescprit, he can make another execution. C. 59 #1.

Great care and necessary knowledge is also necessary for

39. Gasparri, P. op. cit. vol. I. #346, p. 235.

the execution of rescripts that concern the internal forum. The clauses will have to be studied carefully and an investigation made to ascertain whether the causes are true or not. This latter onus is imposed by the S. Poenitentiaria. If the impediment affects only one of the parties, e. gr. in the case of a vow of chastity, it will suffice to dispense only this one party. If it affects both, or was brought about by the delinquency of both, both parties will have to approach the pastor to receive their dispensation. If one of the parties goes to a confessor different than the one who received the rescript, the rescript should be given to that party so that he or she could give it to the confessor approached and ask for the dispensation from him. (40.) As is evident, the dispensation is made for both parties, for, since an impediment is indivisible, a dispensation for the one frees the other also. The reason, why both of the parties concerned are told to approach the confessor in some cases. is that a salutary penance might be imposed upon them.

Finally the pastor must record or have the dispensations recorded. When the impediment is public it is to be recorded along with the name of the parties in the "liber matrimonium." If the dispensation was received from the S. Penitentiary it is to be recorded in the secret archives of the diocesan curia. C. 1047. The S. Penitentiary may make a change in this regard but in such cases the pastor will be told in the rescript himself.

Other matters pertaining to dispensations and their execution must be studied from works on moral theology and canon law, which treat of these matters in detail.

Sect. 8. Extreme Unction.

The administration of Extreme Unction is a function reserved to the parish priest. He has the right of administering this sacrament to all the faithful living within his parochial boundaries. C. 462; C. 938. Consequently, outside of a case of necessity, no one is allowed to confer this sacrament upon those within the parish. unless he has at least the presumed permission of the pastor or the Ordinary of the place. There are, however, several exceptions to this rule. The first is that, when the Bish-

40. S. Poenitentiaria, Nov. 15, 1748.

op is sick and in need of Extreme Unction, the right to administer this sacrament to him belongs to the dignitaries and canons of the chapter. C. 397. Moreover, in clerical religious communities located within the parish, this right belongs to the Superior. He may administer the sacrament to all the professed religious as well as to all the novices and those, who dwell in the house with them night and day, whether as servants, pupils, guests or convalescents. In convents of nuns, situated within the parish, this right belongs to the ordinary confessor or to his substitute. C. 514 #2. In other lay communities of religious the administration of Extreme Unction pertains to the rights of the pastor, within whose parish they are found or to a chaplain, whom the Ordinary appoints for such a community according to canon 464 C. 514 #3. Outside of these cases the pastor has the right to administer Extreme Unction to all the faithful staying within his parish.

The administration of Extreme Unction is not only a right of the pastor but it is also his duty:- "Ordinarius minister ex justitia tenetur hoc sacramentum per se vel alium administrare." C. 939. But "salvo praescripto can. 397, n. 3, 514, #1-3, minister ordinarius est parochus loci, in quo degit infirmus;" C. 938 #2. In cases of necessity every priest is bound to confer this means of grace upon the sick. The importance of this duty on the part of the pastor can be seen from the words of the II. Council of Baltimore:- "Anima Christiani hominis periclitatur tum maxime, cum in summo vitae discrimine versatur. Ut enim Apostoli verbis utamur, "descendit Diabolus" ad eam, ""habens iram magnam, sciens quod modicum tempus habet". (Apoc. XII.-12.). Infirmitas quoque ac dolores corporis intellectum obscurant ac fere obruunt, viresque voluntatis minuunt et labefactant." (1.) It is in this time of trial that the person needs assistance something that would give him strength in his struggle against the powerful onslaughts of the enemies of Christ. The Sacrament of Extreme Unction gives this aid and more, as we know. It is indeed, therefore, an important part of the parochial duties of the pastor. Cardinal Manning speaks of this duty

1. Conc. Plen. Balt. II. Acta et Decreta, #303, p. 162.

in the following terms:- "The chief works of a pastor are the preparing of children for the warfare in life, and the preparing of the sick for the last conflict in death. The school and the sick room are the two chief fields of the priest's charity and fervor." (2.) The New Code stresses the importance of this duty of the pastor again and again. Thus in canon 467 #1 the law states that the pastor must administer the sacraments to the faithful as often as they ask for them reasonably. Then, the Code insists that parish priests take good care of the sick and give them the sacraments (canon 468 #1) and finally, it tells him that, he is bound in justice to administer Extreme Unction "per se vel per alium" to those that are in need of it. C. 939. Although this sacrament is not "per se" necessary "necessitate medii ad salutem," still all care and means are to be employed to have the sick receive it in time, i. e. while they are still in possession of the use of reason. C. 944.

Extreme Unction may be administered to any of the faithful, who, after they come to the use of reason, are found in danger of death either through sickness or through old age. C. 940 #1. When there is a doubt as to the fact of the use of reason, this sacrament may be administered conditionally. C. 941. This will do away with scruples or even with the habit of some priests who thought it inadvisable to confer this sacrament upon children so young. Pope Benedict XIV, already during that time, declared that this means of grace is not to be denied children, who have the use of reason, i. e. those, who are capable of committing sin and of receiving the sacrament of penance. (3.) Pius X in his decree "Quam Singulari" says:- "Detestabilis omnino est abusus non ministrandi Extremam Unctionem pueris post usum rationis." (4.) The New Code goes even further than this and says that, when it is doubtful whether the child has attained the use of reason or not, extreme unction is to be conferred "sub conditione". C. 941. The same concession is made when there is doubt whether the person is really in danger

2. Cardinal Manning. The eternal Priesthood c. XVII, p. 234.
3. Pope Benedict XIV. De Synodo Diocesana, tom. I. lib. VIII. c. VI. p. 249.
4. Quam Singulari, Aug. 10. 1910.

of death or not and also whether the person is dead or alive. If the sick person remains contumacious and impenitent in an open grievous sin unto the end, this sacrament may not be given him. If this is doubtful the person is to be anointed conditionally. C. 942. Noldin says of this canon:- "Canonem 942, qui nonnullis contra doctrinam et praxim huc usque ab omnibus admissam offendere videtur, recte interpretatur Alb. Schmitt affirmans, ibi non de dispositione, sed de intentione sermonem esse, proindeque in dubio sacramentum sub conditione conferri debere. Ratio enim, propter quam contumaciter impenitentibus sacramentum conferendum non est in defectu intentionis consistit." (5.)

But what is the pastor to do when, upon arriving at the bedside, he finds the sick person unconscious? The following canon i. e. C. 943, answers this question for us. If the person asked for the sacrament, at least implicitly, while he had the use of reason, or if he presumably would have asked for it had he foreseen his present state, such a one may be anointed absolutely. C. 943. Father Augustine in his commentary on this canon says:- "This agrees with the advice given to the American Bishop, who asked which sacraments may or should be given to consuetudinarii or recividi or such as are utterly careless of their spiritual welfare. The answer came: If they have given signs of repentance, Extreme Unction may be administered. (6) Broadly speaking it may be said that, unless positive refusal, lasting up to the moment of unconsciousness can reasonably be assumed, this sacrament may be administered." (7.) Even in a refusal we must distinguish between a refusal proceeding from a natural dread of recognizing the immediate approach of death and a refusal, which indicates a disbelief in the efficacy of the sacrament or implying an alienation from the Catholic Faith." A dangerously sick person does not always share the assurance of those around him that he is in imminent danger of death; hence, the desire to defer the reception of what is often regarded as a

5. Noldin, H. op. cit. vol. III. lib. VI. quaest. 5. p. 520. (In doubt regarding the disposition, it is to be conferred absolutely. Noldin l. c. p. 519.)

6. Congr. of the Holy Office, May 9, 1821.

7. Augustine, op. cit. vol. IV. p. 404.

last resort. Under this impression good Christians at times decline extreme unction, though they have no doubt of its virtue nor wish to be deprived of the sacrament in their last hour. Whether this is the motive of the refusal or not must be judged from the general character, previous life, and attitude of mind of each individual. Where faith in the efficacy of the sacrament can be justly assumed, the unconscious person should be given the benefit of the doubt as to his actual desire to receive extreme unction in his great need. On the other hand the absence of such a presumption would forbid the administration of the sacrament." (8.) Whenever it is possible to confer this sacrament on those destitute of reason it should be done since, for such persons extreme unction is a means of salvation much more secure than sacramental absolution. (9.)

Extreme unction is to be given to those only who are in danger of death. However, this danger need be only probable. The pastor should not wait until the patient is near death's door. Genicot expresses this danger of death in these words:- "ut de eorum morte timeatur" and goes to say:- "is timor ex mente Ecclesiae rationabiliter ita intelligendus est:- statim atque probabile fit aegrotantium ex praesenti morbo seu periculo esse moriturum, licet forsan adhuc probabilius sit eum sanatum iri. Tale igitur iudicium, elicitum sive a medico, sive ab alio experientia edocto, requiritur et sufficit, ut extrema unctio conferri possit." (10.) We must distinguish between what is said about danger when the sacrament *must* be administered and about the state of the patient when extreme unction *may* be administered. Consequently, as the New Code says, the sacrament may be conferred, although only conditionally, even when there is a doubt about the fact of the existence of real danger. It is expedient, in order that all the effects be secured more certainly, that this sacrament be received as soon as the first danger of death is noticed. One is not to wait until the last minute, when all hope of recovery is practically given up by the doctors, and

8. Amer. Eccl. Review. vol. LX, 1919, p. 573.

9. Noldin, H. op. cit. vol. III, lib. VI. quaest. I. p. 504.

10. Genicot, op. cit. vol. II.tract. XVI. cap. III. p. 388.

when the patient begins to loose the use of his senses and reason. To defer it until then is contrary to the nature of this sacrament. One of the effects of extreme unction is to restore health to the body "ubi saluti animae expedierit", as the Council of Trent says. (11.) But this cure of the body is not effected by a miracle but by special helps by which nature and free causes are directed to the restoration of health to the infirm. Wherefore, we hope in vain to secure *this effect* after a person is so sick that only a miracle can cure him. Consequently, those who postpone this means until the person is in such a state, differ from the mind of Christ, who instituted the sacrament. (12.) Moreover, the spiritual fruits will not be as great if the person is anointed only after he loses the use of reason. The Code insists that the sacrament be received "dum sui plene compotes sunt." C. 944.

Another point that must be carefully kept in mind is that this sacrament may be conferred only when the person is in danger of death on acount of *some sickness* or *on acount of old age* and not from any other causes. C. 940 #1. The danger must come from an intrisic disposition or infirmity of the body, "videlicet, ex morbo vel ex causa quae morbo aequiparari soleat." (13.) Consequently a person could not be anointed when in danger of death from any of the following causes:- if he is about to enter a battle, if he is about to be executed for crime, when about to undertake a perilous journey, when a woman is to give birth to a child, even in the first instance. Of course, the case is different if, for instance, a soldier is gravely wounded and then wishes to go back to the front again, or if a person hearing the sentence of death pronounced over him is seized with a dangerous fever, which puts him in danger of death. Likewise, a woman suffering extraordinary and dangerous pains in giving birth to a child should be anointed. In these cases the danger of death comes from bodily infirmity and not from something outside of the body as in the cases quoted above. In regard to surgical operations, Noldin has the following to say:-

11. Conc. Trid. ses. 14. De Extrema Unctione, c. 2.
12. Genicot, op. cit. vol. II. Tract. XVI. cap. I. p. 385.
13. Genicot. op. cit. l. c. p. 387.

"Qui difficilem operationem chirurgicam subeunt, ante operationem iniungi possunt, si periculoso morbo iam laborant, non item si operatio demum mortis periculum adducit." (14). Genicot moreover, calls it wrong, "perperam," to administer extreme unction to such as are about to undergo a dangerous surgical operation "nisi iam antea ex infirmitate periclitentur." (15.) Lehmkuhl says:- "Ergo (Extrema Unctio) dari nequit — — · — ante operationem chirurgicam periculosam nisi iam aliunde valetudo periculosa affecta sit." (16.)

Extreme unction cannot be repeated during the same illness unless the patient recovers and then suffers a relapse. C. 940 #2. Such recoveries and relapses occur especially in such cases as heart disease, consumption and typhoid fever. But the pastor must not be scrupulous in this regard even if he has to anoint the same person on several occasions within the space of a few months. (17.) The following is given by Doctor Stang as a rule that may be followed:- "Whenever a chronic disease, such as dropsy or consumption, enters a new phase or state, extreme unction may and ought to be repeated. In case of a positive doubt about this change or turn of the same disease, the priest should incline to the repetition of the sacrament." (18.) The same danger is considered as remaining even when the patient feels better for a few days, unless, of course, one can see otherwise from the nature of the illness. But if the infirm person, in some long illness, feels better, say for a month, the first danger is supposed to have ceased. When the pastor is in doubt whether the first danger still endures or not he should rather anoint again, since this is more in accordance with the old custom of the Church. Naturally, if one notices that a person has recovered from the danger, even if this be within a short time after the first anointing, he may anoint again when the patient becomes dangerously ill after that. But as long as it is certain that the first danger remains, the sacrament cannot be

14. Noldin, II. op. cit. vol. III lib. VI. quaest. V. p. 518.
15. Genicot, op. cit. 1. c. p. 387.
16. Lehmkuhl, Aug. op. cit. pars. II. lib. I. tract. VI. cap. 2. p. 309.
17. Schulze, Fred. op. cit. p. 249.
18. Stang. op. cit. p. 183.

repeated, although this first danger be augmented by some additional ailment. The pastor can also take the following words as a rule for his guidance:- "In cases of chronic illness, extreme unction is not to be repeated unless there has been a recovery and relapse. But moral certainty is not required in regard to either event. It will be enough if, in the opinion of an ordinarily reasonable man, who has had a fair chance of appreciating all the facts, there is a sound probability that both have occured. Both may occur in a very short time — say half an hour or less; on the other hand, it may be obvious enough that, even after several months, neither has occured. What period may be fixed on as a general standard? The experts select a month. They do not claim anything approaching mathematical accuracy. There is nothing especially sacrosanct about the period: it just represents a rough estimate based on intelligent experience. In particular cases it may have to be modified; but, as a rule, and apart from strong evidence to the contrary, it gives as good results as can be reasonably hoped for until the world becomes wiser than it ever was. This is the practical rule." (19.)

The parish priest must see to it that he always has all things, necessary for sick calls, at hand. The Holy Oils must be blessed by the Bishop and should not be old ones, but of this year. Old oils are not allowed to be used except in an urgent case of necessity. C. 734. This oil must be kept with the others in the church, in a safe and fitting place, under lock and key so that no one could tamper with it. C. 946. It may not be kept in the parish house, except in a case of necessity or for some good reason and then only after the permission of the Ordinary has been secured. C. 735.

The anointings are to be made according to the formula prescribed by the approved rituals. C. 947. The anointing of the loins is always to be omitted, while the feet need not be anointed if there is reason for this omission. C. 947 #2-3. The hand and not an instrument should be used in administering the oils. An exception may be made only, in case of grave necessity. C. 947 #4. The eyes, ears, nose, mouth and hands are al-

19. Kinane, J. D. C. L. apud Irish Eccl, Record. vol. XIV-1919, p. 485.

ways to be anointed. In case of urgent necessity, the sacrament may be conferred by one anointng and that on any of these five parts of the body ,but rather on the fore-head. But the obligation of supplying the other anointngs still remains. C. 947 #1.

PART V.

SACRAMENTALS.

Besides the seven sacraments, the Church has in her possession certain rites and ceremonies, which on account of their resemblance to the sacraments, are called sacramentals. These rites and ceremonies are used by Her to gain certain effects, especially spiritual ones. The sacramentals do not operate "ex opere operato' as the sacraments do, but produce their effects through the prayers and the blessings of the Church, i. e. "ex opere operantis Ecclesiae". C. 1144. The right to constitute, interpret, change and abolish the sacramentals is reserved altogether to the Holy See. C. 1145.

The legitimate minister of the sacramentals is the cleric endowed with power from competent ecclesiastical authority and not forbidden to excercise that power. C. 1146. In the first place he must, therefore, be a cleric. Consequently, a lay catechist or even an abbess cannot administer any of the sacramentals. Hence, the blessings imparted by the female religious superiors are not sacramentals in the proper sense. (1). The cleric must also have power from competent ecclesiastical authority before he can administer these rites and ceremonies. This power is received in the different orders. Finally, he must not be forbidden to exercise this power. When a cleric is excommunicated or suspended completely from office, the use of these powers is forbidden. The same holds true when a priest is under a personal interdict. C. 2279; C. 2261; C. 2275 #2.

The person usually called upon to administer the sacramentals is the pastor. Consequently, it will be of practical value to treat here his rights and duties in this regard. Every parish priest should possess a holy reverence and respect for all these rites and ceremonies. As Father Stang remarks:- "a lively faith is wanting either in the priest or in his people at a church where the sacramentals are ignored and neglected." (2.) Frequent in-

1. Augustine, l. c. vol. IV. p. 560.
2. Stang. Pastoral Theology. p. 200.

structions concerning these things will help wonderfully in a-wakening the people to the consciousness of how much good can be gained through them. Opportunities must also be given the people to receive them.

Sacramentals are divided into exorcisms, consecrations and blessings. An exorcism is defined by Ferrerres as " imperata adjuratio daemonis, invocato nomine Dei, ut ipse daemon ex-pellatur ejusque potestas excludatur." (3) Blessings are divided into constitutive and invocative. The invocative blessings are those which "are intended to confer a spiritual or temporal favor, through the bounty of God, upon persons or objects, without however, changing their condition or natural state. The constitutive blessings are those by which persons or objects are dedicated to the ministry or service of God or religion and become permanently separated from profane use, having received, as it were, a higher or sacred existence." (4.) The constitutive blessings are again divided into verbal and real. The former are those constitutive blessings which are given without any sacred oils, the later are imparted with the sacred oils. These latter are properly called consecrations. Keeping these divisions in mind we may proceed.

The use of the power of exorcising is restricted to those only, who have a special, express permission of the Ordinary. C. 1151. Consequently, the parish priest cannot use this power unless he obtains this permission. Consecrating is also forbidden to him except in such cases as are permitted by law or by a special Apostolic indult. C. 1147 #1. This leaves the pastor only those blessings, which are preformed without the use of the sacred oils. But even here the field is not unlimited. There are certain blessings even of this kind which are restricted to the Ordinary or to the Holy Father. C. 1147 #2. However, if such blessings are imparted by the pastor either by mistake or through carelessness, the blessings, although illicit, are valid, unless the contrary is expressed in the reservation by the Holy See. C. 1147 #3.

3. Ferrerres, Compendium Theol. Moralis. vol. II. p. 141.
4. Augustine, 1. c. vol. IV. p. 565-566.

The rites that are to be used and which are prescribed by the Church must be strictly observed. C. 1148 #1. Moreover, the formula prescribed is so necessary that a consecration or blessing imparted without it is invalid. C. 1148 #2.

Blessings may be given not only to Catholics and catechumens but, unless the Church forbids it ,also to non-catholics, in order that the light of Faith or, together with it, bodily health, might be gained for them. C. 1149. It is well to let such people know that the blessings are not absolutely certain signs that they will receive the effect desired and that the sacramentals are not to be considered as superstitious practices. According to the Sacred Congregation of Rites non-catholics may be admitted to receive the public blessings, for instance, to receive the ashes, palms, candles, etc. (5.) However, relics or any other objects, that have been touched by the holy oils, should never be left in the hands of non-catholics. The houses of schismatics or other non-catholics may also be blessed by the pastor. (6.) Exorcisms, when permitted to be performed, may be pronounced also over non-catholics and even those excommunicated. C. 1152.

Whenever an object has been consecrated or merely blessed, but with a constitutive blessing, it should always be handled reverently and never be used for profane or foreign purposes. This is true even when a private person is in possession of such an object. C. 1150.

The faculties granted to priests in former years used to be very extensive. They were secured from the Ordinary. But the Bishops of the United States are not able any longer to grant these extraordinary faculties as they were wont to. The old faculties possessed by our Bishop have been withdrawn and consequently, it is not within their power to communicate them now. The blessing of religious articles such as rosaries, medals etc. cannot, therefore be performed by the parish priest anymore unless new faculties are received. But the Church has been very generous in granting very wide privileges and faculties to all

5. S. Congr. Rituum, March 9, 1921.

6. S. Congr. de Prop. Fid. April 17, 1758. apud Collectanea #411, p. 2263.

those priests who belong to the Holy Name Society. The faculties granted to such are found in a rescript of the 8th of June 1920. They are as follows:-

"(a) fruendi quater in hebdomada Indulto altaris privilegiati personalis, vita ipsorum durante, dummodo huiusmodi Indultum pro alia die non obtinuerint;

(b) Apostolicam Benedictionem cum Indulgentia plenaria, applicabili quoque per modum suffragii animabus in Purgatorio detentis, impertiendi Christifidelibus qui spiritualibus Exercitiis seu sacris Missionibus, ab iisdem sacerdotibus, de consensu Ordinarii, peragendis, ultra medietatem interfuerint, et Benedictioni cum Cruce in fine postremae concionis ab ipsis sacerdotibus dandae vere poenitentes, confessi et sacra Communione refecti adstiterint;

(c) benedicendi coronas Beatae Mariae Virginis cum applicatione Indulgentiarum quae a Crucigeris in Belgio, Apostolica facultate, concedi solent; (crozier indulgences to beads.)

(d) benedicendi, unico Crucis signo, coronas, rosaria, cruces, crucifixos, parvas statuas, numismata, eisque applicandi Indulgentias a S. Sede concessas." (7.)

There are certain sacramentals which are strictly parochial i. e. in the sense that, the pastor alone has the right to administer them to the exclusion of any other priest within the parish. These are: 1. The Nuptial blessing; 2. blessing of the corpse; 3. the blessing of homes on Holy Saturday or any other day according to the custom of the place; 4. the blessing of the baptismal font on Holy Saturday; 5. blessing with pomp and solemnity outside of the church (unless in the capitular church the chapter performs these blessings contained under the last two numbers.) C. 462 #4, 5, 6, and 7.

The pastor, who has the right to the marriage also has the right to impart the nuptial blessing. But he need not give it himself. He is permitted to authorize another to take his place if he chooses. C. 1101 #2. This blessing is called a solemn

7. From a rescript of the S. Congr. for extraordinary affairs. June 8, 1920, found in The Amer. Eccl. Review. vol. LXIII no. 3. p. 282. Sept. 1920.

blessing and may be given even a long time after the parties have been married, if it was not given at the time of their marriage. C. 1101 #1. The blessing consists of the prayers: "Propitiare Domine" and "Deus qui potestate" after the Pater Noster, and the prayer "Deus Abraham" said before the "Placeat". It may never be imparted outside of Mass. Even when the nuptial Mass cannot be said, these prayers are to be inserted into the Mass of the day. The solemn Nuptial Blessing may not be given during the forbidden time i. e. from Ash Wednesday to Easter Sunday inclusive and from the first Sunday in Advent up to Christmas Day inclusive. C. 1108. The Ordinary may, however, allow this blessing to be given even during this time when conditions expressed in C. 1108 #3 are observed. A woman, who has once received this blessing, cannot receive it again even if she marries the second time. C. 1143.

The blessing of the corpse is to be done by the pastor of the subject. "By common law the corpse of the departed Catholic is to be brought to the parish church of the deceased, unless he lawfully chose another church before his death." C. 1216 #1. (8.) If the deceased person had more than one parish the funeral is to take place in the parish church of the place within which he died, if that be one of his parishes. C. 1225. Exceptions to the first rule and other information about the pastor's rights and duties in connection with funerals will be set forth later.

The blessing of the homes of the faithful is not of frequent occurence in the United States except in a few Italian and Slav parishes. When, however, it is performed, it is a strict right of the pastor. C. 462 #6.

Blessing the Baptismal Font on Holy Saturday is another function reserved to the pastor. C. 462 #7. The blessing of the font on Pentecost Day is not mentioned among these parochial rights and, therefore, is not to be classed as such.

As to blessings that may be given by the pastor with pomp and solemnity outside of the church not much need be said. He has the right of blessing buildings, bridges, shops, banners, etc. within his parish limits to the exclusion of any other priest. Be-

8. Augustine 1. c. vol. VI. p. 116.

sides, if he has the faculty from the Ordinary, he may also bless solemnly images that are exposed to the public veneration of the faithful. C. 1279 #4. Before the pastor attempts to impart any blessings whatever, he should first consult his powers and see whether this or that is allowed him. Moreover, even when the pastor has the faculty of giving these solemn blessings outside the church, he will not be allowed to do so if the church is a capitular church and the chapter wishes to give them. C. 462 #7.

Other blessings which are not strictly parochial functions but with which the parish priest will often come in contact are such as the blessing of holy water, ashes, palms, incense, bread on the feasts of St. Blase, St. Agatha and St. Gebhard and at Easter time, wine on the feasts of St. John the Evangelist, fragrant herbs on the feast of the Assumption, the blessing imparted to women after child-birth and the blessing given "in articulo mortis". This last named is not merely a faculty granted to the pastor but also a duty that he must fulfill. C. 468 #2. The blessing of sacred places is reserved but may be delegated by the Ordinary or by the religious superior, as the case may be. C. 1156. The blessing of the "sacra suppelex" i. e. those things used in divine services, which have to be blessed before they are to be used may also be blessel by the pastor as long as these things are for the church or oratory situated within the parish limits. C. 1304 #3. This refers to those blessings only in which the sacred oils are not used. The consecration of a chalice and paten is included in the prohibition. This is clear from the many decisions of the S. Congr. of Rites, e. x. from the decree of the 27th of Sept. 1659, (#18 and 19. vol. I. of Decr. Auth. Congr. S. Rituum, p. 234 #1131.) When other priests not pastors receive the faculty of blessing objects used for divine services, they must be certain to look to the wording of the faculties. If the term "sacra suppelex" is used it includes all the things allowed to the pastors, but if the faculty reads: "benedicendi sacerdotalium imdumentorum" this would not include any vessels nor the altar linens, corporals, palls, etc.

It is also well to remember when a vesel or a vestment loses its blessing or consecration. A vestment or vessel loses its blessing or consecration when it is so badly torn or broken that its original form is wanting and it becomes unfit for further use. The same holds true if such objects are given over to indecent uses or when they are put up for public sale. C. 1305 #1 n. 1-2. But, of course, in many cases the form does not have to be lost entirely. Thus, if a chalice is broken at the bottom so that it will not hold wine any longer, the consecration is lost. Not so if a break would be found at the top. By indecent uses here is meant such as using the sacred vessels at a wedding banquet, etc. If heretics used the vessels for drinking purposes the blessing is also lost. (9.) According to the old law, when a chalice lost its gold and had to be regilded the consecration was lost thereby. This is not so any longer. The law expressly states that "calix et patena non amittunt consecrationem ob consumptionem vel renovationem auraturae". C. 1305 #2. If the gilding is lost the pastor must have the vessel regilded. This is a grave obligation on his part. C. 1305 #2.

9. Augustine l. c. vol. VI. p. 286.

PART. VI.

DIVINE WORSHIP.

All services taking place in the parish church are to be guarded and carefully watched over by the parish priest. Although the administrative board has certain competency when there is question of the administration of temporal affairs of the parish, they have absolutely nothing to say in matters pertaining to the spiritual care of the parish or to the manner in which this is to be carried out. C. 1184. This belongs to the pastor's care and he is dependent solely upon the ecclesiastical superiors for his guidance. C. 1260. It depends upon him to see that all the services are carried on according to the approved books and that no prayers, or practices be introduced, which are not expressly approved by the Ordinary of the place. C. 1259 #1. Care must be taken lest superstitious practices creep into this worship. Rules issued by the Ordinary for the preservation of the approved practices and excercises must be observed by all the pastors, secular or religious. C. 1261 #2.

The parish priest is the one to warn his parishioners not to attend the services of non-catholics without grave reasons, and to tell them how to act even on such occasions when present. C.1258.

The old custom of the Church, of placing men on one side of the Church and women on the other, is still desired by the law. C. 1262 #1. Men are to assist with heads uncovered, while the women should assist with heads covered. C. 1262 #2. Moreover, the women are to be dressed modestly when coming to divine services. This is the more true when they are to approach the Communion Table.

The pastor is the guardian of the music that is rendered in the parochial church. Liturgical laws concerning it are of obligation and should, therefore, be observed wherever this is possible. A careful guard must be kept over the music used lest some lascivious or otherwise improper renditions be given in the House of the Lord. C. 1264. The word lascivious here means, as Pope Alexander said, music that suggests rather the profane than the ecclesiastical ideal. Every pastor ought to read the "Motu Proprio" of Pope Pius X. given on the 22nd of Nov. 1903, so as to have an idea of what the Holy Father tried to bring home to all those, who have anything to do with Church music. Therein the Holy Pontiff says:- "Ne quid igitur occurat in templo necesse est, unde fidelium pietas ac devotio avocetur, vel tantum imminuatur, nihil imprimis quod sacrarum caeremoniarum gravitatem sanctitatemque offendat, atque ideo Domus Orationis Deique maiestate indignum evadet." (1.) The music and its presentation are to be such as would increase the devotion of the faithful. At times the music is good but the presentation is such as might befit the stage rather than the Lord's House. The proper language, moreover, of the Church is Latin and consequently, songs in modern tongues cannot be used at solemn services. The choir, if possible, should be composed of male voices only. (2.) The wishes of the Holy Father will be realized only when the pastors and others having charge of Church music make themselves acquainted with the text of his masterpiece and put it's directions into practise.

Every parish church should keep the Blessed Sacrament regularly upon it's altar. C. 1265 #I. n. I. The usual place for reserving it is the tabernacle of the main altar, which should be so decorated so that it moves the faithful to devotion by it's very appearance. C. 1268-1269. The tabernacle should be an irremovable case placed in the center of the altar and should be so constructed and guarded that there be no danger of sacrilegious profanation. C. 1269 #1-2. Only in certain grave cases may the Blessed Sacrament be kept outside of the tabernacle, and then it must repose on a corporal and in a safe and decent place. C. 1269 #3. A light should be kept burning night and day before it here as well as when it is found in the tabernacle. C. 1269 #3; C. 1271. The lamps used before the tabernacle are to burn olive oil or beeswax and nothing else unless this prescribed material is not available. Even then the Ordinary is to be consulted and his permission secured. C. 1271. The use of electric lights for this purpose is not mentioned here and, consequently, we will be forced to stand by former rulings in this regard. The

1. "Motu Proprio" Pii X. Nov. 22, 1903. apud Collectanea S. C. de P. F. vol. II, p. 445 #2182.

2. Motu Proprio, sect. III-V.

decree of the S. Congregation of Rites given on the 23rd of February 1916 is still in force today. But the pastor must have the Bishop's consent in those cases.

Proper material must be used in the making of altar breads and genuine Mass wine. The sacred species should be renewed frequently and a sufficient supply always kept on hand. Any instructions given by the Ordinary concerning the renewal of the sacred species are to be observed by all the pastors. C. 1272. They should be renewed at least every week. (3.) Devotion to the Blessed Sacrament is to be fostered among the people and they should be exhorted to come to Mass and visit the Lord not only on Sundays and Holydays of obligation but as frequently as possible.

The next two canons treat of the exposition of the Blessed Sacrament and the Forty Hour Devotion. The law states that private exposition of the Blessed Sacrament can be had for any just cause without the permission of the Ordinary. Father Augustine says that "a case of sickness or the mere desire of pious persons or of a religious community would be a private cause sufficient to justify private exposition." (4.) Public exposition of the Blessed Sacrament may be made only on the feasts of Corpus Christi and within the octave of this feast, at Mass and at Vespers. If the pastor wishes to have a public exposition on other occasions he must secure permission from the Ordinary who can grant it for a grave and legitimate cause, especially a cause of a public nature. C. 1274. The distinction between private and public exposition is this:- "when the cause for which it takes place is a public one and the Sacred Host is taken from the tabernacle and exposed to the view of the faithful in attendance and benediction given with it before it is replaced it is a public exposition." It is private when the cause is of a personal or private character. In this case the Host is not taken from the tabernacle nor in any way exposed to the view of those present but is left enclosed in the ciborium — — — and drawn forward to the door of the tabernacle, where it remains to the end of the function." (5.)

3. Ceremoniale Episcoporum, lib. I. c. VI. n. 2.

4. Augustine, op. cit. vol. VI. p. 229.

5. Schulze, F. Pastoral Theology, p. 56.

Forty Hour devotions are to be held in every church that keeps the Blessed Sacrament. This should be done once a year. The Ordinary names the date for each church and that date is to be observed with the greatest solemnity. C. 1275. If, for some grave reason or other, the Blessed Sacrament cannot be exposed in this manner for forty hours, the Ordinary should see to it that the Blessed Sacrament is exposed at least on certain successive hours during stated days.

Passing over to another title ot the New Code we come to the veneration of Saints, sacred images and relics. The Church has ever honored her saints, their relics and images and voices her mind accordingly in the first canon of this title saying:- "Bonum atque utile est Dei Servos, una cum Christo regnantes, suppliciter invocare eorumque reliquias atque imagines venerare; sed prae ceteris filiali devotione Beatissimam Virginem Mariam fideles universi prosequantur." C. 1276. Frequently instruction on these matters will be of great value to the parishioners. They should be told whom they may venerate publicly, (C. 1277.) how this is to done and with what confidence.

The pastor will have to be on guard against the introduction of unusual images into the church, unless this is done with the permission of the Ordinary. C. 1279. Pictures or images, of great value on account of their antiquity or artistic finish or on account of the great public veneration paid to them, when in need of repairs cannot be repaired without the consent of the Ordinary. C. 1280. This is a precaution taken by the Church in order to save those articles from falling into the hands of unskilled men who might spoil the picture or image altogether or at least destroy its beauty. The permanent transference of such pictures and images to another church cannot be done without the permit of the Holy See. C. 1281 #1.

The following decree in regard to certain images was given out recently by the S. Congr. of the Holy Office:-

"Imagines sacras cuiusdam novae scholae pictoricae, quarum specimen exhibetur in opusculo cui titulus: *La Passion de Notre Seigneur Jesus Christ* par Cyril Verschaeve (ornee de compositions d'Albert Servaes. Bruxelles et Paris. Librairie Nationale d'art et d'histoire G. van Oest et Cie Editeurs, 1920), ad praescriptum canonis 1399, n 12, prohiberi ipso iure ,ideoque statim removendas esse ab Ecclesiis, Oratoriis, etc., in quibus forte ex-positae inveniantur." (5a.)

Relics must be held in great veneration. The pastor should always see to it that there is some proof of the genuineness of the relics possessed by the parish. If there be no such document, the Ordinary is to be consulted, since only genuine relics may be exposed to the public veneration of the people. C. 1283. This notification of the Ordinary must take place when the relic is known to be genuine, but the papers are lost. The Vicar General cannot pass judgement, unless he has a special mandate from the Bishop to this effect. C. 1285 #1. If the relic is an ancient one and the people are very much attached to it, it may be retained, unless solid arguments can be brought against its genuineness. C. 1285 #2.

All relics exposed to the public veneration of the faithful must be placed in a capsule and sealed with the seal of the prelate, who authenticated the relic. C. 1287 #1. The relic of the True Cross cannot be kept in the same capsule with other relics, i. e. of the saints and blessed. Moreover, when the relic of the True Cross is carried in procession, "no other relic can be carried in procession under the canopy at the same time." (3.) The relics of the True Cross and of other instruments used in the crucifixion and passion in general, may be carried about during a procession under a canopy. But other relics can never be carried under this canopy. (4.) The same canon also legislates in regard to the veneration of the relics of the blessed in the following words:- "Beatorum reliquiae, sine speciali indulto, in processionibus ne circum ferantur, neve in ecclesiis exponantur, nisi ubi eorum officium et Missa celebretur ex Sedis Apostolicae concessione". C. 1287 #3.

Large relics such as the whole body, the head, a leg, an arm, a hand, etc., and those parts of the body in which the martyr suffered, as long as they are entire and not too small, cannot be alienated validly nor transferred permanently to another church without the permission of the Holy See. The same holds true

5a. S. Congr. S. Officii, 30 Martii, 1921 Martii. apud Acta Apost. Sedis. vol. XIII. p 197.

3. Augustine, op. cit. vol. VI. p. 252. C. 1287 #2.

4. S. Rit. C. Decretum Generale. Die 27 Maii, 1826. apud Decreta Authentica Congr. Sacrorum Rituum. vol. II. #4620a, p. 216-217.

with regard to other relics which are held in high esteem by the people. C. 1281. Nor may such large relics, as those mentioned above, be kept in private houses or even private oratories without the express permission of the Ordinary. C. 1282. All other relics when kept in private places must be treated with proper respect. Furthermore, no relics may be sold and the pastor must take care that none, especially those of the True Cross, fall into the hands of non-catholics or be profaned in any manner or perish. C. 1298.

Processions also make up a part of the divine worship. They are divided into the ordinary and the extraordinary processions. The former are such as are held on certain days throughout the year according to the instructions of sacred liturgy or according to legitimate customs. The latter are those held on other days for some public cause. Among the ordinary processions are found those held on Candlemas Day, Palm Sunday, Rogation Days, funeral processions, etc. Extraordinary processions are such as are held in order to call upon God for rain, fair weather, the aversion of a calamity etc. The Ordinary of the place can, after having consulted the cathedral chapter, order extraordinary processions to be held.

On Corpus Christi only one solemn procession may be held in the public streets of the same town or city. Immemorial custom or peculiar local circumstances, with the permission of the Ordinary, may allow a deviation from this rule. But, unless this permission is given or said custom exists the "ecclesia dignior" of the town or city has the right to lead the procession on this day. "All the clergy and male religious orders, including the exempt, as well as the confraternities of laymen, must attend it." (5.) This refers to the clergy, etc. of the whole town or city and exempts only those regulars, who live in perpetual strict enclosure or at least three thousand paces from the place i. e. from the town or city. C. 1291 #1. The other parish churches will have their procession during the octave, on the day and hour and along the route set by the Ordinary of the place. C. 1291 #2. The pastor cannot introduce any new processions nor transfer or abolish the old, unless he has the Ordinary's permission. C. 1294.

5. Augustine, op. cit. vol. VI. p. 257.

The pastor will not only concern himself about the rites and time of divine worship, but will also care for the vessels and other articles used in the services. Scrupulous care must be taken that they be clean and in good condition and that they be kept in a safe place when not in use. He must remember that all these things are used in the worship of God and, consequently, should be taken care of in the best possible manner. It certainly does not speak well of a pastor when the linens, vessels, etc., are found in a dirty, even unsanitary state. Moreover, he must see to it that those vessels and other articles, which must be blessed, receive this blessing before they are used. Rules regarding the loss of blessings are given in canon 1305.

If a certain parish be very poor the Ordinary may allow that priests, who say Mass there for their convenience, give a small sum to help defray the expense of the "sacra suppelex" required for the celebration. C. 1303 #2. The Ordinary alone to the exclusion of the Vicar General and the Vicar General, can determine the amount of this small fee. C. 1303 #3.

Every pastor is asked and ordered to make a last testament or other valid legal instrument in which he would name a certain person of good standing who, upon the pastor's death, will take temporary charge of all the things belonging to the pastor and to the church and deliver them to the lawful claimants. C. 1301. It will suffice if he merely names the person in this testament. In another letter he can tell this person, designated in the testament, to whom the things should be given. Consequently, the pastor will have to leave an inventory of everything that the church and he possess, stating to whom each article belongs. Moreover in regard to things pertaining to the sacra suppelex he will have to state when the article was purchased, how it was bought, i. e. whether with his own money or with that of the church. Otherwise all such things will be presumed to belong to the church. C. 1299 #3.

PART VII.

THE PASTOR AND ECCLESIASTICAL BURIAL.

The Catholic Church strictly prohibits the cremation of the bodies of her faithful. C. 1203. They are to be buried in cemeteries that are blessed according to the rules of prescribed liturgical books. C. 1203 #1; C. 1205. The ordinary faithful are not to be buried in churches but in the cemetery. Every parish should have its own burying place unless the Ordinary assigns a common cemetery for two or more parishes. C. 1208. If there is no Catholic cemetery in the vicinity and none can be had, the Ordinary is to be consulted about the blessing of a part of the civil cemetery for the use of Catholics. C. 1206.

The Church instructs its members to take the bodies of deceased faithful to the church where the services prescribed shall be carried out. C. 1215. Only a grave reason can excuse from this ruling, for it is more important to bring the corpse to the church than to accompany it to the cemetery, as long as the grave is blessed. The church to which the body is to be taken is the parochial church, unless the deceased selected another church. C. 1216. If the person deceased had more than one parish, he is to be buried from the parish church of the place in which he died, if that church was one of his parish churches. C. 1216 #2. In doubt as to the rights of certain churches to these funeral services, the parish church has the first right. C. 1217. If the person died outside of his own parish, he is nevertheless to be taken to his nearest parish church if he can be carried there conveniently on foot; otherwise to the nearest parish church of the place wherein he died. C. 1218. The Ordinary may decide about the distance and all other circumstances which would make the transportation of the body inconvenient. C. 1218 #2. But notwithstanding the fact that the transference may be very difficult, the relatives and heirs and others interested have the right of transporting the body to the parish church of the deceased if they so desire and are willing to stand for the expenses. C. 1218 #3.

Bodies of resident beneficiaries are to be buried from the church of their benefice unless they choose another church. C. 1220.

Religious are to be buried from the church or oratory of their own house or religion. Novices may select another church if they wish, but the right of removing the body and accompanying it to church always belongs to their religious superior. C. 1221 #1. If the place of death is so far from the religious house that the deceased religious cannot be transferred there conveniently nor to a church of his order or congregation, they are to be buried from the parish church of the place in which they died. Even in such cases the religious superior of the deceased has the right of removing and transporting the body to the religious house if he so desires and pays the expenses of transportation. Of course, if the novice selects another church, he or she are to be buried in that church. C. 1221 #2. The funerals of servants who are actually employed by and stay within the religious house, i. e. janitors, farm-laborers, teachers, etc., are to take place according to the rules just quoted for novices. C. 1221 #1. If they died outside of the religious house this privilege does not hold and they are to be buried according to the rules for the ordinary faithful i. e. according to Canons 1216 and 1218. Nor does this privilege hold for students in houses or colleges even of regulars or for those who die in hospitals. Such are to be buried as the other members of the laity according to canons 1216-1218. Guests and sick persons living in religious houses are also comprised in this rule. A particular law or privilege may exempt all such from the common law and introduce a change here. C. 1222. Seminarians, however, are to be buried by the authorities of the seminary, unless the Holy See itself should determine otherwise for some seminaries. C. 1368.

As was said, a person is to be buried in the parochial church unless he selects another church. The choosing of a church for the funeral services and the place of burial is allowed to any one except to those to whom it is expressly forbidden by law. Thus a wife may choose her place of burial and the church from which she is to be buried, separately from her husband. This is also allowed to children who have reached the age of puberty. C. 1223. But children who are not of the age of twelve and fourteen respectively for girls and boys, cannot select a church or cemetery for their burial. Neither is this allowed to professed religious unless the religious be a Bishop. C. 1224.

Although a person may have the right of selecting the church for his funeral services, he cannot choose any church. As the Code says a person may select any parochial church ,any church of regulars or any other church which has the "jus funerandi" i. e. the right to funeral services. C. 1225. The patron of a church which is a church "juris patronatus" can choose that church. Note that the law does not allow a person to choose any church of-religious except those of regulars. Moreover, the churches of nuns, i. e. "moniales" (sisters with solemn vows) cannot be validly chosen by outsiders. The only persons who can be buried from there are the sisters themselves and those women "quae famulatus, educationis, infirmitatis aut hospitii causa intra clausuram eiusdem monasterii non precario commorabantur." C 1.225. But what are the other churches mentioned here under the term "aliam ecclesiam funerandi iure praeditam?" From Canon 1191 #2 we know that ecclesiastical functions not prohibited by the rubrics may take place in all public oratories which are dedicated to the perpetual public worship of God according to canons 1155-1156. The same privilege is granted to all legitimately erected semi-public oratories unless the Ordinary forbids some of these functions to be held there. C. 1193. But the funeral service is an ecclesiastical function. Consequently, such services can be held in any public or semi-public oratory, as long as it is not forbidden by the Ordinary.

The cemetery selected may be any one in which the faithful in general may be interred. However, if the cemetery is another than the parochial cemetery the negative consent at least of authorities of that cemetery is necessary. C. 1228 #1. If the cemetery selected be one that belongs to religious, the consent of the competent religious superior must be obtained. The religious superior must be aware of the constitution of the order or congregation in this regard. C. 1228 #2.

If the person dies without selecting a church or cemetery he will be buried from the parochial church and in the parochial cemetery, according to canons quoted above. If the deceased has an ancestral tomb or grave in some cemetery he is to be buried in that tomb or grave, if transportation can be effected with convenience. C. 1229 #1. A wife who dies without a special choice of a cemetery is to be buried in the ancestral tomb of her husband. If she had two or more husbands she is to be interred in the ancestral tomb of the last husband. When a person has more than one ancestral tomb and dies without a special choice of any certain one, the members of the family and his heirs have the right to select any one of them. C. 1229 #3.

The pastor is not to induce anyone to select the parochial church for his funeral services nor the parochial cemetery for his interment. Nor is he to induce anyone to change from another church or cemetery to his own. If this were done the selection or change is null and the party will have to be buried in the cemetery and from the church of his own parish as the other canons rule. C. 1227. Freedom of choice is to be respected in all who possess this right and consequently, the Church does not want any of her ministers to meddle in this matter by inducements, etc.

The choice of the church and cemetery may be made "per se vel per alium cui legitimum mandatum dederit." C. 1226. If it was made through another, this person has the right to demand its fulfillment, and he can use any legitimate means of proving that the mandate was given him and that it is genuine. Two witnesses attesting under oath will be sufficient proof.

Now we come to the important canon which treats of the pastor's rights and duties in regard to funerals. The canon is divided into seven sections and it will be best for us to observe that order.

I. The pastor of the deceased subject has not only the right but also the duty of removing (levandi) the body from the house, accompanying it to his parish church and there performing the prescribed funeral rites. Only a grave reason can excuse him from doing this either "per se vel per alium." If, however, the deceased person had more than one proper pastor, this right and duty belong to that proper pastor within whose parish the person died. C. 1216, #2.

II. If the subject dies in a parish of which he is not a member and can be transported conveniently to his own parish, the pastor of the deceased has the right to go into that other parish and to remove the body from the house and accompany it to his own parish church, after notifying the pastor of that other parish. Of course, if the place where the person dies is exempted from the pastor's jurisdiction and has the right of burying, the pastor cannot interfere with this right. Thus a hospital may be exempt from the jurisdiction of the pastor of that place and have the right of funeral services in its' own chapel for all such as die within that hospital. In such cases unless the deceased desires another church for his funeral services, the functions will be carried on there.

III. If the church chosen by the deceased is that of regulars or any other that is exempt from his jurisdiction, the pastor cannot perform the funeral rites in that church, but he has the right of removing the body from the house and accompanying it to that church of the regulars or others under the cross of this exempt church. The rector of that church has the right of performing the funeral services although the deceased is a member of the pastor's congregation and was removed from the parish. It remains understood that the church, which was chosen, is situated within the parish. Otherwise the pastor could not perform these rights whether the church be one of regulars or of the secular clergy.

IV. If the church situated within the parish is under the jurisdiction of the pastor i. e. "Ecclesia no-exempta", and the deceased is a subject of the pastor, the latter may take the body from the house to that church which was chosen and perform there the rites prescribed. This right, however of funeral services may be reserved by a special privilege of the rector of that church.

V. This section treats of female religious and novices. If such die within the enclosure, the body is to be carried to the threshold of that inclosure by other religious of that house, from where the chaplain or the pastor of the territory will conduct the funeral to the church or oratory where the services are to be held. The chaplain has this right only when the religious are exempt from the jurisdiction of the pastor. Otherwise, the pastor of that territory has the right to conduct the procession and hold the services in his own parochial church. If a female religious or novice passes away outside of the religious house, "serventur canonum praescripta". C. 1230 #5.

VII. If the corpse of one of the faithful is shipped to a place where the deceased had no proper parish nor even a church selected by him for the funeral services, the right of receiving the body and performing all exequial functions and conducting the body to the cemetery belongs to the cathedral church of the place. If there be no cathedral church there, this right falls to that parish within whose limits the cemetery is situated. Diocesan statutes or local customs may have some other arrangement which is, then, to be followed. C. 1230 #7.

After the services have been performed in the church, the body is to be conducted by the officiating priest or his substitute to the cemetery of that church for burial. C. 1231 #1-2. This is binding unless a grave necessity excuses. If the deceased chose another cemetery than the parochial one the burial is to take place there. In any case the officiating priest at the funeral services also has the right of passing through any other parish or diocese with stole on and cross elevated while he is on the way to the place of burial. He needs no permission of the pastors through whose territory he passes nor of the Ordinary of another diocese if he passes through that place. C. 1232 #1. But this right cannot be claimed by such an officiating priest in a cemetery to which the body cannot be transported conveniently. C. 1232 #2.

The pastor has no right to exclude members of the secular clergy or pious societies, invited by the relatives or heirs of the deceased, from taking part in the procession to the church and cemetery and from assisting at the funeral and burial services, unless he has a serious reason for doing so and this reason has been approved by the Ordinary. C. 1233. Societies or emblems manifestly inimical to the Church should be barred by the pastor. C. 1233 #2. The pastor also has the right of arranging the funeral procession and he should be obeyed. He must, of course, have regard to the rights of precedence. C. 1233 #3.

The pastor is not allowed to demand more than is allowed by the diocesan rules for performing the funeral and burial services. And when there is question of those who are poor, he should bury them gratis. In these cases he is not to omit any of the rites just because he is doing it for nothing but should make use of all exequies which liturgy and the diocesan statutes may prescribe. C. 1235.

According to the New Code and, when there is no contrary particular law, the "portio paroecialis" i. e. the pastor's portion, must be given to the pastor of the deceased whenever the funeral is held outside of the parochial church. It makes no difference whether the deceased chose another church or not. If, however, the subject died in a place from which he could not be transferred to the parochial church conveniently, this rule does not bind. C. 1236 #1. In cases where the deceased had more than one proper pastor the pastor's portion is to be divided among them all whenever the funeral took place in another church than one of these and the deceased could have been conveniently transported to any one of these churches. C. 1236 #2.

The pastor's portion, which is to be determined by the synodal tax, is to be taken from all the fees established by the synodal statutes for the funeral services and for burial. C. 1237 # 1-3. If the parish church and the church which held the funeral services belong to two different dioceses and the funeral fees are different in each, the "portio paroecialis" will be determined according to the tax of the diocese in which the church that held the funeral services is situated. If the solemn funeral services were not held on the day the deceased was buried but within a month from the time, the pastor of the deceased has the right also to the "portio paroecialis" from the belated funeral service. C. (1237. #2.) e. g. suppose a man dies of the influenza on Nov. 6th, and cannot be taken to the church then but must be taken directly to the cemetery and buried after the priest blessed the grave. On Dec. 1st the relatives of the deceased person wish to have the services held solemnly in some other church than the subject's parish church. The pastor of the subject is in this case also entitled to a share in the regular stole fee which was paid then. "But" as Father Augustine remarks," the stole fee was supposed to have been offered only for the solemn function, which means not a sung Mass, but the funeral service, with either low or high Mass, and the absolution or Libera". (1). The following solution of a doubt regarding this part of canon 1237 has been given by the Pontifical Commission for the authentic interpretation of the New Code:-

"1. Utrum officium funebre quod non intra mensem a die tumulationis celebratur, sed intra mensem a die notitiae obitus alicujus qui in regione longe dissita decessit (v. g. in America),

1. Augustine, op. cit. vol. VI. p. 149.

haberi debeat officium sollemne, de quo in can. 1237 quoad effectus paragraphi secundae illius canonis.

2. An Ordinarius, ad vitandos abusus eorum qui ultra mensem protrahunt officium funebre eo animo ut Parochus emolumenta non percipiat, possit statuere quod officium a parentibus celebratum pro defuncto publice et cum cantu habeatur uti officium sollemne funebre quoad omnes suos effectus.

Resp. Ad Ium et 2um: Recurrendum ese ad S. C. Concilii. (Ia.)

Rules regarding the denial of ecclesiastical burial must also be known to the parish priest. He must know that ecclesiastical burial cannot be given to those who are not baptised and that it must be granted to all those who were baptized and to those catechumens, who, without their fault, died without baptism, as long as the law does not expressly forbid this burial to such. Canon 1240 tells us to whom ecclesiastical burial must be denied. They are the following:- "Ecclesiastica sepultura privantur nisi ante mortem aliqua dederint poenitentiae signa:- 1. Notorii apostatae a christiana fide, aut sectae haereticae vel schismaticae aut sectae massonicae alliisve eiusdem generis societatibus notorie addicti; 2. Excommunicati vel interdicti post sententiam condemnatoriam vel declaratoriam; 3. Qui se ipsi occiderint deliberato consilio; 4. Mortui in duello aut ex vulnere inde relato; 5. Qui mandaverint suum corpus cremationi tradi; 6. Alii peccatores publici et manifesti." C. 1240 #1. If there be any doubt as to whether a person should be given ecclesiastical burial or not the Ordinary should be consulted, if time allows. If the doubt cannot be dispelled ecclesiastical burial should not be denied but it must be given so as not to give scandal. Thus, if the fact that the person gave signs of repentance is made public the danger of scandal will be done away with. Moreover, if a person who was an "excommunicatus vitandus" is buried among the faithful he should be removed from there and buried on the plot reserved for such as must be denied ecclesiastical burial. Of course, if it cannot be done without serious inconvenience the removal may be omitted. The permission of the Ordinary must be secured even for exhumations of this nature. C. 1242 .

1a. Apud Acta Apost. Sedis. vol. XII. p. 576.

After the funeral services have taken place the pastor is to make the proper entries into the "Liber Defunctorum". The data to be recorded is the following: 1. Name of deceased; 2. the age of the deceased; 3. names of the parents of the deceased or, if the deceased was married, then the name of the consort is recorded instead; 5. who administered the sacraments to the person when sick and which of the sacraments were administered; 6. the date and place of burial; 7. date of death. C. 1238.

PART VIII.

TEMPORAL ADMINISTRATION.

"A pastor must have in mind that as "custos ecclesiae" he is responsible not only for the souls entrusted to his care, but also for the temporal goods which belong to the parish, since they are the means by which the spiritual end, the eternal salvation of men and their spiritual welfare, is effected." (1.) Although the Church is of divine institution and it's end is a spiritual one, still that part of it known as the Church militant, needs property, temporal goods, to carry on its work toward this end. This property must, of course, be properly administered by some one, and this some one is as a rule the parish priest. Business tact and practical prudence must, consequently, be his if he wishes to do justice to this position. With an ever watchful eye he must care for all the temporal affairs of the parish and see that they are safe and in good condition.

That the Church has the right of acquiring, holding and disposing of temporal goods independently of the civil power cannot be doubted. C. 1495 #1. The individual churches are also endowed with this right. C. 1495 #2. But this right would not be of practical value if the Church did not have the right to demand that her subjects contribute to Her support and to that of Her clergy. For unless the people, belonging to the Church, contributed of their means, the Church would have no property and its right of acquiring would be a dead letter, theoretically of value but practically of no use. Consequently, the law states that the Church has this right to demand support from its members for its clergy and other ministers as well as for all things necessary for divine worship and other proper ends. C. 1496.

The administration of all Church property belongs in the first and highest place to the Roman Pontiff. He is the supreme administrator and chief steward of all the property possessed by the Church. C. 1518. The Ordinary is placed over the property found within his diocese and the pastor over that within his parish. The Ordinary may issue special rules for the administration of the property over which he has jurisdiction, but all this is done under the authority of the Roman Pontiff, and, conse-

1. Schulze, F. op. cit. p. 358.

quently, the common law must be followed in all matters of this kind, having due regard also for legitimate customs and peculiar circumstances. C. 1519 #2. Peculiar statutes issued by the Ordinary according to the common law must be observed by every pastor since the pastors are, again, under the authority of the Ordinary of the diocese.

The new law tells the Ordinary to establish a diocesan board of administrators in the episcopal city and special administrators for the individual institutions. C. 1520-1521. Here in the U. S. such special administrators are not appointed for parishes because the pastor, aided by the trustees, is the one who is charged with the duty of administering the temporal affairs of the congregation. Consequently, it may be well to mention some of the special duties of a special administrator which also bind the parish priest.

In the first place, before the pastor enters into the office, he is to take an oath before the Ordinary or the Vicar Foraneus, swearing that he will administer the goods well and faithfully. C. 1552. This is not absolutely necessary for the pastor since it is included in the oath which he takes before entering upon his duties as pastor wherein he promises to care for the parish to the best of his ability. Secondly, the pastor will take an inventory, accurately and distinctly, of all the immovable goods as well as of the more valuable movable goods, giving therein a complete description of such things and an appraisal of them. After signing this inventory he sends one copy to the diocesan archives and the other to the archives of the administrative council established by the Ordinary according to C. 1520. C. 1522. It will also be well to keep a special copy in the parochial archives, so that he can check up on these things from time to time. If he finds such an inventory at the parish upon his arrival he should re-check all the goods and see whether anything has been sold or lost since the time that inventory was compiled and if anything has been added to the temporal goods of the parish. C. 1522 #2. This should be done before the pastor takes up his charge or if it was omitted then, at least, as soon as possible thereafter.

The pastor is to administer the parochial temporal goods with as much care as a father takes of his family property. Consequently, he must "vigilare ne bona ecclesiastica suae curae concredita quoque modo pereant aut detrimentum capiant; 2. Praescripta servare iuris tam canonici quam civilis, aut quae a fundatore vel donatore vel legitima auctoritate imposita sunt; 3. Reditus bonorum ac proventus accurate et iusto tempore exigere exactoque loco tuto servare et secundem fundatoris mentem aut statutas vel normas impendere; 4. Pecuniam ecclesiae, quae de expensis supersit et utiliter collocari potest, de consensu Ordinarii, in emolumentum ipsius ecclesiae occupare; 5. Accepti et expensi libros bene ordinatos habere; 6. Documenta et instrumenta, quibus iura ecclesiae in bona nituntur, rite ordinare et in ecclesiae archivo vel armario convenienti et apto custodire; authentica vero eorum exemplaria, ubi commode fieri potest, in archivo vel armario Curiae deponere." C. 1523. Besides, he is instructed to pay all the servants fair wages, give them sufficient time to perform their religious duties and not deter them from their domestic duties or from habits of thrift. C. 1524. Naturally, the pastor will not be such as to overlook the servants concerned nor give them such jobs which they are not able to perform. At the end of the year the pastor is to give an account of his administration to the local Ordinary. C. 1525.

Lawsuits may not be started or contested by the pastor before he has the permission of the Ordinary of the diocese. This refers to the starting of lawsuits in the name of the church or to the contesting of a lawsuit brought against the parish. If the case urges, the pastor need only ask the permission of the foraneus vicar C. 1526. If the parish priest starts or contests a lawsuit without this permission and the case is decided against the church, he will be held for the losses which the church sustains thereby. The Church is not responsible for the contracts entered into by the administrator concerning affairs outside of their jurisdiction unless they have the written permission of competent ecclesiastical authority, i. e. the Ordinary or Holy See or unless the contract is favorable to the Church. C. 1527. The acts are also invalid when the administrator oversteps the bounds and the mode of his ordinary administration.

The civil law concerning contracts must also be observed unless the Code states otherwise and as long as the regulations are not contrary to the divine law. C. 1529.

In the alienatoin of church property the following rules must be observed. Large relics and precious images as well as those relics and images which are held in great veneration by the people cannot be alienated without the express permission of the Holy See. C. 1281 #1. All other goods of the Church, whether movable or immovable, "quae servando servari possunt", may be alienated only after, 1. an appraisal of the goods by a conscientious expert has been made. 2. a just cause is present and 3. the necessary permission has been secured from competent ecclesiastical authority. C. 1530. Without this permission any alienation of church goods is invalid. Moreover any other precautions that may seem necessary are to be used by the Superior who gives the permission. C. 1530 #2. The competent authority mentioned here is either the Holy See or the Ordinary as follows: The Holy See must be petitioned: in cases of alienation of precious articles of any kind or amount; in the alienation of property valued above 30,000 lire or francs. (2.) When the property to be alienated does not exceed the sum of 1,000 francs or lire the Ordinary after consulting with the board of administrators — — unless the sum is of little value, — and with the consent of the parties concerned, may give this permission. If the value of the property is between 1,000 and 30,000 lire or francs the Ordinary may give the consent only after he has 1. the consent of the cathedral chapter (or diocesan consultors), which is to be given by vote in a meeting, 2. the consent of the board of administrators and 3. of the persons concerned in the alienation. C. 1532 #2-3. When the property is divisible and a part of it has been disposed of before, this must be mentioned in the request for the permission; otherwise the consent given is null. C. 1532 #4. This last part of the canon refers to a petition of any kind whether sent to the Holy See or to the Ordinary.

The just cause mentioned above means an urgent necessity or evident utility on the part of the church, or piety. This utility must be measured according to the value of the thing alienated and must be evident. The cause is not necessary for the validity

2. The lire and the franc must be computed according to their normal value and not according to what they are worth in these unsettled times. The foreign exchange in normal times was about 5 francs or lire to $1. Consequently the sum in our money would be about $6,000 at all times unless a change is ordered by the Holy See

of the contract. If, however, an alienation takes place without this cause and the church suffers loss therefrom, the pastor would be held responsible. Sufficient causes for making alienation of some kind would be the paying off of a debt, redeeming a mortgage, repairs of the church, buying land necessary for the other buildings, aid to the poor, etc. (3.) Piety is another reason for alienation. This as Father Augustine says may be gratitude to someone from whom favors have been received, help to the poor and captives and other works of Christian mercy and charity. Urgent necessity may also induce alienation.

According to the common law of the Church all alienations are to be made by means of advertising or public auction. C. 1531 #2. When this has taken place the property should be given to the highest bidder after considering all things carefully. It should not be given for less than the appraisal made by the expert. C. 1531 #1. When articles that were blessed are sold, the fact of their being blessed should not induce the pastor to ask a higher price for them. C. 1539. Nor may immovable property of the church be sold or leased to the administrator (or pastor) himself, or to persons who are related to him in the first or second degree of consanguinity or affinity, unless a special permit has been secured from the Ordinary of the place. C. 1540. Circumstances may persuade another manner of alienating church property than that mentioned above

The formalities spoken of in canons 1530-1532 must be observed in all contracts through which the condition of the church might become worse. C. 1533. If these formalities are omitted the church may bring personal action against the pastor or even his heirs. And if property has been alienated without the permission of the competent Superior, according to canon 1532, or in any other manner, so as to make the contract invalid, the church may take real action also against those who acquired this property invalidly. The person who received the church property in this manner will then have the right of action against the pastor through whom the property was thus invalidly secured. C. 1534 #1. The parish priest has the right to revoke any invalid alienation which he himself has made. C. 1534 #2. The Bishop and the successor of the pastor may also take this action as well as any cleric ascribed to the church which suffers the loss.

3. Augustine, op. cit. vol. VI. p. 595.

A pastor is not allowed to make large donations from the movable church goods for any cause unless there be a just reason for it and it be done for the sake of reward, piety or christian charity. If he does, the successor has the right to recall that donation. Small donations may be made according to the legitimate custom of the place. C. 1535. Immovable goods cannot be given away by the parish priest. In making the donations in the cases allowed, the pastor must observe a proportion between the merits of the person or cause receiving the gift itself. Moreover, the condition of the church must be remembered and the gifts meted out accordingly.

Donations made to the pastor of the parish are presumed to be offered to the church itself, unless the contrary is proven. C. 1536 #1. For this reason it will be necessary for the pastor to have solid proofs of the intention of the giver when the gift is made to himself. The pastor cannot refuse donations offered to the church without the permission of the Ordinary. And if he makes such a refusal he may be held for the loss which the church suffers thereby. C. 1536 #2-3. Any donation once made to a church is entirely out of the power of the giver and, consequently, cannot be recalled at any time. C. 1534 #4.

The Code sets down an absolute rule regarding the loaning of ecclesiastical goods which have been blessed or consecrated. None of these things may be loaned to anyone for any purpose repugnant to the nature of the thing in question. C. 1537. Consequently, as Father Augustine says, " a church should never be turned into a concert hall, a chalice is not to be used for banquets, even though it were only for a transitory loan and the money were sorely needed." (4.) The loaning of such articles to be used for purposes for which they are destined is not forbidden. Thus, there would be no wrong in lending a chalice to another priest while he is having his own regilded.

Church property cannot be pawned, mortgaged or placed in a state of debt without the permission of the proper competent superior. C. 1538 This holds good in all debts about to be contracted. Nor may the pastor even exchange notes payable which the church possesses into other titles or investments, even when the latter are safer than the former, unless the consent of the

4. Augustine, op. cit. vol. VI. p 603.

Ordinary, the administrative board and the parties concerned is secured. C. 1539 #2.

The pastor should always keep in mind the fact that a thing is blessed or consecrated must not make any difference in exchanges of sacred articles. C. 1539 #1.

Renting of parish land must be done according to the formalities mentioned in canons 1531-1532, i. e. proper permission must be secured beforehand, it must be done in public auction or by means of advertising, etc. The rental contract must include the following information and conditions: the amount to be paid and when, the use to which the land is to be put, the exact boundaries of the land rented, the safeguards necessary for the fulfillment of all these conditions, etc. C. 1541 #1. Moreover, the pastor cannot ask that rent be paid for more than six months in advance, without the permission of the Ordinary of the place. C. 1479; 1541 #2. Again, if the sum of the rent exceeds 30,000 francs or lire and the lease was for more than nine years, an apostolic indult will be necessary. If the contract is for less than this time the local Ordinary may give the permission after securing the consent of the cathedral board (or diocesan consultors), and of the administrative board established by him, and also of those concerned. If the amount of the rent is something over 1,000 francs or lire and less than 30,000 and the contract is to run for more than nine years, the Ordinary can grant the necessary permission with the consent of the cathedral chapter (or diocesan consultors), the administrative board and those interested. If a contract of this kind runs for a shorter time, the Ordinary need only consult the administrative board and receive the consent of the parties concerned before he grants the permission. Finally, if the rental does not exceed 1,000 lire or francs and the contract runs for more than nine years, the Ordinary may give permission after consulting with the board of administrators and receiving the consent of the parties interested; if the contract is made for nine years or less the administrative board itself can grant the necessary permission "monito Ordinario." C. 1541.

Canon 1542 treats of emphteusis while the following canon takes up interest and says that "it is not "per se" forbidden to make loans under the usual legal conditions, provided no excessive interest is charged; nor is it forbidden to stipulate a higher rate of interest if a just and proportionate reason can be advanced." (5.) If, however, a fungible thing is given to another in such a way that it is his, no interest can be demanded by reason of the contract itself when the thing is restored in kind to the same amount because this would be usury and, consequently, forbidden by the Church. (6.)

Instructions in reference to pious foundations, the safeguards against accepting too many of them, their acceptance, constitution and administration, the formalities in making them out, etc. are contained in title XXX of the third book, embracing in all canons 1544-1551 inclusive. As is stated there the Ordinary, and not the pastor, has the right of determining the minimum amount of the endowment as well as one manner in which the fruits of the endowment are to be distributed. C. 1545. Consequently, no one may accept any foundation of lesser amount than that fixed by the Ordinary of the place. No moral person can accept an endowment without the written consent of the Ordinary. C. 1546. All endowments ought to be made in writing. But even when they are made orally they are to be recorded in writing and signed. One of these records is to be sent to the diocesan archives while the other remains in the place where the foundation's obligations are to be fulfilled. C. 1548. The Church, which has any such pious foundations must keep a record of the obligations coming from them in a safe place, designated by the rector or pastor of the church. C. 1549 #2. Just as the pastor is to keep a record of all the Mass intentions received and said, so also are the obligations of these foundations to be entered in a special book, giving also the time when they were fulfilled and the amount of the alms received. This must be done so that the Ordinary could be given an accurate account of these things. C. 1549 #2.

When pious foundations are made and accepted by churches in charge of religious who are exempt, the rights and obligations, spoken of here in Canons 1545-1549 as referring to the Ordinary, belong exclusively to the major Superior. All con-

5. Augustine, op. cit., vol. VI. p. 609.

6. Benedict XIV. "Vix Pervenit" Nov. 1, 1745; S. C. de Prop. Fide, 1873. Both apud Collectanea S. C. de Prop. Fide vol. II. #1393, p. 60.

trary privileges granted to any order are revoked and annulled by the Constitution "Nuper" of Innocent XII. from which these laws are for the most part taken. (7.)

The patron has no right in the acceptance, constitution and administration of pious foundations spoken of here under this title. C. 1546 #2.

Unless the charter contains some express provisions to the contrary, no one but the Holy See can reduce the obligations arising from a pious foundation. C. 1551. This is the general rule and has but one exception. When the obligations imposed by the pious foundations cannot possibly be fulfilled on account of some reason, which is not due to faulty administration of the foundation, the Ordinary of the place may, after consulting those concerned in the matter, diminish the obligations, except the Mass obligations. But even in these cases the Ordinary should keep as close as possible to the founder's will. C. 1517 #2.

When an indult has been received from the Holy See, the pastor or whoever is concerned must read it carefully and interpret it strictly. The reduction of foundation Masses must not be extended to the reduction of Masses arising "from some other species of contract differing from that by which the foundation is accepted, nor to other works imposed by a pious foundation." (3.) When a general indult of reducing the pious works of a foundation has been received it should rather be interpreted to the reduction of other obligations than the Masses. Of course, if it is evident from the Indult that it refers to the Masses also, the case is different. C. 1551 #3.

The pastor should always follow this general rule. Keep a record of all the transactions so that you have something tangible to prove the existence of such transactions. Without these records the parish priest may meet with many difficulties and the church may suffer losses therefrom.

In order to maintain the temporal affairs of the parish, the pastor will need money. And, as a rule, it is up to the pastor to see to it how and where this is to be secured. There are many legitimate ways in which money can be gotten for church purposes.. In some countries the governments supply at least part

7. Augustine, op. cit. vol. VI. p. 615. C. 1550
8. Augustine, op. cit. vol. VI. p. 616.

of the financial support. But here in the United States it must come altogether from the people. Consequently, the pastor will have to seek a system, best suited to the people of that place, through which the necessary funds will be obtained. Some parishes use the system of pew-rent, others the school tax, still others depend upon collections, while some secure the means through a combination of several of these systems. Respecting the general law and the diocesan statutes in this regard the par ish priest will make a wise and prudent choice of the manner in which funds are to be collected in his parish, seeking to distribute the burden proportionately among the parishioners.

But while the parish priest is busily engaged in securing new funds he must not become oblivious of the fact that property deteriorates in time and that repairs will be necessary. The church goods, which the parish has, will have to be preserved and this necessitates constant watching over everything so that repairs, etc., may be made in time. The money necessary for repairs is to be taken from the sources and in the manner mentioned in canon 1186 #2. If a church becomes so dilapidated that it cannot be used anymore for services, the parish priest should try to raise sufficient funds for repairs or for a new building. When no funds of this kind can be secured, the Ordinary is to be consulted about the best step to be taken. C. 1197.

The school and the rectory are other objects of the pastor's care. They, as well as the church, must be kept in good order and condition. Proper ventilation, sanitation and lighting facilities are to be provided in all. The furnishings need not be works of art; practicalibity and suitableness are the chief requisites. The children of the school are to be reminded that the property is church property and should be treated as such and not be abused by carving and cutting on chairs, desks boards, etc.

If a parish has a cemetery this will also have to be supervised by the parish priest. The law instructs him to fence it in well so that no animals could pass through it and that it be separated from other land. C. 1210. When the parish cannot afford to hire a care-taker for the cemetery, the pastor will have to use his influence with the people and ask them to keep the place, where their deceased relatives and loved ones rest, in order. Moreover, all epitaphs, inscriptions and ornaments not in conformity with Catholic ideals and teaching should be barred from the cemetery. C. 1211. A certain portion of the cemetery ought to be set aside for the burial of such to whom ecclesiastical burial will have to be denied. C. 1212. The section should be separated from the rest of the cemetery by a fence and is not to be blessed. In case an "excommunicatus vitandus" has been buried among the faithful, the pastor should see to it that his body is removed from there and placed in this portion of the cemetery which is set aside for such. But if this cannot be done without serious inconvenience the law does not bind. C. 1242. If the diocesan statutes contain any instructions regarding cemeteries, they must be observed.

Finally church property should be covered by sufficient insurance. This is to be taken out with some reliable company so that in case of fire, etc., some financial aid will be forth-coming. Diocesan statutes regulating such matters are to be kept in mind.

At the end of each year an account of the temporal administration must be given to the Ordinary. C. 1525 #1. Even if there is some special law, which demands, that such an account must be rendered to others, the Ordinary cannot be excluded from inspecting those accounts. C. 1525 #2.

CHAPTER VI.

THE REMOVAL AND TRANSFER OF PASTORS.

Although the parochial office may be lost in many ways, I do not intend to treat of them all here but shall limit myself to the two that occur most frequently — removal and transfer. A transfer simply means a change from one parish to another, while a removal means the forcible taking away of a pastor from his parish, whether he be given another parish or not. Both of these are negotiated by competent authority. In reserved parishes the Holy See alone is competent to make such changes and removals, while the Ordinary is the competent superior with other parishes. While a transfer can be made for any reason, as long as it is demanded for the good of souls, (C. 2162) a removal cannot take place, (except with religious pastors,) unless the parish priest is unable to govern the parish properly. This inability does not have to be caused by any fault of the pastor. But before either the transfer or the removal can be made validly a certain formality prescribed by law must be observed. It is of these formalities and of the causes that I shall treat in this the concluding chapter of this dissertation.

The New Code states that all pastors are to be established permanently, "stabiles in ea (paroecia) esse debent." C. 454 #2. Still, both can be removed. But this seems to be a contradiction, "irremovable" and "possibility of removal". The terms would be contradictory if used in their strict sense. But irremovability here does not mean impossibility of removal. The term is used to distinguish the two classes and to indicate the greater stability of one over the other. Neither does the law say that pastors are irremovable. It states that they are called by that name, — "appelari solent." Although the Church desires to give all pastors a certain degree of security while in office it does not wish to stretch this to such an extent that it would work injury to souls. This is clear from the constitution of Pope Pius X. "Maxima Cura" on which a large part of the present legislation in the New Code in this regard, is based. The Pontiff says there:- "Quamvis autem, ut hi rectores quae paroeciae utilia aut necessaria esse iudicarent alacriore possent animo suscipere soluti metu ne ab Ordinario amoverentur pro libitu, praescriptum generatim fuit, ut stabiles in suo officio permanerent; nihilomnius, quia stabilitas haec in salutem est inducta fidelium, idciro sapienti consilio cautum est, ut eadem non sic urgeatur, ut in perniciem potius ipsorum cedat." (1.)

Sect. I. Removal of parish priests.

The New Code gives us two formulas for the removal of pastors and one for their transfer. The formulas are divided so as to apply to the removal of both irremovable and removable parish priests, while the form prescribed for transfers is that for removable pastors since an irremovable pastor cannot be transfered against his will unless the Ordinary secures special faculties from the Holy See. C. 2163 #1. The causes for removals are also given.

Speaking of causes for the removal of both irremovable and removable pastors the New Code states the following:-

"#1. Parochus inamovibilis a sua paroecia amoveri potest ob causam, quae ipsius ministerium, etiam, citra gravem suam culpam, noxium aut saltem inefficax reddit.

#2. Hae causae sunt praesertim quae sequuntur:

1°. Imperitia vel permanens infirmitas mentis aut corporis, quae parochum suis muneribus rite obeundis imparem reddit, si, iudicio Ordinarii, per vicarium adiutorem bono animarum provideri nequeat ad normam can. 475;

2°. Odium plebis, quamvis iniustum et non universale, dummodo tale sit, quod utile parochi ministerium impediat, nec brevi cessaturum praevideatur,

3°. Bonae existimationis amissio penes probos et graves viros, sive haec oriatur ex levi vivendi ratione parochi, sive ex antiquo eius crimine quod nuper detectum eximatur iam poena ob praescriptionem, sive ex facto familiarium et consanguineorum quibuscum parochus vivit nisi per eorum discessum bonae parochi famae sit satis provisum;

4°. Probabile crimen ocultum, parocho imputatum, ex quo Ordinarius prudenter praevidet magnam in posterum oriri posse fidelium offensionem;

5°. Mala rerum temporalium administratio cum gravi ecclesiae aut beneficii damno, quoties huic malo remedium afferri

1. "Pope Pius X. "Maxima Cura" August 20, 1910. apud Acta Apostolicae Sedis, vol. 2, 1910 p. 66 sqq.

nequeat sive auferendo administrationem parocho, sive alio modo, quamvis aliunde parochus spirituale ministerium utiliter exerceat." C. 2147.

Now let us take up these causes one by one and see what they mean. In the first place the law mentions "imperitia". This term embodies both ignorance and inexperience. If the pastor is so ignorant of his duties that he cannot hope to perform his ministry with fruit to souls in his charge, he has no place in that position. So also with a pastor so wanting in experience i. e. practical knowledge. The second section speaks of chronic infirmity of body or mind. Such would be insanity from which the pastor, according to the prudent judgement of a skilled physician, will never fully recover, or at least not so that there would be no danger of relapses. Blindness, dumbness, deafness and other such defects, which make the pastor permanently (or for a long time) incapable of performing his duties properly and with fruit to his parishioners, are sufficient to remove him as long as the Ordinary does not think that this inability on the pastor's part could be supplied by a vicar according to canon 475. But if the Ordinary thinks that the pastor's ignorance, inexperience or other defects could be supplied by appointing a "vicar adiutor" according to canon 475; there would not be cause for removing him.

"Odium plebis". This is another cause for removal of irremovable pastors. This hatred need not be that of the whole community nor need it arise through the pastor's fault. As long as a large number of people bear this attitude toward the parish priest, even if it be unjustly, he may be removed, as long as the cause cannot be forseen to cease in the near future and the pastor is not able to perform his ministry with fruit while he is under this disadvantage.

"Bonae existimationis amissio." This loss of reputation or esteem must be found with good and prudent men and not only with some tale-bearers and light-headed parishioners. It matters not whether this state of things arises from the pastor's manner of living or from some crime which he may have committed years ago and is now exempt from punishment on account of prescription or whether it comes through the conduct of his house-keeper or relatives, who live with him. But if the good name of the pastor can be restored by dismissing the house-keeper or relatives from his abode this is to be done and then there will be no cause for removing him.

"Probabile crimen occultum." Consequently, even when the pastor is prudently suspected of some crime, which he never committed and this causes an impediment to fruitful ministry in that parish, the pastor can be removed. So also if the Ordinary judges that this suspicion may cause grave scandal in the parish later on if the pastor remains.

"Mala rerum temporalium administratio," although his ministry in spiritual affairs may be properly carried on. Not any mis-administration of the temporal affairs of a parish is sufficient to remove a parish priest. It must be coupled with grave damage to the parish or benefice. But the removal should not take place until other means of remedying this state of affairs are of no avail. Thus, if the pastor could be deprived of the administration of the temporal goods while retaining the spiritual care of the parish, this should be done or if this defect in the pastor can be supplied by a vicar etc, these remedies should be made use of. As the law states when this cannot be remedied in any manner whatever, then only is it a sufficient cause for removing an irremovable parish priest.

These, then, are the canonical causes set down by law. But they are not all. As the first part of the same canon says an irremovable pastor can be removed for any cause which makes his ministry in that parish injurious or inefficacious. Consequently, it is left to the Ordinary and those concerned to see whether any such cause is present before use of the law is made against him.

Before we speak of the different formalities that are to be used in removing any of the pastors or in transferring them to other parishes it will be well to make a few general remarks about some of the proceedings etc, used in these processes of removal and transfer.

When any of the proceedings to be mentioned take place a notary must always be at hand, who will draw up in writing all the documents which have to be signed by those concerned and preserved in the diocesan archives. C. 2142. When any monitions are to be made these must, as a rule, be in writing and sent by a special messenger. If this cannot be done for some reason, the Ordinary may send them by mail as long as the letter is registered and a receipt signed by the party receiving the letter is secured. If there be some other safer way of sending this monition, that should be made use of since the law demands that the safest manner, according to the laws and conditions of the place, be used in the transmission of such monitions. C. 2143 #I and C. 1719. If the monition is made orally it must be done before the chancellor or another official of the curia or before two witnesses. C. 2143 #1. An authentic copy of all monitions is to be preserved in the acts of the case. C. 2143 #2. When the party to whom the monition was sent or given refuses to accept it or impeeds its course to him, the monition is considered as made. C. 2143 #3. In proceedings of this kind the summary form is to be used but the Ordinary may admit two or three witnesses, who may be called "ex officio" or by request of the pastor concerned, as long as the Ordinary does not think that these witnesses are being introduced solely for the purpose of prolonging and delaying the proceedings. C. 2145 #1. As in civil cases all witnesses and experts are to be placed under oath before they are allowed to testify. C. 2144 #2.

When a definite sentence had been passed the pastor has no other recourse than that to Rome, in which case all the acts of the case in question must be sent there. During this recourse the pastor must refrain from the office of which he was deprived and the Ordinary cannot appoint another pastor to that place until the case is setlled by the Holy See. C. 2146.

Now let us proceed to take up the treatment of the formality to be used in the removal of a irremovable parish priest as set down by the New Code.

When the Ordinary, in his prudent judgment, thinks that one of the causes, mentioned in canon 2147, is present in a certain case, he shall call into consultation two of his diocesan examiners. According to the constitution "Maxima cura" of Pope Pius X these examiners were to be the two seniors by reason of their election to this office, or, if they were all the same in this regard, those who were priests the most number of years were to be selected and if even such a distinction could not be made the older members in age were to be chosen. (2.) In the New Code no such a distinction is made nor is any such selection prescribed and, consequently, the Ordinary is free to choose whom he may

2. "Maxima Cura" Pope Pius X. can. 5 #I. apud 1. c.

desire. The examiners having been called, the Ordinary will go over the case with them in order to ascertain, if possible, whether the cause really exists and its gravity is sufficient. When, after this consultation with the examiners (he needs not their consent), the Ordinary feels that the cause is there and that it is sufficiently grave for proceeding against the pastor in question, he shall invite this parish priest, either orally or in writing, to tender his resignation within a certain time. This invitation must also include the cause which makes this invitation necessary and the arguments on which the charge is based. C. 2148. This mention of the cause, which moves the Ordinary to such action, and the arguments on which the charge is based, is necessary for the validity of the acts. If the pastor is mentally defective no such invitation need be made. C. 2148 #1.

If a pastor renounces his parish after having received such an invitation from the Ordinary, the latter will proceed to declare the parish vacant. C. 2150 #1. The law tells us that the pastor need not resign the parish for the reasons alleged in the invitation, but may give his own reasons for doing so, e. gr. some reasons which are less odious or grave, as long as they are true and legitimate. Thus, the pastor may make his resignation for the reason that he wishes to comply with the wishes of the Ordinary. C. 2150 #2. Moreover, this renunciation may also be made conditionally as long as the Ordinary can accept such a resignation and in fact does so. C. 2150 #3. Every resignation may be made in writing or orally before two witnesses or even through a procurator by giving him a special mandate to that effect. If the renunciation is made in any other manner it is invalid. C. 186. An authentic written document of the renunciation is to be preserved in the archives of the diocesan curia. C. 186.

The irremovable pastor, however, may not wish to resign but attacks the charges brought against him in the invitation. In this case he may also ask for a prolongation of the time set in the invitation to resign so that he could collect proofs. The Ordinary may extend the time according to the pastor's wishes as long as this delay does not work injury to the souls of the faithful. C. 2151. When the reasons and arguments of the irremovable pastor have been received by the Ordinary he must call the same examiners that acted in the first place and with them go over the judgment. This consultation is again necessary for the validity of the proceedings. After the consultation, the Ordinary will either approve or reject the reasons and arguments of the pastor and make known his decision to the pastor by means of a decree. C. 2151 #1-2.

If the decree was one of removal the irremovable pastor can take recourse, within ten days, to the same Ordinary. The latter will again be forced, so that the proceedings be valid, to call in others for consultation. This time it is the parochial consultors, (two of them,) that he must call in. C. 2153 #1. With them the Ordinary must examine the reasons of the pastor. Thereupon he must either reject or approve these arguments and give his decision to the pastor by means of another decree. C. 2153 #1 and 3. The pastor has a right to call in special witnesses, who could not be gotten in the first attempt to prove his reasons against the invitation to resign during the acts of this recourse to the Ordinary, as long as the Ordinary does not think that these witnesses are being brought in solely for the purpose of delaying the proceedings. C. 2153 #2. But the burden of proof, that these witnesses could not be gotten during the first part of the proceedings, falls upon the pastor. C. 2153 #1.

But if the pastor, to whom the invitation to resign has been sent, completely ignores this invitation by not answering during the time set for the resignation (nor asking for more time nor attacking the reasons and arguments of the Ordinary) the latter will have to ascertain whether the invitation reached the pastor and whether he was not kept from answering by some legitimate impediment. If he finds that the pastor received the invitation and that he could have answered had he cared to do so, the Ordinary may proceed to remove him at once. Nor is the Ordinary bound by canon 2154 in such cases. C. 2149 #1. If, however, the Ordinary finds that the pastor did not receive the letter or that he could not have answered within the time set because he was hindered by some legitimate impediment, he should either send another invitation or prolong the time set in the first one. C. 2149 #2. The same is true when the Ordinary cannot make certain whether the invitation has been received or whether the pastor could have answered. C. 2149 #2.

When a pastor has finally been removed, the Ordinary is to consult the examiners or consultors, used in the case, as to the end of the pastor and see whether the removed irremovable pastor should be given another parish, benefice, or office, if he is fit, or whether he should be placed on the pension list. C. 2154 #1. A pastor, who resigns is to be favored over the one, who had to be removed. C. 2154 #2. This new provision should be made known to the pastor as soon as possible. It can be made in the same decree which determines his removal.. C. 2155.

After the irremovable pastor receives the decree of removal from the Ordinary he must leave the parish house and all that pertains to the parish to the priest sent there to take his place. C. 2156 #1. This must be done as soon as possible unless the pastor in question be infirm and cannot be moved conveniently. In that case the Ordinary may leave him there and give him the exclusive use of the parish-house until such a time as he will be able to be transferred therefrom. C. 2156. #2.

This then is the formality to be used in the removal of irremovable pastors. The removable pastor is moved in very much the same way. The same causes are required to remove a removable pastor as those mentioned for the irremovable one. C. 2157 and 2147. Of course, as was stated before, if the pastor be a religious no canonical cause or formality need be used in proceeding to remove him. C. 2157.#2; C. 454 #5. The form of removing a removable pastor is the following:-

After the Ordinary judges that one of the causes mentioned in canon 2147 is present he should write to the pastor in question and admonish and exhort him in a fatherly manner to resign that parish within a certain time, stating at the same time the cause which makes his further work there undesirable, because it is injurious to the souls of that place or at least unfruitful. C. 2158. We may notice that while in the case of an irremovable pastor the Ordinary was forced to consult two diocesan examiners before he made the invitation of resignation, here he may ask the removable pastor to resign without consulting anyone before that. The invitation here can also be made orally.

If the removable pastor ignores the admonition during the time set therein by not resigning nor asking for more time in order to secure proofs against the charges made in the admonition of the Ordinary nor by attacking the charge, the Ordinary may remove him at once and declare the parish vacant. C. 2159 and 2149. If the Ordinary is not certain whether the pastor received the admonition or whether he could have answered, he is to send him another such admonition and exhortation to resign or he may prolong the time set in the first. C. 2149.

When the pastor refuses to resign the parish after the first admonition and sends his reasons and arguments against the charge to the Ordinary, the latter must call in two diocesan examiners, as stated for irremovable pastors, and with them go over the matter sent in by the removable pastor against the first admonition. This is necessary for the validity of the proceedings. C. 2159. If, after this consultation, the Ordinary does not judge the reasons of the pastor legitimate, he should repeat the first admonition and exhortation to resign within the time prescribed in this document. C. 2160. When the time set in this second admonition elapses without a renunciation on the part of the removable parish priest in question the Ordinary may either prolong the time set or remove him at once. C. 2161 #1. The decision that he is removed is to be sent the removable pastor by means of a decree.

When the pastor has resigned or has been removed, provision should be made for him in the same manner as in the case of the irremovable pastor. C. 2161 #2.

Transfer of Pastors.

While the Code names many distinct causes for removing a pastor it includes all those sufficient for transferring him under the one phrase "si bonum animarum postulet." C. 2162. Consequently, it will be left to the Ordinary himself to decide whether such a cause is present so that he could start proceedings against the pastor in question. When he deems such a reason present in a certain case, he should propose the charge to the pastor in question and persuade him to consent to the change. C. 2162. If the pastor refuses to make the change and he is an irremovable pastor, the Ordinary cannot change him unless he first secures special faculties from the Holy See. C. 2163 #1. If the pastor refuses and is a removable parish priest and the parish to which he is to be transferred is not much inferior to the one in which he is at present, the Ordinary can transfer the pastor even against his will. But the following prescriptions of the law must be made use of.

The pastor who refuses to abide by the exhortation of the Ordinary must give his reasons in writing and send them to the

Ordinary who desired the change. C. 2164. The Ordinary will examine these reasons sent in and see whether they justify a change from the first proposal. If he does not think so, he will, in order to make the proceedings valid, call in two diocesan parochial consultors and go over the whole matter with them, considering the cause for the transfer, the conditions of the two parishes, i. e. the parish "a qua" as well as the parish "ad quam", and the reasons of the pastor for refusing to make the change. C. 2165. If, even after this consultation, the Ordinary wishes to make the change, he is to repeat the paternal exhortation to consent to the transfer, according to the will of the superior. C. 2166. If even this second exhortation is of no avail and the Ordinary still judges that the change should be made, he will order the removable pastor to leave the present parish within a certain time and take another parish. He should also tell him in this written notice, that after the time set within this notification elapses. the parish will be vacant ipso facto. C. 2167 #1. If the time set here passes and the pastor still remains there the Ordinary shall declare that parish vacant. C. 2167 #2.

FINIS.

Sources of Bibiography.

SOURCES.

Acta Apostolicae Sedis, Commentarium Officiale, Romae.
Catechismus ex Decreto Conc. Tridentini. Romae-Tornaci. 1902.
Catholic Mind, The. America Press, New York.
Catholic Encyclopedia, Encyclopedia Press. New York.
Codex Juris Canonici, P. J. Kennedy & Son, New York. 1918.
Collectanea S. Congr. de Prop. Fide. Romae. 1907.
Concilii Plen. Baltimorensis II, Acta et Decreta. J. Murphy. Baltimore. 1880.
Concilii Plen. Baltimorensis III, Acta et Decreta. J. Murphy Co. 1886.
Concilii Tridentini, Canones et decreta, cum appendice Theologiae Candidatis perutili, editio Novissima. Typ. Polyglotta S. C. P. F. Romae. 1904.
Congregationis Concilii, Thesaurus Resolutionum. Ex typ. Vaticana. Romae.
Congregationis S. Rituum, Decreta Authetica. Typ. Polyglotta S. C. P. F. Romae.
Constitutiones Dioc. Bostonensis. Ex Syn. Dioc. VI. Boston. 1919.
Ecclesiastical Review, The. Philadelphia.
Homiletic and Pastoral Review, The. Wagner. New York.
Irish Ecclesiastical Record. Brown & Nolan. Dublin.
Rituale Romanum Pauli V. Pont. Maximi.-Editio 2a Taurinensis juxta typicam Taurini Sumptibus et Typis Eq. P. Marietti. 1917.
Synodo Diocesana Superiorensis I, Acta et decreta. Superiore. 1907.

AUTHORS.

Andrea, Valerius. Synopsis Juris Canonici per Erotemata. Lovanii. 1669.
Augustine, Chas. A Commentary on the New Code of Canon Law. B. Herder Book Co., St. Louis, Mo. 1918-1921.
Ayrinhac, H. A. Marriage Legislation in the New Code. Benziger Bros. N. Y. — Cincinnati, O. 1918.
Penal Legislation in the New Code. Benziger Bros. N. Y. — Cincinnati, O. 1920.
Barbarosa, Augustine. De Officio et Potestate Parochi. Romae. 1774.
Summa Apostolicarum Decisionum extra ius commune vagantium. Editio ultima aucta et recognita. Romae. 1658.
Bargilliat, M. Praelectiones Juris Canonici. Edit. tricesima. Parisiis. 1915.
Benedict XIV., Pope. De Synodo Diocesana. Romae. 1806.
Blat, Fr. Alb. Commentarium Textus Codicis. Jur. Can. Lib. II. De Personis. Ferrari. Romae. 1919. — Lib. III. De Rubus. ex typ. Pont. Instituto Pii IX. Romae. 1920.
Bouix, D. Tractatus de Parocho. edit. 3a. Parisiis. 1880.
Callan, C. The Four Gospels. J. F. Wagner Co., New York. 1917.
Capello, Felix. De Censuris iuxta Codicem Juris Canonici. Aug. Taurinorum. Typ. P. Marietti. 1919.
Cavagnis, Felix. Institutiones Juris Publici Ecclesiastici. Romae. 1882.
Craisson, D. Manuale totius Juris Canonici. edit. 4a. Pictavii. 1875.
Creusen-Vermeersch. Summa Novi Juris Canonici Commentariis aucta. Brussells. 1919.

De Fargna, Fr. Commentaria in singulos Canones de Jure Patronatus. Romae. 1719.

De Luise, Gaspare. Codex Canonum Ecclesiae. C. Pedone Lauriel. Neapoli. 1873.

Devoti, Joan. Institutiones Canonicae. Romae. 1825.

Fagnani, Prosp. Commentaria in quinque libros Decretalium. Apud P. Balleonium. Venetiis. 1696.

Ferraris, F. Lucius. Prompta Bibliotheca Canonica, Juridica, etc. J. P. Migne. Paris. 1865.

Ferreres, P. Joannes B. Compendium. Moralis ad normam novissimi Codicis Canonici. editio Subirana. Barcinone. 1919.

Garcia, Nicolas. Tractus de Beneficiis Amplissimus et doctissimus. Apud. Phil. Albertum. Coloniae Allobrogum. 1636.

Gasparri, Petrus. Tractatus Canonicus de Matrimonio. edit. 3a. Parisiis. 1904.

Tractus Canonicus de Sanctissima Eucharistia. Parisiis. 1897.

Genicot, Eduardus. Institutiones Theologiae Moralis. ed. 8a. Brussells. 1919.

Giraldi, Ubaldus. Animadversiones et additamenta — ad Aug. Barbosa De Officio et Potestate Parochi. Romae 1774.

Grisar. Disputationes Tridentinae. F. Rauch. Oeniponte. 1886.

Kubelbeck, Wm. The Sacred Penitentiaria and its relations to faculties of Ordinaries and Priests. Somerset, Ohio. 1918.

Lapide, Cornelius a. Commentarius in Evang. SS. Lucae et Joannis. Venetiis. 1717.

Lehmkuhl, Aug. Theologia Moralis. Freiburg. Herder. 1884.

Leurenius, Petrus. Forum Beneficiale. J. B. Ricurti. Coloniae. 1742.

Liguori, St. Alphonsus de. Theologia Moralis. Aug. Taurinorum H. Marietti. Romae. 1891.

Manning, Card. H. E. The Eternal Priesthood. Benziger Bros. 1907

Maschat, Remigius. Institutiones Canonicae. Romae. 1757.

Micheletti, Pr. De Pastore Animarum. Pustet. Romae. 1919.

Summula Theologiae Pastoralis. F. Pustet. Romae. 1919.

Millet-Byrne. Jesus living in the Priest. Benziger Bros. 1901.

Moran, Wm. The Government of the Church in the 1st Century. Benziger Bros. 1913.

Murray, Wm. The Present Juridical Status of Parishes in the U. S. C. U. A. 1919.

Nardi, Luiga. Dei Parrochi, Pesaro. 1829.

Noldin, H. Summa Theologiae Moralis. editio X. H. Rauch. Oeniponte. 1912.

Summa Theologia Moralis. editio XII. Pustet. Romae. 1920.

O'Malley, A. The ethics of medical homicide and mutilation. Devin-Adair. N. Y. 1919.

Pallen, Conde. The education of Boys. America Press. 1916.

Pasqualigo, Z. De Sacrificio Novae Legis. Apud. P. Balleonium. Venetiis. 1707.

Pastor, Melchior. Tractatus de beneficiis ecclesiasticis ad usum utriusque fori. Tolosae, 1675.

Petavius, Dionisius. Dogmata Theologica. Parisiis. 1867.

Petrovits, Jos. The New Church Law on Matrimony. J. McVey. Philadelphia. 1919.

Pirhing, Enricus. Jus Canonicum nova methodo explicatum. Dilingae. 1722.

Pycia, M. Momentum iuris civilis romani in formando iure ecclesiastico publico. Kielciis. 1907.

Reclusius, Fr. Ant. Tractatus de Concursibus collationibus, et vacationibus parochiarum. Salomoni. Romae. 1774.

Reiffenstuel, A. Jus Canonicum Universum. Apud A. Bartoli. Venetiis. 1735.

Richter, A. L. Canones et decreta Concilii Tridentini ex editione Romana A. MDCCCXXXIV repetiti. Lipsiae. 1853.

Sabetti-Barrett. Compendium Theologiae Moralis. F. Pustet & Co. edit. 22a. New York. 1915. — Editia 27a. F. Pustet & Co. 1919.

Santi, Fr. Praelectiones Juris Canonici. F. Pustet. New Yoork. 1898.

Scherer, Rudolf Ritter von. Handbuch des Kirchenrechts. Graz. 1886.

Schmalzgruber, Fr. Jus Ecclesiasticum Universum. Romae. 1844.

Schmidt, G. T. The American Priest. Benziger Bros. N.Y.—Cincinnati. 1919.

Schulze, Fred. Mannual of Pastoral Theology, Diedrich-Schaeffer. Milwaukee, Wis. 1906.

Sebestiani, Nic. Summarium Theologiae Moralis. Aug. Taurinorum. ed. 4a minor. Romae. 1919.

Smith, S. B. Compendium Juris Canonici. Benziger Bros. 1891.

Stang, Wm. Pastoral Theology. Benziger Bros. 1907.

St. Thomas Aquinas. Summa Theologica. Ex typ. Forzani et S. Romae 1894.

Tauton, Ethelred. The Law of the Church. Herder. 1906.

Thomassinus, Lud. Vetus et Nova Ecclesiae Disciplina. Parisiis. 1688.

Valuy, F. B. Directorium Sacerdotale. M. G. Gill & Son. Dublin. 1879.

Vechiotti, Sept. Institutiones Canonicae. edit. 19a. Aug. Tauinorum. H. Marietti. 1886.

Wapelhorst, Innoc. Compendium Sacrae Liturgiae. edit 9a. Benziger Bros. 1915.

Wernz, F. X. Jus Decretalium. Orati. 1911-1915.

UNIVERSITAS CATHOLICA AMERICAE

WASHINGTONII, D. C.

S. FACULTAS THEOLOGICA

1920—1921

No. 11

Tituli.

D E U S L U X M E A

T I T U L I

Quos Ad Doctoratus Gradum In

J U R E C A N O N I C O

apud

UNIVERSITATEM CATHOLICAM AMERICAE

Consequendam Publice Propugnabit

C A R O L U S J O S E P H K O U D E L K A
Sacerdos Diocesis Superiorensis
Juris Canonici Licentiatus.

Hora XI. A. M. DIE 25 MAJI. A. D. 1921

TITULI.

1. Canones.............. 25—30
2. Canones.............. 31—35
3. Canones.............. 63—79
4. Canones.............. 80—86
5. Canones..............111—117
6. Canones..............152—159
7. Canones..............183—195
8. Canones..............222—229
9. Canon................249
10. Canones..............339 & 466
11. Canones..............356—362
12. Canones..............385—390
13. Canones..............445—450
14. Canon................459
15. Canon................462
16. Canon................463
17. Canon................465
18. Canones..............471—478
19. Canones..............487—491
20. Canones..............632—636
21. Canones..............702—706
22. Canones..............738—754
23. Canones..............762—769
24. Canones..............782—789
25. Canones..............824—844
26. Canones..............853—866
27. Canones..............871—892
28. Canones..............908—910
29. Canones..............938—944
30. Canones..............873—982
31. Canones............1019—1034
32. Canones............1059—1067
33. Canones............1076 & 96
34. Canones............1077 & 97
35. Canones............1094—1103
36. Canones............1110—1117
37. Canones............1172—1177
38. Canones............1239—1242
39. Canones............1243—1249
40. Canones............1250—1254
41. Canones............1290—1295
42. Canones............1329—1336
43. Canones............1385—1394
44. Canones............1484—1488
45. Canones............1544—1551
46. Canones............1556—1568
47. Canones............1572—1579
48. Canones............1585—1590
49. Canones............1594—1596
50. Canones............1661—1666
51. Canones............1756—1759
52. Canones............1770—1781
53. Canones............1960—1965
54. Canones............2038—2041
55. Canones............2147—2156
56. Canones............2157—2161
57. Canones............2168—2175
58. Canones............2236—2240
59. Canones............2286—2290
60. Canones............2350—2359

VIDIT

† THOMAS J. SHAHAN, S. T. D.
Rector Universitatis

JOANNES A. RYAN, S. T. D.
p. t. Decanus

PETRUS GUILDAY, Ph. D.
p. t. Secretarius

CONTENTS

ERRATA

p. 15. l. 23. "or" instead of "of".

p. 55. l. 6. "pastor" instead of "parish"; l. 19. "concedendam" instead of "consedendam".

p. 56. l. 18. "nullum" instead of "nullium".

p. 59. l. 17. "poet" instead of "pet".

p. 66. l. 25. "lenocinio" instead of "lenocino".

p. 107. l. 13. a comma to be placed after the word "recourse".

p. 117. l. 35. Instead of line 35 read: "plication. In the first place we were told that before the pas-"

p. 172. l. 17. should read: "of the Vicar General and the Vicar Capitular".

p. 189. l. 14. "the" instead of "one".

VITA

Charles Joseph Koudelka was born of Catholic parents in Reedsville, Wis. on January 30, 1894. He received his elementary education in St. Mary's Catholic school and the Reedsville graded school, both of Reedsville, Wis. Thereupon he entered St. Procopius College, an institution under the direction of the Benedictine Fathers at Lisle, Ill. After the usual college course he was adopted for the Green Bay diocese in Wisconsin and sent to St. Francis Seminary, St. Francis, Wis. for the courses in Philosophy and Theology. Six years later he was ordained to the Priesthood for the diocese of Green Bay, Wisconsin, by the Right Rev. Joseph M. Koudelka, D. D., Bishop of Superior, Wisconsin, April 27, 1919. Shortly after he was transferred to the Superior diocese. After six months of parish work he was sent to Washington, D. C. for a post-graduate course in the Sacred Sciences at the Catholic University of America. His major subject was Canon Law under the direction of Rt. Rev. F. Bernardini, S. T. D., J. U. D. His minor studies were Dogmatic and Moral Theology under the direction of the Very Rev. Edmund T. Shanahan, Ph. D., S. T. D., J. C. L. and the Very Rev. John A. Ryan, S. T. D. respectively.

He desires to express at this opportunity his most sincere thanks to his professors and the members of the faculty of Sacred Sciences for their kind assistance.

www.ingramcontent.com/pod-product-compliance
Lightning Source LLC
LaVergne TN
LVHW050239080826
844660LV00012B/562

* 9 7 8 0 8 1 3 2 2 2 0 2 8 *